THE NEW CONSERVATIVES

RESTORING AMERICA'S COMMITMENT TO FAMILY, COMMUNITY, AND INDUSTRY

edited by **Oren Cass**

Founder of AMERICAN COMPASS

RADIUS

Radius Book Group
A division of Diversion Publishing Corp.
www.radiusbookgroup.com

Copyright © 2025 by American Compass Inc.

Most essays in this volume were published initially by American Compass and are reprinted here with permission of the authors. The following essays, initially published elsewhere, are reprinted with permission from the copyright holders:

Oren Cass, "The Working Hypothesis," adapted from *The Once and Future Worker* (Encounter Books, 2018).

Oren Cass, "Comparative Disadvantage," *Law & Liberty*, January 15, 2020.

Oren Cass, "A New Conservatism: Freeing the Right from Free-Market Orthodoxy," *Foreign Affairs*, March/April 2021.

Robert Lighthizer, "Robert Lighthizer on the Need for Tariffs to Reduce America's Trade Deficit," *The Economist*, October 5, 2021.

Wells King & Dan Vaughn, Jr., "The American Camry," *National Review*, October 17, 2022.

Wells King, "Myth-Busting Silicon Valley," *American Conservative*, November 28, 2022.

Gabriela Rodriguez, "How Airbus Took Flight," *American Conservative*, April 12, 2023.

Oren Cass & Gabriela Rodriguez, "The Case for a Hard Break with China," *Foreign Affairs*, July 25, 2023.

Oren Cass, "This Is What Elite Failure Looks Like," *New York Times*, July 6, 2024.

Oren Cass, "Rebuilding Worker Power," Economic Innovation Group, August 2024.

All rights reserved, including the right to reproduce this book or portions thereof in any form whatsoever. No part of this publication may be reproduced or transmitted in any form or by any means, electronic or mechanical, including photocopying, recording, or any other information storage and retrieval, without the written permission of the publisher.

Radius Book Group and colophon are registered trademarks of Diversion Publishing Corp.

For more information, email info@radiusbookgroup.com.

First Radius Books Group Edition: June 2025
Hardcover ISBN: 979-8-89515-050-4
e-ISBN: 979-8-89515-051-1

Printed in the United States of America

10 9 8 7 6 5 4 3 2 1

Radius books are available at special discounts for bulk purchases in the US by corporations, institutions, and other organizations. For more information, please contact admin@diversionbooks.com.

The publisher does not have any control over and does not assume any responsibility for author or third-party websites or their content.

For the American worker.

Contents

Editor's Note	vii
Prologue *The Working Hypothesis* by Oren Cass	xi
Introduction *This Is What Elite Failure Looks Like* by Oren Cass	xxii

PART ONE: PRINCIPLES

CHAPTER ONE: THE MARKET	3
A New Conservatism by Oren Cass	5
What Happened to Capitalism? by Oren Cass	15
CHAPTER TWO: THE STATE	22
Rediscovering a Genuine American System by Wells King	24
Removing the Blinders from Economic Policy by Oren Cass	33
CHAPTER THREE: LABOR	45
Jobs Americans Would Do by Oren Cass	46
CHAPTER FOUR: CAPITAL	64
Planning for When the Market Cannot by Julius Krein	65
The Rise of Wall Street and the Fall of American Investment by Oren Cass	75

PART TWO: PRODUCTION

CHAPTER FIVE: GLOBALIZATION	91
Searching for Capitalism in the Wreckage of Globalization by Oren Cass	92
The Need for Tariffs by Robert Lighthizer	106
CHAPTER SIX: CHINA	114
Trading It All Away by Marco Rubio	115
The Case for a Hard Break with China by Oren Cass & Gabriela Rodriguez	125
After Hegemony by Elbridge Colby	134

CHAPTER SEVEN: Industrial Policy 143
   Comparative Disadvantage by Oren Cass   145
   The American Camry by Wells King & Dan Vaughn Jr.   152
   Myth-Busting Silicon Valley by Wells King   161
   How Airbus Took Flight by Gabriela Rodriguez   170
   Rebuilding the Supply-Side Platform by Chris Griswold   174

PART THREE: PEOPLE

CHAPTER EIGHT: Worker Power 185
   Conservatives Should Ensure Workers a Seat at the Table (joint statement)   187
   Labor's Conservative Heart by Brian Dijkema   190
   Rebuilding Worker Power by Oren Cass   198

CHAPTER NINE: Education 208
   Teach for America by Oren Cass   209
   The School of Self-Rule by Bruno V. Manno and John Sailer   214
   Making Meritocrats Moral by Yuval Levin   222

CHAPTER TEN: Family 230
   One Generation Away by Oren Cass   232
   Why Bother with Family? by Helen Andrews   236
   A Plan for Supporting Working Families by Oren Cass & Wells King   242

CHAPTER ELEVEN: The Public Purse 253
   The Government Should Keep Its Hands Off Your Medicare by Michael Lind   254
   The Return of the Fiscal Conservatives by Oren Cass   265

CONCLUSION: The Center Cannot Hold..279

Acknowledgments   283
About American Compass   287

Editor's Note

We founded American Compass in 2020 with a mission to restore an economic consensus that emphasizes the importance of family, community, and industry to the nation's liberty and prosperity. A blind faith in markets had come to dominate right-of-center economic thinking, at great cost to conservatism's political prospects and the common good. This market fundamentalism left policymakers and pundits unable or unwilling even to admit the serious challenges that Americans were facing, let alone craft a responsive agenda. Tax cuts, deregulation, and free trade were the only items on the menu; cheap labor and rising corporate profits were the goals. Government's only task was to get out of the way, and anyone who suggested otherwise was, as former South Carolina governor and United Nations ambassador Nikki Haley put it, taking "the slow path to socialism."

The legacy institutions of establishment conservatism—think tanks, editorial pages, congressional offices, and so on—had become complacent, preferring to suppress or gloss over disagreement in the interest of preserving their existing arrangements. A wide variety of lazy platitudes, indefensible assumptions, and unacknowledged trade-offs demanded exploration and debate. New questions had emerged that demanded new answers.

We believed that, like the boy calling attention to the emperor's state of undress, a simple willingness to speak clearly about the obvious weaknesses in the unchallenged orthodoxy could have immediate and dramatic effect. An enormous opportunity to construct a compelling new agenda lay untapped. But we needed to apply conservative principles to contemporary problems, rather than page repeatedly through a dog-eared 1980s playbook.

None of us would have dared predict we would come this far this quickly.

In just a few years, our organization has become "a policy nerve center for the party's younger, more populist generation" (Ezra Klein, *New York Times*), a "slaughterhouse for Republican sacred cows" (*The Economist*), "ground zero in a fierce conservative clash over Trump-era economics" (*Politico*), and "the most influential New Right group on Capitol Hill" (*Wall Street Journal*). The ideas that we introduced, initially mocked and condemned as "progressive" and "socialist," have become not only acceptable but, in many cases, the accepted position. Prominent elected leaders and key institutions have become skeptical of corporate power and financial engineering and optimistic about a renewed labor movement; actively hostile to globalization and enthusiastic about industrial policy; averse to entitlement cuts and eager to expand support for working families. The one organization in all of American politics responsible for advancing that set of ideas is American Compass.

How did we accomplish this? We have none of the resources available to the enormous think tanks with scholars dedicated to every issue able to release countless op-eds and talking points and meet with every relevant congressional staffer. Nor do we have armies of lobbyists on our side, whose nonsensical arguments succeed simply because they are in both the speaker's and listener's interest to accept. To the contrary, our team has only just become ten people strong; our budget has only just reached $2 million. At the beginning of 2025, we finally moved into real office space from a converted yoga studio above a chiropractor and next door to a liquor store.

We are prevailing only because the quality of our ideas and our work is undeniable. We have built a robust foundation for a compelling agenda supported by reams of research, the best writing, and a growing coalition of elected leaders and young policy professionals eager to carry it forward. We are charting an intellectually coherent and politically persuasive course for where American politics, economics, and public policy ought to go. And importantly, for both our popularity and our prospects of success, our heterodox and inclusive approach has attracted supporters and adherents from across the political spectrum.

This volume serves as an anthology documenting *how* we have revitalized conservative thinking and as a primer on *what* that new thinking is. The data, quotations, anecdotes, and arguments that the authors draw upon repeatedly in so many different contexts are the ones that have proved most formative for a new generation of policy professionals. The seminal ideas in the essays are the ones that are winning debates on the national political stage, defining the contours of the conservative coalition, and spawning an enormous range of legislative proposals. Have you noticed conservative political leaders sounding strange new notes about Wall Street, labor unions, trade deals, antitrust enforcement, industrial policy, and so many issues where the GOP position had always been so uncomplicated and predictable? Have you wondered, "What are they talking about?" This is what they are talking about.

The volume's first part, "Principles," examines the core commitments of conservatism and their implications for the key conceptual debates of modern politics. The first chapter, "The Market," traces the descent of conservative economic thinking into market fundamentalism and charts a course to a more coherent approach that celebrates and relies upon markets while also recognizing their limits. The second chapter, "The State," addresses similar questions as they pertain to the role of government. What is public policy good for and when has it traditionally been used? The third and fourth chapters, on "Labor" and "Capital," define the roles of these countervailing forces and interests in a well-functioning capitalist system and the conditions under which their interaction generates positive outcomes.

Part Two, "Production," focuses on the errors that have led to deindustrialization of the American economy, the consequences of the imbalances that have ensued, and the types of policy responses needed. Chapter Five, "Globalization," shows how and why free trade has proved destructive rather than complementary to free markets. Chapter Six, "China," considers specifically the problems of the U.S.–China relationship and the need for the United States to execute a "hard break" from it. Chapter Seven discusses "Industrial Policy," a concept that came to be associated with "central planning" in the conservative mind but in fact is a vital economic tool that has been used frequently and to great effect in American history.

Finally, under the heading "People," the volume's final part addresses the role that conservative policy must play in sustaining supportive communities and creating the conditions for human flourishing. Chapter Eight, on "Worker Power," makes the case that a strong labor movement is vital to capitalism and should be a conservative priority. Chapter Nine, on "Education," interrogates the purpose of public education and argues for much greater emphasis on preparing people to build decent lives as productive contributors to their communities. Chapter Ten, on "Family," explains the sudden conservative interest in family policy broadly and the creation of a more generous family benefit in particular. The last chapter, on "The Public Purse," works through the conservative turn against cuts to entitlement programs like Medicare and Social Security and the prospects for moving beyond a "starve the beast" strategy of tax cutting that has succeeded only in driving the nation further into debt.

Taken as a whole, this collection of more than thirty essays from more than a dozen scholars and policymakers represents where the cutting-edge of conservative thinking is right now, where the center of gravity in the conservative movement will be in the coming decades, and the only plausible foundation in modern American politics on which to build a durable governing majority.

Oren Cass
Lenox, Massachusetts
January 2025

Prologue

An important point of departure for the new conservative thinking is a turn away from a single-minded focus on maximizing consumption, which has traditionally been the focus of economists and policymakers. People are workers as well as consumers, and their own health, the health of their families and communities, and ultimately the security and the prosperity of the nation depend as much on what they contribute through their production as on what they enjoy in consumption. That shift in perspective has enormous consequences for how we understand what has happened in America in recent decades and for what responses we might consider.

The case for this renewed focus on production was the central argument of *The Once and Future Worker*, the book I published in 2018 while a senior fellow at the Manhattan Institute for Policy Research. The key lines of argument and their implications are woven together in this adaptation from the book's first part, which foreshadows the approach that American Compass would go on to advance.

THE WORKING HYPOTHESIS

by Oren Cass

Adapted from *The Once and Future Worker* (Encounter Books, 2018); a version of this adaptation appeared in the *American Interest* on October 15, 2018.

Since the middle of the past century, our political economy has relied upon the insidious metaphor of the "economic pie," which measures success by the amount of gross domestic product (GDP) available to every American for consumption. When serving a pie, each portion's size depends on both the size of the dish and the share allocated to each slice. Likewise, the thinking goes, each person's consumption depends on the size of the overall economy and the share he receives. Fighting over shares is a zero-sum game, but if we concentrate on baking an ever-larger pie, then everyone's slice can grow. If some slices are too small, pie can be redistributed among the plates. And who doesn't like pie?

The phrase *economic pie* first appeared in the presidential lexicon in 1952, when Harry Truman quoted from a *Business Week* article that used the term. John F. Kennedy used it when addressing the U.S. Chamber of Commerce. Presidents Lyndon Johnson, Gerald Ford, Ronald Reagan, George H. W. Bush, Bill Clinton, and Barack Obama used it, too. The media and think tanks across the political spectrum bandy it about with ease.

On its own terms, this "economic piety" has delivered. The overall economy has grown enormously: From 1975 to 2015, the nation's GDP increased threefold. Redistribution has widened the smaller slices: During the same period, spending on programs targeting lower-income households increased fourfold. For Americans of all socioeconomic strata, material living standards, access to technology, and consumer variety all marched steadily higher.

But the things America thought she wanted have not made her happy. Her troubles are by now well known: decades of stagnant wages, a labor-force exodus, too many unstable families, and crumbling communities. Years before the financial crisis that sparked the Great Recession, a majority of Americans began telling Gallup that they are, "in general, dissatisfied with the way things are going in the United States at this time."

Understandably embarrassed by these results, many economists and policymakers now point the finger for these troubles at phenomena like "automation." But that is no explanation. Technological innovation and automation have always been integral to our economic progress, and in a well-functioning labor market they should produce gains for all types of workers. The economic data these days all point to declining productivity growth, suggesting that progress is "destroying jobs" more slowly than ever.

Another defense holds that conditions are much better than the data indicate or people perceive. Incomes look better or worse, depending on the measure of inflation. Poverty levels look higher or lower, depending on the accounting for government benefits—for instance, Harvard professor Steven Pinker highlights our progress lifting people above the "consumption poverty line." And so many people have iPhones! Such observations aren't persuasive, though, because neither readjusted data nor celebration of gadgetry does anything to improve the reality of deteriorating individual, family, and community health. Claims that overall growth is robust and wages not so bad don't remedy ongoing social collapse, reverse workforce abandonment, or lessen government dependence—they only underscore the disconnect between conventional economic measures and the quality of life for which those measures are supposed to provide proxies. If policy analysts ask, "Who are you going to believe, me or your lyin' eyes?" Americans will—rightly—choose the latter.

IN MAKING GDP growth and rising consumption the central objectives of public policy, economic piety represents a truncated and ultimately self-undermining concept of prosperity. Workers have no standing in this view of the economy; neither do their families or communities. Households that see their economic prospects plummet or their livelihoods vanish should ask for a government check and be placated when they get one. Towns that can no longer sustain themselves become places that people should just leave. Politicians will pay lip service to the importance of education and retraining, but they will not hold themselves accountable for such programs actually working. The economic pie's expansion, regardless of what or who gets left behind, is the goal; maintaining a healthy, inclusive society is a hoped-for by-product, not an end in itself.

Economic piety acknowledges the existence of economic losers but holds that any losses are exceeded by gains to winners, which means that with careful redistribution, everyone can emerge ahead. *But what if people's ability to produce matters more than how much they can consume?* That ability cannot be redistributed. And what if smaller losses for those at the bottom of the economic ladder are much more consequential to them than the larger gains for those already on top? Under those conditions, rising GDP will not necessarily translate into rising prosperity.

Such considerations have deep implications for society's longer-term trajectory. Even if gains exceed the costs initially, what happens if the losses undermine stable families, decimate entire communities, foster government dependence, and contribute to skyrocketing substance abuse and suicide rates? What if the next generation, raised in this environment, suffers as well—perhaps reaching adulthood with even lower productive capacity? What if, in the meantime, cheap capital from foreign savings has fueled enormous increases in government and consumer debt, while the industrial policies of foreign governments have left the American economy with fewer opportunities to create well-paying jobs for less-skilled workers? Such costs show up nowhere in GDP—at least initially. Sadly, they appear to have been much more than hypothetical and have proved much costlier than anyone imagined.

The explanation for why economic piety steered the nation off course, and the road map to recovery, are encapsulated in what I call the Working Hypothesis: *that a labor market in which workers can support strong families and communities is the central determinant of long-term prosperity and should be the central focus of public policy.*

Alongside stable political institutions that protect basic freedoms, family and community provide the social structures necessary to a thriving society and a growing economy. Those institutions in turn rely on a foundation of productive work through which people find purpose and satisfaction in providing for themselves and helping others. The durable growth that produces long-term prosperity is the emergent property of a virtuous cycle in which people who are able to support their families and communities improve their own productivity and raise a subsequent generation able to accomplish even more. Conversely, without access to work that can support them, families struggle to remain intact or to form in the first place, and communities cannot help but dissolve; without stable families and communities, economic opportunity vanishes.

Economic growth and rising material living standards are laudable goals, but they by no means guarantee the health of a labor market that will meet society's long-term needs. If we pursue growth in ways that erode the labor market's health, and then redistribute income from the winners to the losers, we can produce impressive-looking economic statistics—for a while. But we will not generate the genuine and sustainable prosperity we want. Growth that consumes its own prerequisites leads inevitably to stagnation.

This shift in perspective from consumer to producer conjures a vision of two constituencies vying for the same resources, but here the dynamic is more complex. Every individual is both a producer and a consumer, the economy an engine of both production and consumption. An emphasis on the consumption lens has long been a tenet of classical liberalism: "Consumption is the sole end and purpose of all production; and the interest of the producer ought to be attended to, only so far as it may be necessary for promoting that of the consumer," wrote Adam Smith in *The Wealth of Nations*. Superficially, at least, consumption seems a sensible focus.

But only through production does the ability to consume exist. Production without consumption creates options; consumption without production creates dependence and debt. Most of the activities and achievements that give life purpose and meaning are, whether in the economic sphere or not, fundamentally acts of production. Yes, material living standards contribute to prosperity, but accomplishments like fulfilling traditional obligations, building strong personal relationships, succeeding at work, supporting a family, and raising children capable of doing all these things themselves are far more important to life satisfaction. What these things have in common is their productive nature not as boosts to GDP but as ways that people invest effort on behalf of others. Our social norms recognize productive activities as essential to a functioning and prosperous society, and so we award respect, dignity, and gratitude to those who perform them.

Without work—the quintessential productive activity—self-esteem declines and a sense of helplessness increases; people become depressed.

Where fewer men work, fewer marriages form. Unemployment also doubles the risk of divorce, and male joblessness appears the primary culprit. These outcomes likely result from the damage to both economic prospects and individual well-being associated with being out of work, which strain existing marriages and make men less attractive as marriage partners.

Work is both a nexus of community and a prerequisite for it. Work relationships represent a crucial source of social capital, establishing a base from which people can engage in the broader community. Communities that lack work, by contrast, suffer maladies that degrade social capital and lead to persistent poverty. Crime and addiction increase, their participants in turn becoming ever less employable; investments in housing and communal assets decline; a downward spiral is set in motion.

The role of family and community in transmitting opportunity to the next generation also depends on work. When parents lose their jobs, their children tend to do worse in school, graduate at lower rates, and have less success as adults. Part of productive activity's worth derives from the dignity and respect that society confers on self-reliance and productive contributions. In a community where dependency is widespread, illegality a viable career path, and idleness an acceptable lifestyle, the full-time worker begins to look less admirable—and more like a chump.

Regrettably, neither of the two major political parties has genuinely concerned itself with work for decades. Politicians on all sides talk incessantly about "good jobs," but the policies they pursue speak louder. What a coincidence that cutting taxes and shrinking government, expanding health care entitlements and fighting climate change, all were supposedly jobs programs as well!

The economic landscape is pocked with the resulting craters. Starting in the 1960s and 1970s, payroll taxes and workplace rules directly and substantially raised the cost of employing lower-wage workers. Aggressive environmental regulation reduced investment in industrial activity and thus the demand for workers whose advantage lay in relatively more physical work, while the education system's obsession with college for all left many students ill-prepared to join the labor force. A system of organized labor that once helped broaden prosperity began instead to hoard it for a dwindling membership, at everyone else's expense. Our immigration system increased the supply of low-wage workers available to employers by millions, while free trade increased the supply by billions—to the advantage of those seeking to use such labor, but not those seeking to provide it. All the while, an ever-expanding safety net provided more benefits to a rising share of the population, reducing work's economic and social value.

LOOKING AHEAD, FORECASTS depict coming economic transformations similar in scale and pace to those of the past. Yes, the latest in artificial intelligence and robotics looks impressive. So did electricity, the assembly line, the computer, the robot, and the internet. Headline-grabbing studies that predict doomsday make ludicrous leaps like suggesting that school bus drivers, fashion models, and real estate agents will all disappear. Conversely, careful studies of how forthcoming technologies will interact with humans indicate that opportunities to replace workers are quite rare, while the typical effect will be to augment their capabilities. As many firms are already discovering, a key limitation on the rate of technology adoption is the ability of workers to use it. Robots can be workers' best friends, if employers find it in their interest to foster the relationship.

What really underlies pessimism about the American worker's future is the assumption that we cannot possibly make concessions on any of our other priorities. True enough, if the preferences of the typical urban professional are always the most valid and important, if the maximization of economic efficiency and material consumption is inviolable, if businesses retain the incentive to find the cheapest possible workers anywhere in the world, then the future of the American labor market indeed looks grim. But all this merely begs the question of what our priorities should be. In the past, our society was much less affluent, and yet the typical worker could support a family. How could it be that, as we have grown wealthier as a society, we have lost the ability to make that kind of arrangement work? Or do we just not really want to?

If work is foundational to our society, then we have a duty to make the changes and trade-offs necessary to support it. If we give workers standing, if we make their productive employment an economic imperative instead of an inconvenience, the labor market can reach a healthy equilibrium. At the very least, we should not dismiss as impossible the renewal of work and family, sustained by a healthy labor market, before we even try. Nor can we dismiss it as too expensive, unless we know the alternative's real cost. Departing from the market's default outcome will always appear expensive if the "efficient" default is defined as the overriding social goal. But if some other outcome is better for society, then the efficient outcome is actually the more expensive one.

Neither economic growth nor economic redistribution will rescue America from its current predicament. If the Working Hypothesis is correct, then we will need to create the social and economic conditions for a robust labor market in which all able Americans can be contributors, achieve self-sufficiency, and support strong families and communities.

A genuine commitment to that kind of inclusive society requires a willingness to shape institutions to that end, even when doing so is for the benefit of others or when it creates tension with other values. Such concessions are of a different character from the taxes and spending that are often confused for compassion in American politics. "Don't tell me what you value," former president Joe Biden liked to say. "Show me your budget and I'll tell you what you value." But taxes are easy, and deficit spending is even easier, compared with reordering social priorities—reconsidering whether to tolerate more pollutants in the air we breathe, determining whose children our schools are oriented toward, deciding what constraints our national borders should impose, and, ultimately, defining what we expect of and owe to one another.

The people needing to accept a departure from some of their preferences if labor market health is to be society's priority are, generally speaking, the highly skilled, college-educated "winners" of the modern economy, who command the nation's economic, political, and social heights. Perhaps it should be no surprise, then, that such an agenda has received little attention from anywhere on the conventional political spectrum.

Rather than acknowledge the need to change course, many people pleased with the status quo have concluded that typical voters must be either too stupid to recognize how good they have it or else too closed-minded to put aside their provincial fears and embrace the wonderful modern world that has been created for them, without anyone having asked them about the particulars. Others took the dissatisfaction more seriously but attributed it to inadequate implementation of existing approaches.

One prevalent narrative emphasized "globalization" as both the catalyst for disruption and the axis of political realignment. "The new divide in rich countries is not between left and right," asserted *The Economist*, "but between open and closed.... Welcome immigrants or keep them out? Open up to foreign trade or protect domestic industries? Embrace cultural change or resist it?" *Washington Post* columnist Fareed Zakaria, among others, endorsed the same open-versus-closed framing, lauding former British prime minister Tony Blair's "remarkably prescient" view to this effect.

As their framing makes clear, those purveying the open/closed dichotomy regard only one of its sides as valid. They elevate the free flow of goods and people as the nonnegotiable underpinning of both economic and social progress. Anyone with other priorities is condemned to the closed camp—closed-minded, even racist.

Yet how does the open agenda, which has already characterized the past generation of American policy, address the critical challenges facing the nation? It does not. Rather, the standard response is that this openness must be paired with a renewed commitment to helping those left behind, as if only a lack of focus and resources has prevented government programs from transforming people's prospects. Invariably, the suggested solution is education. Zakaria calls his approach "open and armed," because it requires "a far more ambitious set of government programs" to equip Americans with "a bristling armory of tools and training."

The vision is supposed to be an inspiring one, in which people are lifted upward to greater opportunity. Its real implications are less exalted: If the economy no longer works for the average worker, it is he who needs to transform into something it likes better. If government programs could change human capabilities to match whatever the market might compensate highly, public policy would become rather easy. But the insufficiency of this approach as a response to the nation's challenges recalls the joke about the economist's solution to finding himself shipwrecked among boxes of canned goods: "First, assume a can opener."

Without education as a *deus ex machina*, a commitment to openness turns out to mean little more than merging together and doubling down on existing programs of growth and redistribution, offering a veritable buffet of warmed-over policies—all served with a heaping side of self-righteousness. "I'm for globalization and a strong safety net" seems likely to become for the next generation of insulated but determinedly respectable professionals what "I'm socially liberal and fiscally conservative" was for the last.

So they have sought approaches in which "everybody wins." This is precisely the premise of economic piety and especially of the "open" agenda—characterized by the priority given to globalization and GDP growth above all other policy goals; the hope that intensive training and education can transform those left behind into those getting ahead; and the backstop of economic redistribution, or even a basic income, if all else fails. That so many Americans feel left behind by this agenda, even as it allows their consumption to rise, is a source of honest confusion.

The irony is that openers are themselves making just the kinds of choices that they struggle to recognize when made by others. They are happy to accept higher taxes and advocate for expansive government programs if it buys peace and quiet. But they will not contemplate any deviation from the borderless, green, multicultural, college-educated, individualistic, consumption-oriented society they prefer. They regard their willingness to part with money (and thus consumption) to preserve their way of life as benevolent. Yet when the targets of their largesse display a comparable hierarchy of priorities, the openers assume the explanation to be ignorance, or worse.

A useful question for programs of reform in today's America is whether the reformer has proposed any concessions whatsoever on behalf of the average American worker. If the only thing on offer is tax dollars, the program is not a serious one. If the path forward is for the workers to change themselves to fit better into the reformer's preferred society, the program is not a serious one. We now have decades upon decades of overwhelming evidence that neither outright redistribution nor investments in education provide the help promised—to the contrary, massive influxes of resources toward both have coincided precisely with the economic and social declines that have brought the nation to its present predicament.

Happily, many, perhaps most, prospering Americans really do care about the fate of their fellow citizens and the quality of their society and are prepared to make sacrifices on behalf of others. For them, the time has come to grapple with the real trade-offs that money can no longer obscure.

Introduction

THIS IS WHAT ELITE FAILURE LOOKS LIKE

by Oren Cass

First published in the *New York Times* on July 6, 2024.

I first learned about the opioid crisis three presidential elections ago, in the fall of 2011. I was the domestic policy director for Mitt Romney's campaign and questions began trickling in from the New Hampshire team: *What's our plan?*

By then, opioids had been fueling the deadliest drug epidemic in American history for years. I am ashamed to say I did not know what they were. Opioids, as in opium? I looked it up online. Pills of some kind. *Tell them it's a priority, and President Obama isn't working.* That year saw nearly 23,000 deaths from opioid overdoses nationwide.

I was no outlier. America's political class was in the final stages of self-righteous detachment from the economic and social conditions of the nation it ruled. The infamous bitter clinger and "47 percent" comments by Mr. Obama and Mr. Romney captured the atmosphere well: delivered at private fund-raisers in San Francisco in 2008 and Boca Raton in 2012, evincing disdain for the voters who lived in between. The opioid crisis gained more attention in the years after the election, particularly in 2015, with Anne Case and Angus Deaton's research on deaths of despair.

Of course, 2015's most notable political development was Donald Trump's presidential campaign launch and subsequent steamrolling of 16 Republican primary opponents committed to party orthodoxy. In the

2016 general election he narrowly defeated the former first lady, senator, and secretary of state Hillary Clinton, who didn't need her own views of Americans leaked: In public remarks, she gleefully classified half of the voters who supported Mr. Trump as "deplorables," as her audience laughed and applauded. That year saw more than 42,000 deaths from opioid overdoses.

In a democratic republic such as the United States, where the people elect leaders to govern on their behalf, the ballot box is the primary check on an unresponsive, incompetent, or corrupt ruling class—or, as Democrats may be learning, a ruling class that insists on a candidate who voters no longer believe can lead. If those in power come to believe they are the only logical options, the people can always prove them wrong. For a frustrated populace, an anti-establishment outsider's ability to wreak havoc is a feature rather than a bug. The elevation of such a candidate to high office should provoke immediate soul-searching and radical reform among the highly credentialed leaders across government, law, media, business, academia, and so on——collectively, the elites.

The response to Mr. Trump's success, unfortunately, has been the opposite. Seeing him elected once, faced with the reality that he may well win again, most elites have doubled down. We have not failed, the thinking goes; we have been failed, by the American people. In some tellings, grievance-filled Americans simply do not appreciate their prosperity. In others they are incapable of informed judgments, leaving them susceptible to demagoguery and foreign manipulation. Or perhaps they are just too racist to care—never mind that polling consistently suggests that most of Mr. Trump's supporters are women and minorities, or that polling shows he is attracting far greater Black and Hispanic support than prior Republican leaders.

Mr. Trump is by no means an ideal tribune of the popular will, especially considering his own efforts to defy it after the 2020 presidential election. But the nation, given full opportunity to assess that conduct, seems to have decided it likes him more than ever, at least compared with the alternatives on offer. Somehow the response of elites to that humiliating indictment of their leadership is a redoubled obstinance: Democracy itself is at stake if the election does not go their way, they lecture, even as they pursue plainly anti-democratic strategies. How's that going?

One mid-2024 poll of swing-state voters found that most see "threats to democracy" as an extremely important issue in the coming election, and that they are more likely to believe Mr. Trump can handle the issue well.

The result is a shockingly irresponsible national game of chicken. Barreling from one side are elites who remain fully committed to their own preferences, to pulling the levers of power for their own benefit and to offering candidates in both parties who would preserve the status quo. Barreling from the other are ordinary people, the majority of Americans, who reject elite preferences but feel unable to assert others, except through the last resort that democracy affords them. Both sides are honking as loudly as they can.

The people do not pull to the side, nor should they. "The administration of the government, like the office of a trustee, must be conducted for the benefit of those entrusted to one's care, not of those to whom it is entrusted," observed Cicero more than 2,000 years ago. Anyone worried about the future of American democracy should be concerned foremost with the elites' bizarre belief that the road is theirs. This is the root cause of present instability and poses the most serious long-term threat to the Republic.

The U.S. Constitution is designed to bend without breaking regardless of any one election's outcome. It has done so before and it will do so again. In words widely attributed to James Madison, "dependence on the people is no doubt the primary control on the government; but experience has taught mankind the necessity of auxiliary precautions." Thus the separation of powers, the checks and balances, the countervailing state and federal power. But no system can save a nation from a ruling class so unresponsive that it would choose to accelerate toward political collapse.

TAKING THE MAJORITY'S preferences seriously, even when they conflict with the preferences of more sophisticated experts, is often disparaged as populism. But while elected officials and their technocratic advisers may have special insight into how the people's goals are best achieved, only the people can determine what those goals should be and whether they are being met.

Opioid deaths are more than a terrible tragedy. They are also a telltale sign of national decay and desperation. Wages for the typical worker have stagnated for decades, and research I conducted at American Compass has found that the typical worker no longer earns enough to provide middle-class security for a family.

We also found that only around one in five young Americans makes the transition smoothly from high school to college to career, and for young men the figure is lower still. The anti-poverty scholar Scott Winship has shown that for men ages 25 to 29, inflation-adjusted median earnings and compensation were lower in 2020 than they were 50 years earlier. The years leading up to Mr. Trump's election coincided with the first time on record that Americans ages 18 to 34 were more likely to be living at home with their parents than independently with a significant other.

Measured in flat-screen televisions owned, health-care treatments received, and calories consumed, Americans have been on an upward trajectory. But while popular media often translates the American dream as being better off than your parents in materialistic terms, polling conducted by American Compass in partnership with YouGov indicates that Americans between 18 and 50 were more than twice as likely to say "earning enough to support a family" is what's most important. Related, our polling has found that the vast majority of American parents consider "being able to support your family on one parent's income" to be an important or essential marker of middle-class life. For all the talk of "upward mobility," more than 90 percent of Americans chose "financial stability" as more important in a 2014 Pew survey.

Note the contrast with the small cohort of upper-class Americans with college degrees and the highest incomes, who see the American dream more in terms of going as far as their talents and hard work take them than as either supporting a family or even getting married and raising children. They prefer having both parents work full-time and using paid child care full-time, and regard the chance for their children to pursue postsecondary education that would offer "the best possible career options but was far from home" as more desirable than one that would offer "good career options close to home." All other groups said they preferred the latter.

The same pattern repeats itself on issue after issue. While policy initiatives so often seek to maximize efficiency and growth, move people to opportunity, and redistribute from the economy's winners to the losers, the typical American has an attachment to place, a focus on family, a commitment to making things, and would accept economic trade-offs in pursuit of those priorities.

Public education devotes disproportionate resources to getting students into and through college as compared to the other pathways most ultimately take. But an American Compass survey found that American parents say nearly three to one that the more important task should be to "help students develop the skills and values needed to build decent lives in the communities where they live," compared with helping students "maximize their academic potential and pursue admission to colleges and universities with the best possible reputations." Most would prefer to have their children offered three-year apprenticeships that lead to good jobs over full college scholarships.

Adam Posen, president of the Peterson Institute for International Economics, remarked in 2022 that concern for American manufacturing reflects "the fetish for keeping white males of low education outside the cities in the powerful positions" he believes they have occupied in America. But to most people, it's just common sense that making things matters.

Another American Compass poll found that Americans agree by 10 to one that "we need a stronger manufacturing sector," most often because it "is important to a healthy, growing, innovative economy." Asked to choose, most say they would much rather pay higher prices to strengthen domestic manufacturing than to combat climate change. Only the upper class was evenly split on this question. Is America a "nation of immigrants"? Perhaps. But while most Americans believe that immigration is a good thing for the country, at no time on record have more than around one-third wanted to increase immigration levels; support for decreasing the level is almost always much stronger.

The important feature of all these preferences is that they are inherently valid. No set of facts or statistical analyses, to which an expert might have superior access, overrides what people actually value and what trade-offs they would choose to make. Leaders might seek to shape public opinion and alter preferences—indeed, that is part of leading—but they must yield to the outcome. Their obligation is to pursue the community's priorities, not their own.

THE DEMOCRATIC PARTY celebrates worker power but has little appetite for enforcing immigration law, let alone reducing the legal level of low-skill immigration. Its education policy strives to pay off the debts of the college-educated while leaving the broken system that created the debts largely untouched and the majority who do not earn college degrees underserved. President Biden's agenda features welcome emphasis on domestic manufacturing, but with a counterproductive and distinctly elite approach to a green transition.

Climate change is a problem worth fighting, but many Americans have been rightly doubtful that the enormous cost of economic transformation is worth the benefits these programs promise. The existing energy sector provides productive blue-collar jobs and a source of inexpensive power. A coherent industrial policy would double down on those advantages; investing hundreds of billions of dollars to jeopardize them may satisfy climate activists, but the trade-off is a poor one for workers and their communities.

As for the Republican establishment: During the Trump administration, a G.O.P.-controlled Congress made its one major accomplishment a tax cut. Wall Street remains mostly off-limits to criticism, let alone constraint. Representative Patrick McHenry, as chairman of the House Financial Services Committee, obstructed efforts to restrict U.S. investment in China and, in fact, argued for expanding it. Former Vice President Mike Pence's organization Advancing American Freedom says that making more working-class families eligible to receive the full child tax credit would transform it "into another welfare program." The party's anti-Trump faction spent eight years plotting its return to power only to rally behind Nikki Haley, the quintessential vessel for the anti-government, pro-globalization ideology already rejected by the party's voters.

The promise—and necessity—of the more populist mode of economic policy gaining momentum in the United States is that it chooses differently on all these fronts. Mr. Trump himself represents that movement imperfectly, and most often just by rejecting the old regime. Like an earthquake triggered by the shifting tectonic plates of American politics, he disrupted a great deal. And in shaking existing structures to their foundations, he exposed and collapsed those that were outdated or poorly constructed. But his manner is not that of a rebuilder.

Look toward the horizon, though, to the next generation of conservatives poised to lead the post-Trump Republican Party, and the signs of a possible sea change are visible. A cadre of young senators, led by Marco Rubio, JD Vance, Josh Hawley, and Tom Cotton, have released a flood of proposals in the past few years for reshaping global trade and confronting China, rebuilding domestic manufacturing, removing environmental constraints on industrial development, enforcing immigration law and reducing the flow of low-wage workers into the country, discouraging mergers and taxing stock buybacks more aggressively, shifting resources from higher education to noncollege pathways, providing financial support directly to working families instead of through child-care subsidies, and so on. (My organization has worked with all four lawmakers on a variety of proposals.) They have done things like join picket lines with striking workers, push to increase the minimum wage, and demand stronger regulation of railroads. Not coincidentally, Mr. Rubio, Mr. Vance, and Mr. Cotton all received attention as potential running mates for Mr. Trump.

They have areas of agreement with Democrats that present enormous opportunities for progress—and have already yielded some bipartisan legislation—but the conservative reformers' positions on immigration, climate, education, and family policies signal a different set of priorities. They also pair this economic agenda with an unapologetic patriotism and more traditional views on hot-button issues such as policing, racial preferences, and transgender athletes.

Two threads run through this more populist, conservative economics, and they offer the best hope of rebuilding a capitalism that first and foremost serves the prosperity, liberty, and security of the American people. The first thread is creating productive markets, which starts with an acknowledgment that many are anything but. The key to capitalism, as Adam Smith observed with his metaphor of the invisible hand, is that private actors pursuing their own self-interest can behave in ways that advance the public interest as well. But this holds true only if the activities that yield the greatest profit are also ones that yield broad benefits. Smith was quite explicit: For the invisible hand to work, the capitalist must prefer "the support of domestic to that of foreign industry" and "direct that industry in such a manner as its produce may be of the greatest value," which would also "give revenue and employment to the greatest number of people of his own country."

Those are substantial constraints, which modern economists managed to miss. When larger, easier profits can be achieved by offshoring production to countries that exploit workers or bringing foreign workers who will accept lower wages into the country, corporations will do just that. When the highest compensation goes to Wall Street speculators and the developers of addictive social-media algorithms, the most promising business leaders will pursue those careers. What share of Ivy League graduates bring their talents to vocations that will improve the productivity, and with it the earning potential, of anyone without a college degree, or create booming new businesses in struggling regions? It should be no surprise that the productivity growth necessary for rising wages has slowed and, in manufacturing, turned negative, that the longtime pattern in American economic development of poorer areas catching up with richer ones no longer holds.

The tragedy, but also the good news, is that these trends are not inevitable. They represent foolish policy choices, which means we can choose differently. Instead of the globalization that cast aside workers like unsold inventory and hollowed out communities, we can structure our trade and industrial policies to ensure the path to profit runs through domestic investment that creates productive jobs throughout the country. Instead of allowing migrants to enter the country illegally and employers to exploit them, we can enforce our laws rigorously and further restrict entry into the labor market's low end, forcing employers to offer good, highly productive jobs to American workers instead of undercutting them.

In the financial sector, deregulation, tax and bankruptcy laws, international agreements, and the mismanagement of public pensions have all encouraged the smart money and top talent to gravitate toward manipulating and trading piles of assets rather than building anything. Capital markets that once served to deploy the nation's accumulated wealth broadly now extract value from enterprises and communities to reaccumulate it in narrow enclaves. The financial sector keeps growing, salaries and profits keep rising, and yet my research has shown that actual investment has been weakening. This is not the capitalism that any coherent economics would celebrate. Some leaders on the right have now joined those on the left in arguing that its excesses must be discouraged, regulated, taxed, and perhaps banned.

The second thread that runs through this new conservative economics is supporting communities. People rely on the institutions around them, beginning with their families, to form them as productive citizens, to help them build decent lives and to prepare them to raise children of their own. But it is the Americans most in need of supportive communities who are often least likely to have them. The elite conception of support for families tends to be paid leave and child-care subsidies that push toward the career-optimizing and G.D.P.-maximizing arrangement of all parents in the work force. Proper family policy, as a range of Republicans have now proposed, would provide funds directly to working families to help with the cost of raising children and let them arrange their lives as they themselves prefer. Public education, likewise, would focus less on filling the high-school-to-college-to-career pipeline that benefits so few and more on improving the range of pathways that most people travel.

Another key institution is the labor union. Organized labor can be a vital force for giving workers power in the labor market, representation on the job, and support in the community. Unfortunately, in the United States, the labor movement now often operates as a force for progressive political activism unrelated to the priorities of most workers, which may help explain why nearly three-quarters of potential union members say they would prefer a worker organization that focused only on workplace issues to one that is also engaged in national politics. Some conservatives are making progress by working directly with less partisan unions and proposing alternative forms of representation that might put worker representatives on corporate boards or encourage industrywide bargaining rather than company-by-company fights.

In 2023, the United States saw 81,000 deaths from opioid overdose. Other forms of drug overdose are climbing faster: Fatal cocaine overdoses rose sixfold in the past decade, to 30,000. Psychostimulant deaths rose tenfold, to 36,000. All told, the rate of drug overdose deaths in the United States is now similar to the average death rate from alcohol use disorders in Russia during the decade after the Soviet Union's collapse.

Are American elites capable of seeing beyond their own preferences? Can they admit that what they value is not what's best for everyone—shoddily constructed rationales notwithstanding? Their moment of decision—the oncoming car—feels like it is fast approaching. The off-ramp is available, but only they can decide to take it.

PART ONE

PRINCIPLES

CHAPTER ONE

The Market

The breakdown in American capitalism over the past half-century is most apparent in its failure to deliver widespread prosperity for the American people. Success requires more than just rising material living standards: For citizens to flourish, they must have access to good jobs that pay family-supporting wages. For the nation to flourish, its growth and opportunities must be broadly shared. Capitalism is unique in its ability to achieve these results, but no principle of economics guarantees that it will.

Conservatives rightly champion the market economy's unparalleled capacity for innovation and growth. But in recent decades, right-of-center economic thinking devolved into a market fundamentalism that takes "economic freedom" as the end unto itself and considers any public policy aimed at shaping market outcomes to be inherently destructive. This view is the antithesis of conservatism, which recognizes that markets are institutions embedded in societies, that their effectiveness depends upon the cultural context and policy framework within which they operate, and that their value lies in their ability to advance the common good. Preserving our free enterprise system requires acknowledgment of its shortcomings and a commitment to strengthening the supports and constraints necessary to its success.

The first essay in this chapter, "A New Conservatism," was my initial attempt in early 2021 to place the new conservative thinking in the broader conservative tradition. Where had the right-of-center gone wrong in its thinking about markets and capitalism, and how could a better understanding of conservative principles and economics help to correct course? The second essay, "What Happened to Capitalism?," is the foreword to American Compass's acclaimed *Rebuilding American Capitalism* handbook, published in the summer of 2023.

Here is the fully developed corrective to market fundamentalism's misunderstanding of capitalism, starting from a proper reading of Adam Smith's famous "invisible hand."

A NEW CONSERVATISM

by Oren Cass

Adapted by permission of *Foreign Affairs*, March/April 2021. Copyright 2021 by the Council on Foreign Relations, Inc. www.ForeignAffairs.com. First published under the title, "A New Conservatism: Freeing the Right from Free-Market Orthodoxy."

The descent into dogmatism is a time-honored tradition in American politics. What makes conservatism's present bout peculiar, however, is its lack of any discernible conservatism. The coalition of economic libertarians, social conservatives, and foreign policy hawks that kicked off the Reagan revolution, vanquished stagflation, and won the Cold War is rightfully proud of its accomplishments. But that bargain—whereby each camp took charge of its own portfolio—left wide swaths of public policy in the hands of a small clique of market fundamentalists. They shared few values or intuitions with conservatives, who were themselves consigned to talking about "social issues." As conservative economic thinking atrophied, libertarian ideas ossified into the market fundamentalism that most commentators today casually call "conservative." The result has been a political crisis, for conservatism especially and for American government broadly. A right-of-center that is neither conservative nor responsive to people's problems is incapable of playing its vital role as the outlet for a nation's conservative impulses and the counterweight to its progressive ones. Nor will it win many elections.

Now is the moment for conservatives to reassert their claim to the right-of-center. In the United States and in the rest of the world, serious problems created in part by the absence of a robust conservatism require conservative solutions. Progressivism, meanwhile, is increasingly obsessed with identity politics and the bugbears of its overeducated elite. That makes it uniquely vulnerable to competition from an ideological message focused on the worries shared by most Americans, regardless of their race or religion, about the foundations of their families and communities. In politics, the odds usually favor incumbents, but the establishment that is flying conservatism's banner has lost its vitality and now hunkers down behind crumbling walls, reciting stale pieties that few still believe. The circumstances today suggest that a realignment around a multiethnic, working-class conservatism might just have a chance.

ESTABLISHMENT THINKING

The hallmark of conservativism is not, as is often thought, opposition to change or the desire for a return to some earlier time. The misconception that conservatives lack substantive preferences and merely reflect their environments leads to some confusing conclusions—for example, that the conservative of 1750 would oppose American independence but the conservative of 1800 would support it, or that today's conservative must favor rapid globalization and deregulated financial markets because that has been the recent tradition. What in fact distinguishes conservatives is their attention to the role that institutions and norms play in people's lives and in the process of governing. "When the foundations of society are threatened," wrote the political theorist Samuel Huntington, "the conservative ideology reminds men of the necessity of some institutions and the desirability of the existing ones."

Edmund Burke, the father of modern conservatism, provided a quintessential illustration of this dynamic. Although he was a member of the British House of Commons, Burke supported the American Revolution in 1776 on the grounds that the United Kingdom, through its overbearing administration and arbitrary taxation, had irrevocably breached its relationship with the Colonies. He thought the Americans could better continue in their tradition of self-government if they freed themselves from King George III's rule. Yet a decade later, Burke reacted with horror to the French Revolution, in which he saw a radical mob tearing away the guardrails and buttresses on which society depended. In both assessments, of course, he was proved entirely correct: the United States became a flourishing democracy, and France descended into chaos.

Burke was at once a "preserver of venerated traditions" and "a reformer of failing institutions," the conservative scholar Yuval Levin has written. As Burke himself put it, "a disposition to preserve, and an ability to improve, taken together, would be my standard of a statesman." This same disposition is easily identifiable in conservatives today. The psychologist Jonathan Haidt, who has spent years testing the foundations of people's moral reasoning, has found that conservatives tend to exhibit a much broader range of moral concerns, giving fairly equal weight to care, liberty, fairness, loyalty, authority, and sanctity. "They believe that people need external structures or constraints in order to behave well, cooperate, and thrive," Haidt has written. "These external constraints include laws, institutions, customs, traditions, nations, and religions." Liberals, by contrast, overwhelmingly prioritize care, particularly care for victims of oppression. Libertarians, for their part, are obsessed with liberty to the exclusion of other values.

As a result, conservatism, more so than other ideologies, sees progress as a process of accumulation rather than disruption, recognizing what is good in society and striving to build on it. Conservatism approaches the project of governing with particular humility, grateful for whatever order a society's traditions have managed to wrangle from imperfect human nature. The problems it identifies and the solutions it proposes give relatively less weight to guaranteeing individual freedom and choice and more to reinforcing obligations and constraints, relationships and norms, and the mediating institutions that shape and channel people's energies toward productive ends.

Viewed this way, the conservative affinity for markets should seem natural. Markets limit the power of a central government and place it instead in the hands of those best positioned to take care of their own interests. They evolve over time in response to real-world conditions rather than at the whim of a technocrat. They are themselves institutions through which people develop informal codes and formal rules to help themselves cooperate and transact more productively. An alliance with libertarians to promote markets was logical in the second half of the twentieth century, during an era of great-power competition against communism and when the domestic market was choked by an exploding bureaucracy and welfare state, a sclerotic system of organized labor, confiscatory tax rates, and raging inflation.

Critically, however, a conservative skepticism of markets is equally natural. Markets reduce people to their material interests and reduce relationships to transactions. They prioritize efficiency to the exclusion of resilience, sentiment, and tradition. Shorn of constraints, they often reward the most socially corrosive behaviors and can quickly undermine the foundations of a stable community—for instance, pushing families to commit both parents to full-time market labor or strip-mining talent from across the nation and consolidating it in a narrow set of cosmopolitan hubs. For conservatism, then, markets are a valuable mechanism for sustaining and advancing a flourishing society. But they should never be an end unto themselves. And their quality is contingent on the norms and rules by which they function and the vitality of the other institutions operating alongside them.

Libertarians have no time for such nuance, and the purportedly conservative establishment has paid it little heed, either. Senator Pat Toomey, Republican of Pennsylvania, has defined capitalism as "nothing more than economic freedom," a sentiment echoed by Haley, who has warned that any interference with that freedom would head down "the slow path to socialism." Jack Spencer, the vice president of the Heritage Foundation's Institute for Economic Freedom and Opportunity, has suggested, "Why don't we look at a policy and just ask, Does it expand economic freedom?" The conservative columnist Amity Shlaes has gone so far as to declare, "Markets do not fail us. We fail markets."

The right-of-center's preeminent public policy institutions displayed these same blinders in their mission statements—or, rather, mission statement, as they all seemed to share the same one. The conservative think-tank world is dedicated to advancing the principles of "limited government, free enterprise, and individual liberty" (the Competitive Enterprise Institute), or "free markets and limited, effective government" (the R Street Institute), or "free enterprise, limited government, individual freedom" (the Heritage Foundation), or "individual liberty, limited government, free markets" (the Cato Institute), or "economic choice and individual responsibility" (the Manhattan Institute), or "individual, economic, and political freedom; private enterprise; and representative government" (the Hoover Institution). What began as entirely justified advocacy for the benefits of markets has mutated into a fundamentalism that throws bad policy after good, unable to distinguish between what markets can and cannot do and unwilling to acknowledge the harm that they can cause. Fortunately, it comes with an expiration date.

ANATOMY OF A FAILURE

It is telling that right-of-center coalitions across Western democracies have all come under pressure simultaneously. The politics and circumstances of course vary by country, but tremors from the same tectonic shifts that triggered an earthquake in American politics can be felt far and wide. Three major trends seem responsible for the fall of the old orthodoxy, and all point toward the promise of a conservative resurgence.

The first is a changing world. Few observations are more trite than "the world changes," yet analysts cling to outdated economic claims with religious tenacity, as if each insight represents an eternal and universal truth. Perhaps this is because economists, play-acting at science, pretend that their models offer just that. Those models rely on countless unstated assumptions about the world as it happens to be, and they stop working when it becomes something else. Purveyors of the myth that free trade is always good and more is always better are eager to dismiss the havoc wreaked by the introduction of China's aggressive mercantilism into the global market as an outlier or the exception that proves the rule. But economic models and policy recommendations are of little use if they cannot account for a near-peer economy of 1.4 billion people dominated by the state-controlled enterprises of a communist, authoritarian regime.

Another change in the world has been the unmooring of ownership and management from the communities in which firms operate. In *The Theory of Moral Sentiments*, the economist Adam Smith emphasized how societal expectations shape people's incentives. A person's "desire of being what ought to be approved of," he wrote, is "necessary in order to render him anxious to be really fit" for society. Such considerations for the traditional business owner lose their effect if he is replaced by a set of institutional investors or a consortium of private equity funds on another continent deploying capital held in trust by some government for workers' pensions. In his seminal case for the now prevalent doctrine of shareholder primacy, Milton Friedman, a leader of the Chicago school of economics, disregarded Smith's nuanced view of the prerequisites for a well-functioning society and celebrated instead a world in which the desires of owners "generally will be to make as much money as possible." If the character and constraints of capital ownership change, it should not be surprising that outcomes do, too.

The list goes on. Changes in cultural norms and expectations—"what ought to be approved of," in Smith's formulation—should cause policymakers to rethink economic assumptions. Instead, conservatives have developed the habit of saying, "that's a cultural problem" as an excuse to do nothing, for instance, when growing numbers of young men cannot find and hold steady jobs. Growth, investment, and what passes for innovation have become concentrated in a technology sector that defaults toward natural monopoly. Trillion-dollar tax cuts seem not to spur capital spending, and trillion-dollar deficits seem not to raise interest rates. Playbooks published in the 1980s do not contain answers.

The second trend responsible for the failing consensus is overreach. In technocratic fantasies, careful regulators fine-tune their policies, asymptotically approaching the ideal formula for delivering the best outcomes. In practice, politicians and their advisers land on ideas that seem to work and then push them ever further. A reduction in too-high marginal tax rates rarely sates the appetite for tax cuts. Few policymakers go partway on liberalizing the cross-border flow of goods, people, and capital and conclude that the time has come to stop. Likewise, issues that have been deemed undeserving of concern do not receive attention at the first sign of trouble; they remain ignored until they no longer can be. Even as risk built up in the United States's deregulated financial system, nothing was done until after the 2008 meltdown.

Policies will tend to experience diminishing returns that eventually turn negative—until the case for changing direction becomes undeniable.

Even the best thinking contains within it the seeds of its own undoing, with inevitable excesses driving a necessary cycle of failure and reform. The West, now well into a postwar period filled with extraordinary achievements, can double down on the solutions of 40 or 60 years ago only so many times before going bust. Defusing the hypernationalist tensions of the early twentieth century was wise; proceeding to eviscerate solidarity within the nation-state was not. Requiring pollution controls and considering the environmental impacts of new projects made sense in the 1970s; tightening the ratchet afterward until industrial investments faced prohibitive risks and costs did not. Expanding the pipeline of talented students attending college has always been a worthy aspiration; converting high schools into college-prep academies is not.

The third factor undermining the old economic orthodoxy is its failure to update its own rules. An analogy to sports is instructive. The goal of a professional sports league is to entertain paying customers, but the league does not accomplish this by directing how each player moves around the field to create maximum drama. Instead, it establishes rules and trusts that players competing under those rules will yield an entertaining product. The unpredictability of the outcome is key to the spectators' enjoyment. Likewise, the rules that the government establishes for economic actors are designed to facilitate competition that will redound to the benefit of all. And because those actors are free agents working within a system of rules, rather than performers following a script, they can respond creatively to changing conditions. But no framework of rules is perfect. Designed based on how the game is being played at the time, it works well at first. But the athletes and teams evolve their own strategies in ways that the rule-makers could not have anticipated. When competition fails to yield the desired benefits, the leagues modify the rules—pushing back the three-point line in basketball, lowering the pitcher's mound in baseball, or adding the forward pass in football.

The same thing has happened in the U.S. economy, except that the rule-makers haven't kept up. Businesses and investors exploit ever more obscure opportunities for efficiency, and their most successful strategies tend to diverge from those that produce desirable results for the nation.

One such effect is the economy's financialization, which has directed an increasing share of talent, investment, and profits toward firms that excel at speculative transactions rather than productive contributions. Another is the labor market's trend toward workplaces in which many functions are outsourced and many employees are replaced with independent contractors, as firms maximize their flexibility and profit margins by minimizing their attachments and obligations to workers. Surging profitability may signal success for the capitalist, but as Smith recognized in *The Wealth of Nations*, the opposite holds true for capitalism. "The rate of profit does not, like rent and wages, rise with the prosperity, and fall with the declension, of the society," he wrote. "On the contrary, it is naturally low in rich, and high in poor countries, and it is always highest in the countries which are going fastest to ruin."

A NEW APPROACH

These trends are the product not of too much conservative thinking but of too little. American politics, guided by the neoliberal consensus between progressives and libertarians, has focused on a blinkered set of moral concerns and blindly pursued the unquestioned priorities of personal freedom and consumption. No wonder the prevailing consensus struggles to respond to the problems facing society today. Conservatism, however, is well suited to addressing them. Conservatives have an appreciation for the nation-state, the rules and institutions necessary to well-functioning markets, and the strength of the social fabric. That starting point provides a better foundation for addressing great-power competition with China, monopolies in the technology sector, failing communities, and rising inequality than does the libertarian faith in markets or the progressive reliance on redistribution. Whereas progressives and libertarians both exhibit an inclination to reason from abstract principles toward absolute commitments and thus encourage overreach, the conservative begins by looking at real-world conditions. Burke knew this well. "Circumstances ... give in reality to every political principle its distinguishing color and discriminating effect," he wrote. "The circumstances are what render every civil and political scheme beneficial or noxious to mankind." Accepting the rule book's inherent imperfection and striving to update it over time as conditions change—that is the quintessential conservative approach to policymaking.

A conservative economics would recognize the power and value of markets but insist on analyzing them within their human context rather than as abstract engines of efficiency. For instance, it would recognize the pernicious effects that high levels of economic inequality can have on the social fabric, the functioning of markets, and people's well-being, regardless of absolute material living standards. It would give weight to the value of diffuse and widespread investment, not just the value of agglomeration. It would consider the benefits that locally owned establishments bring to their communities, alongside the benefits that hyperefficient conglomerates can deliver. It would recognize the importance of nonmarket labor performed within the household and the community, such as caretaking and volunteering, rather than assuming that the higher monetary incomes in a society of two-earner families must indicate progress.

Conservatives are right to look skeptically at the ability of the government to supplant markets, but they must appreciate both what markets do well and what they will not do on their own and thus embrace the indispensable public role of channeling investment toward long-term national priorities. This was long the American tradition. Indeed, it was a pillar of the "American System" of investment in domestic industry and infrastructure proposed by Alexander Hamilton, championed by Henry Clay, and endorsed by Abraham Lincoln, a plan that helped transform the United States from a colonial backwater into the leading global power. A modern equivalent would sponsor innovation, mandate domestic sourcing in critical supply chains, and discourage the financial speculation that goes by the name "investment" but bears little resemblance to the work of building productive capacity in the real economy.

A conservative coalition built around economic priorities such as these, plus a merely nonradical set of cultural concerns, attracts a broad range of voters. As of about 5:00pm eastern time on Election Day 2024, one could still find pundits opining that the Republican Party would have done better nominating Ambassador Nikki Haley, who would surely have held together the GOP coalition more effectively than Donald Trump, appealed more to women, and so on. *The Dispatch*'s Jonah Goldberg tweeted proudly that he had written in Paul Ryan, the former Speaker of the House best known for a tax cut that added nearly $2 trillion to federal deficits and his subsequent work launching SPACs and promoting cryptocurrency. The future direction of American conservatism seemed likely to face sharp contestation in the coming years.

By midnight, all that was over. Trump was going to win the popular vote, the first time a Republican had done so in twenty years. He was going to win more electoral college votes than any Republican since 1988. And while narrow victories in every single one of the swing states would hand him the presidency, the massive shifts among young and non-white voters and accompanying double-digit gains in urban areas were the story with the longer-term implications. Democratic strongholds appear headed toward swing-state status: Virginia, Minnesota, and New Jersey all had margins below six points. After years of Democrats talking about "turning Texas blue," Republicans are now closer to turning Illinois and New York red.

The path for conservatives to a durable governing majority runs forward from here, toward solidifying and expanding this multiethnic, working-class coalition. Will a serious Old Right candidate even bother running for president on a free-trade, open-borders, anti-worker agenda in 2028? Perhaps. Certainly there will be no shortage of wealthy donors eager to set their money on fire supporting the effort, no shortage of commentators with careers dedicated to market fundamentalism who will cheer along. But as a political matter, such campaigning is dead on arrival. The relevant question for the next several years is how to deliver for the ordinary Americans who swung the 2024 election and create a political movement, message, and agenda capable of building on that success.

WHAT HAPPENED TO CAPITALISM?

by Oren Cass

Adapted from the foreword to *Rebuilding American Capitalism* (American Compass, June 2023).

What has happened to capitalism in America? Businesses still pursue profit, yes, but not in ways that advance the public interest. Over the 50 years from 1972 to 2022, corporate profits rose by 185%. Wages rose by 1%. American industry lost its technological edge, from semiconductors to commercial aerospace to robotics. Investment stalled, so much so that the entire corporate sector became a net *lender*, handing money back to financial markets faster than it tapped those markets for capital to invest. As *American Affairs* editor Julius Krein has observed, if $1 trillion in annual stock buybacks are to be taken at face value and "there are in fact no better investments to be made, . . . it calls into question the viability of the free market capitalist system itself."

Managers are supposed to be accountable to owners, but the latter's identity is no longer discernible. Most shares are held by passive funds, often on behalf of pension plans on behalf of retirees and taxpayers, or else overseas, often in sovereign wealth funds. Comparative advantage is supposed to allow a developed economy like America's to focus on the most advanced technologies, but the U.S. trade balance in advanced technology products has swung from a $60 billion surplus in 1992 to a $190 billion deficit in 2020. Innovation is supposed to drive productivity but, in the manufacturing sector, productivity growth has turned negative, with factories producing less per worker in the early 2020s than the early 2010s.

The economic system's malfunction has dire human consequences. Whereas 40 weeks of the typical male worker's income in 1985 could provide the middle-class essentials for a family of four, by 2022 he needed 62 weeks of income—a problem, there being only 52 weeks in a year. Nearly half of Americans report having fewer children than they want and, outside the most highly educated and compensated households, affordability is the most frequently cited obstacle. The average American can no longer expect to earn more than his father did at the same age. Poorer regions can no longer expect to catch up with wealthier ones. The bottom 50% of households had less wealth in 2019 than in 1989, though the top 10% added $29 trillion. Life expectancy is falling.

In *The Wealth of Nations*, Adam Smith described conditions under which the private pursuit of profit advances the public interest. "By preferring the support of domestic to that of foreign industry" and "directing that industry in such a manner as its produce may be of the greatest value," the capitalist "promote[s] an end which was no part of his intention." That is, *if* capitalists see the expansion of domestic value creation as their best route to profit, *then* the nation will benefit.

The "invisible hand" is an explanation of how capitalism *can* work, not a promise that it *will*. If the hard, capital- and labor-intensive work of extracting natural resources, raising agriculture, building infrastructure, and manufacturing products consistently offers a less attractive investment profile than developing a cloud-based application that might scale to millions of users in just a few years with just a few employees, capitalism does not work. If firms facing pressure to raise wages or improve conditions or otherwise invest in American workers can instead offshore production to foreign labor or bring that labor into America for "jobs Americans won't do," capitalism does not work. If top business talent finds it can earn more money trading piles of assets in circles than making productive investments in the real economy, capitalism will not work. The market will deliver the profits, as America has learned, but also national decay.

WHAT HAPPENED TO CONSERVATIVES?

Rebuilding American capitalism is a quintessentially conservative task. Libertarians cannot understand the many supports that capitalism requires or countenance a role for government in supplying them. Progressives are disdainful of a system that leaves so much to private ordering and are eager to use public programs to provide whatever the market does not. Only conservatives have the necessary gratitude for what has worked before, preference for a free enterprise system that both grants liberty and imposes obligations, and comprehension of the need for institutions to shape market actors and constraints to channel productively their ambition.

Conservatives value the unique ability of the free market to allocate resources efficiently and empower people to meet one another's needs, to limit the power of a central government and place it instead in the hands of those best positioned to take care of their own interests, and to evolve over time in response to real-world conditions rather than at a bureaucrat's whim. Markets are themselves institutions through which people develop informal codes and formal rules for cooperating and transacting more effectively. But conservatives also recognize that markets have drawbacks and limitations. The free market can reduce people to consumers and relationships to transactions. It prioritizes efficiency over resilience, and individual self-interest over the common good.

Unfortunately, conservative economics was supplanted on the American right-of-center for the past 40 years by a market fundamentalism that saw capitalism as "just another word for economic freedom," in former Senator Pat Toomey's words. The task for policymakers, then, was simple. To quote Jack Spencer, vice president of the Heritage Foundation's Institute for Economic Freedom and Opportunity, "Why don't we look at a policy and just ask, does it expand economic freedom?"

Conservatives relinquished any right to advance a positive vision beyond free individuals exercising free choice in the market, each presumably able to optimize his own life. The failure of families to form reflected merely a preference for other pastimes. "Americans have voted with their wallets," according to Scott Winship, director of the American Enterprise Institute's Center on Opportunity and Social Mobility, "for more stuff, smaller families, and less time devoted to housework, raising kids, and investing in communities."

Underlying this blind faith in the market was an assumption stated most clearly by Professor Glenn Hubbard, chairman of President George W. Bush's Council of Economic Advisors: "The goal of the economic system [is] optimizing consumption." Thus, what Americans made, or whether America could make anything at all, did not matter. Michael Boskin, chairman of the elder Bush's Council of Economic Advisors, famously quipped, "Computer chips, potato chips, what's the difference?" Michael Strain, director of economic policy studies at the American Enterprise Institute, said of America becoming a manufacturing center again, "we cannot, and we should not want to be."

The accompanying agenda of tax cuts, deregulation, and free trade was well suited to an ideology of freedom disconnected from any conception of flourishing, but as economic policy it was a disaster for the nation. Globalization crushed domestic industry and employment, leaving collapsed communities in its wake. Financialization shifted the economy's center of gravity from Main Street to Wall Street, fueling an explosion in corporate profits alongside stagnating wages and declining investment. The decline of unions cost workers power in the market, voice in the workplace, and access to a vital source of communal support. These trends, actively cheered on the Right, contributed to rising inequality, slowing innovation, narrowing of opportunity, and loss of middle-class security.

As with any fundamentalism, this reality was reframed to fit a happy and coherent narrative. Any market outcome, no matter how socially corrosive, was the right one: Broad regions of the country experiencing economic decline was natural and beneficial "creative destruction," and a cue for left-behind residents to "move to opportunity" in a coastal city. Business talent flocking to hedge fund and private equity paydays was "efficient" and reflected the "enormous social value" created by financial engineering and trading assets in circles. If China's state-owned enterprises dump cheap products into the American market, pulling investment and expertise and supply chains across the Pacific in the process, American consumers could enjoy the bounty at the Chinese Communist Party's centrally planned expense.

The American Dream was not dead—cars, after all, now had seat warmers. Televisions were larger and cheaper than ever. And anyway, if economic freedom were the only goal, what else could be done? Watching a global pandemic bring the American economy to a standstill, former South Carolina Governor Nikki Haley remarked, "As we are dealing with changes in our economy, tax cuts are always a good idea."

CAPITALISM, PROPERLY UNDERSTOOD

Conservative economics, unlike the fundamentalism that supplanted it for a time, begins with a confident assertion of what the market is *for* and then considers the public policies necessary for shaping markets toward that end. The conservative conception of the common good requires a free-market economy in which all people can choose their own life course and through their own efforts contribute productively to their communities, support their families, and raise children prepared for the same. This is a richer notion of freedom, attached to obligation, recognizing that with economic rights come economic responsibilities.

In this conception, the economy serves not only the family and community, but also the nation. Efforts to dissolve borders and construct a more efficient global market devalue the nation-state, weaken its sovereignty, and reduce the citizenry's democratic control. And notwithstanding liberalism's one-world ideals, leaders in many other countries remain firmly committed to operating on behalf of their own national interests. If America pursues global supply chains while China pursues national ones, the result will be Chinese supply chains.

The conservative vision thus requires that markets not only allocate capital to productive uses and serve consumers at the lowest possible price, but also create the range of secure and dignified jobs in which people of varying aptitudes, with varying interests, in varying places can build decent lives. Over time, the market must produce growth that is widely shared and sustainable—a term co-opted by the environmental movement but applicable as well to other foundations of a free and prosperous nation that market forces will tend to erode. The industrial commons requires protection, to ensure that its capital base, talent pool, and centers of innovation fuel productivity gains and provide for the national defense. So does the labor market, to ensure that the nation's workers are essential to economic success and prepared for contributing to it. So does the social fabric, to ensure a sense of place, caring relationships built on mutual obligation, and the solidarity to solve problems and counter threats.

Capitalism, properly buttressed and constrained, can do all this. One need only look at the first 200 years of American history, as a backwater colonial republic grew into a continent-spanning industrial colossus and home of the world's middle class, to have confidence it is possible. A robust national economic policy promoted this development through aggressive public investment in both industry and infrastructure, heavy involvement in the financial system, regulations for safe and equal access to vital services, the pioneering of public education and organized labor, and high tariffs to insulate the domestic market. These were not exceptions to American capitalism; they were its scaffolding.

In the 21st century, capitalism itself, and the public policies supporting it, will necessarily look different. Rebuilding American capitalism is not a nostalgic exercise in re-creating the past. The effort is more akin to what occurs after an earthquake levels parts of a city. The disaster causes great suffering, but it also exposes poor construction, crushes unsuitable structures, and provides the opportunity to modernize. Rebuilding does not mean recreating the old city, but rather building something that retains its character while preparing to better serve its residents for the decades to come.

The task begins with an emphasis on productive markets—ones in which the conditions and constraints channel investment toward the uses most valuable for workers, the broader economy, and the nation. Globalization must be replaced with a bounded market that restores the mutual dependence of American capital and labor and invites the trade and immigration that benefit American workers. Financialization must be reversed, so that both talent and capital in pursuit of profit find their best opportunities in productive investment rather than extraction and speculation. Policymakers must embrace the principle that making things matters and boost investment in critical industries.

Likewise, policymakers will need to help reinvigorate supportive communities—the institutions that operate alongside and within the market. The American labor movement has devolved into a dysfunctional and sclerotic collection of unions that fail to advance workers' interests effectively or represent very many at all. But a strong labor movement is vital for capitalism to function well. Public education has become obsessed with college prep, and does it poorly, but what Americans want it to do is help students develop the skills and values needed to build decent lives in the communities where they live. At the foundation of it all, families must form and flourish. For capitalism to succeed, the jobs it creates must be ones that support families and allow them to thrive.

This is true partly because families are important to a well-functioning capitalist system, but more so because they are its proper end. Families do not exist to support capitalism; capitalism exists to support families. The fundamental task of rebuilding American capitalism is establishing those constraints and strengthening those institutions that will create a market and reinforce a culture supportive of family life. The decision to form a family and raise children is not a consumption choice—an experience, to be weighed against a nice vacation or more time for gardening. It is the basic obligation of life and citizenship, incurred by virtue of having been born and raised oneself, and of enjoying liberty and prosperity in a nation built through that same work performed countless times across generations. A capitalism that avows neutrality on the importance of this pursuit compared to others, rather than holding it up as the highest good, has no future, and does not deserve one.

CHAPTER TWO

The State

T he mirror image of the debate over what markets can and cannot do is the debate over what role public policy can and should play. Of course, both markets and public policy will in all cases perform imperfectly, and the appropriate reliance on one or the other will always depend upon circumstances and require prudential judgment. But looming large in the market fundamentalism of recent decades, indeed a hallmark of the fundamentalism, has been the contrary assumption that the market is always the right choice and government can only make things worse. An entire mythology arose, in which the United States was founded on libertarian principles of free trade, freedom of contract, minimal government intervention in the economy, and so on. A suggestion to use public resources or regulation to focus investment in vital industries would earn a rebuke that "we cannot beat China by becoming more like China."

So it is important, especially for conservatives—who take most seriously the question of traditional practice in guiding contemporary decisions—to emphasize that, in fact, the American tradition is one of robust national economic policy. Conservative principles call for a substantial public role in making markets work. The essays in this chapter are two of the three that American Compass published on the day that we launched. The collection was titled *Rebuilding the American System*. (The third essay, Julius Krein's "Planning for When the Market Cannot," appears in Chapter Four.) Wells King's "Rediscovering a Genuine American System" tells the fascinating story of American economic policy since the founding era. My own "Removing the Blinders from Economic Policy" provides the rationale and scope for government involvement in markets based on a conservative understanding of their purpose.

REDISCOVERING A GENUINE AMERICAN SYSTEM

by Wells King

Mr. King was the research director at American Compass.

First published by American Compass on May 4, 2020.

On February 2, 1832, Henry Clay rose on the Senate floor to defend a bold national economic agenda that he had christened eight years earlier "a genuine AMERICAN SYSTEM" (emphasis in original). He had already advanced a number of measures critical to his vision: the Second Bank of the United States, protective tariffs for burgeoning industries, and infrastructure to connect commercial centers to the expansive frontier. But the political revolution in 1828 that drove Clay's National Republican party from power and installed a backcountry populist in the White House was threatening to undo these projects.

Speaking over the course of three days, Clay documented the "unparalleled prosperity" that the American System had produced. He explained how this "long established system" was "patiently and carefully built up, and sanctioned, ... by the nation and its highest and most revered authorities." His opponents' alternative, he alleged, was vacuous at best: "When gentlemen have succeeded in their design of an immediate or gradual destruction of the American System, what is their substitute?" Clay asked. "Free trade! Free trade! The call for free trade, is as unavailing as the cry of a spoiled child.... It never has existed; it never will exist."

Clay lost this particular round in the never-ending fight over America's economic aspirations and the role of government in fulfilling them. President Andrew Jackson vetoed the re-chartering of the national bank that summer and then soundly defeated Clay's challenge in the presidential election that fall. But he was not the first great American statesman to champion a robust role for public policy in shaping the national economy. Nor would he be the last. The efforts of that coalition, from Hamilton to

Lincoln to Eisenhower, kept alive the spirit of the American System from the nation's founding to the middle of the twentieth century. Through its various expressions, the System helped to deliver the "unparalleled prosperity" Clay once heralded and made American industry the envy of the world.

Conservatives abandoned that tradition in recent decades and then forgot its existence altogether, concocting the myth of a laissez-faire America and conceiving of capitalism as little more than "economic freedom." The ensuing political struggle between a Left committed to globalization and redistribution and a Right that would do nothing at all, has ignored the actual needs of the nation's citizenry and its economy. We need more Henry Clays. Conservatives could provide them, if they recognized that the history of American political economy furnishes a rich tradition worthy of conserving.

HAMILTON'S TRIUMPH

The very framing of the Constitution emphasized the limited but positive role for government in the American economy. Indeed, the inadequacy of the Articles of Confederation for dealing with essential matters of political economy—international trade, interstate commerce, and public finance—spurred the formation of the Constitutional Convention in the first place. As Article 1, Section 8 makes clear, the Framers understood not only the importance of these economic powers, but also that each one—to lay and collect taxes, to borrow money, and to regulate commerce—was distinct and deserving of enumeration. Such powers were reportedly not a matter of controversy at the Convention.

Still, the proper scope and ends of federal power were open questions. The ensuing public debate was shaped—and still is shaped—by an overarching conflict of visions about the ideal American republic: between the Hamiltonian vision of a commercial republic driven by industrialization and a robust financial system and the Jeffersonian vision of an agrarian democracy of small, free-holding yeomen farmers.

Alexander Hamilton proposed an aggressive economic agenda to President Washington and the First United States Congress. In his first act as the nation's first Treasury Secretary, he advised Congress to pass a general tariff to fund the government's debt and operations. He later devised a plan to establish the creditworthiness of the United States by assuming the states' debts and paying creditors at face value. Against the objections of Secretary of State Thomas Jefferson, Hamilton also persuaded Washington in 1791 to sign a twenty-year charter for the Bank of the United States, a national bank for which "public utility [was] more truly the object . . . than private profit."

Later the same year, Hamilton submitted the *Report on Manufactures* to Congress, outlining a plan to support industrialization through federal "bounties" (subsidies). He argued that the "independence and security" of the United States were "materially connected with the prosperity of manufactures" but that private capital would not be sufficient to support its development. The national interest would "therefore require the incitement and patronage of government." To modern ears, such state-sponsored industrialization may sound like a response to market failure, but Hamilton's case was broader: that investment was an affirmative obligation of the federal government. "In a community situated like that of the United States," he maintained, "the public purse must supply the deficiency of private resource. In what can it be so useful, as in prompting and improving the efforts of industry?"

Though not fully implemented in his tenure as Treasury Secretary, Hamilton's vision of political economy ultimately triumphed. Following its humiliating experience in the War of 1812, the country pursued a number of Hamiltonian reforms. Congress had failed to renew the charter of the First Bank of the United States in 1811, but chartered the Second Bank in 1816. A series of tariffs, beginning in 1816, were also instated with the express purpose of protecting infant domestic industries. In 1817, Congress passed the *Navigation Act* requiring that interstate trade be conducted with American-owned ships.

Hamilton did not live to see his vindication, but he would especially have appreciated the concessions of his erstwhile opponents. Thomas Jefferson later admitted that "experience" had demonstrated that manufacturing was "as necessary to our independence as to our comfort." He was emphatic. The person "who is now against domestic manufactures," he wrote after the War, "must be for reducing either to dependence on that foreign nation [Britain], or to be clothed in skins, and to live like wild beasts in dens and caverns. I am proud to say, *I am not one of these*" (emphasis in original). James Madison likewise came to defend state-sponsored industrialization through protective tariffs. "Unless aided in its nascent and infant state by public encouragement and a confidence in public protection," he wrote, entire industries "might remain . . . for a long time unattempted, or attempted without success."

"There is no Hamilton memorial," George F. Will has noted. "But if you seek his monument, look around. This is Hamilton's America." This was already true when Henry Clay spoke in 1832. Only the Hamiltonian project went by a new name: the American System.

THE AMERICAN SYSTEM AND ITS SCHOOL

The American System emerged from crisis and the young nation's sudden awareness of its own mortality. As the United States entered the War of 1812, Henry Clay emerged as a leading War Hawk in the Congress. Economic nationalism was a natural outgrowth of his anti-British posture and would become a common lesson from the experience of war. Its primary aim was self-sufficiency. "We should thus have our wants supplied, when foreign resources are cut off," Clay advised his fellow lawmakers, "and we should also lay the basis of a system of taxation, to be resorted to when the revenue from imports is stopped by war."

Clay's American System integrated three mutually supporting priorities: tariff-based protection of infant industries, a national financial system, and "internal improvements," which we would today call infrastructure. In 1816, Clay led the passage of an expressly protective tariff for the nation's burgeoning manufacturing industry, averaging 40 percent on all imported manufactured goods. He also advocated the creation of the Second Bank of the United States and federal funding of canal and railroad projects with revenue generated from land sales.

The American System's development was supported by political economists whose thinking came to be known as the American School. Like Clay, the thinkers behind the American School were engaged not only in a battle of ideas, but a contest between nations. They were contemporaries of the great British classical economists like David Ricardo and John Stuart Mill and took part in a transatlantic debate over the laws of economics and the role of government. They rebutted the arguments of these "British School" advocates for free trade and *laissez-faire* and outlined policies to protect America's interests from what they deemed to be hostile British policy.

Daniel Raymond (1786–1849), for example, established his reputation after publishing criticism of Adam Smith's *Wealth of Nations*. Raymond objected to Smith's very definition of national wealth as the sum of all private wealth, arguing that its distribution mattered and that national wealth ought to reflect "the condition of the whole nation" such that "general prosperity and happiness" would be maximized.

Another leading light of the American School was Friedrich List (1789–1846), a German émigré who developed and systematized a "national system" of economics that stressed the importance of industrialization in the emerging global economy. "To attain the highest degree of independence, culture and material prosperity," List argued, a country "should adopt every measure within its power to defend its economic security." For the still-developing United States, this meant tariff-based protection and import substitution for the nation's infant industries. Once the nation had industrialized, however, List's system advised switching to a reciprocal trade strategy with other industrialized nations, cautiously opening American markets in exchange for access to others.

These were common themes of the American School: treating the nation—rather than the individual—as the principal unit of economic analysis and incorporating social and geopolitical factors that today might seem beyond the scope of economics. The British "dismal science" could not satisfy the optimism and liberality of the still young American republic.

The American School struck its mid-century crescendo in the work of Henry Charles Carey (1793–1879). He warned that the purpose of British free trade policy was to "secur[e for] the people of England the ... monopoly of machinery" and argued for an aggressive policy of support for infant industries to "break down this monopoly" and "restore the natural tendency" of balancing manufacturing with agriculture to support "stabler self-sufficient communities." "The Americans, and few more so than Henry Carey," writes historian Gabor S. Boritt, "made political economy the beautiful science."

Yet Carey's greatest contribution to the American tradition may not have been his writing, but his service as an advisor to an ambitious young statesman from the frontier—an admirer of Henry Clay and a student of the American School named Abraham Lincoln.

From his very first campaign manifesto in 1832, Lincoln confessed that "my politics are short and sweet.... I am in favor of national bank... in favor of the internal improvements system and a high protective tariff." By the time he occupied the White House, his economic policy seemed to have changed little: "I have always been an old-line Henry Clay Whig," he proclaimed in 1861.

As the Civil War raged, Lincoln pursued an American-System agenda on an epic scale. Having long advocated for protective tariffs, he raised them two times in the course of just three years. From Lincoln's presidency through World War II, the American home market was the most protected in the world. Lincoln also re-created a federal financial system. With the Legal Tender Act, he granted Treasury the ability to issue "greenbacks," paper money backed by federal debt. With the National Currency Acts, he taxed state banknotes out of existence and established a network of nationally chartered banks approved to issue U.S. Treasury banknotes. As with protective tariffs, Lincoln had supported ambitious infrastructure projects throughout his political career, and in 1862 he signed legislation to spend millions on what would become the First Transcontinental Railroad.

But Lincoln also expanded the American System's scope—in both concept and deed. Less than three months after the Battle of Fort Sumter, Lincoln addressed a special session of Congress commemorating the eighty-fifth anniversary of the Declaration of Independence. At the close of his remarks, the President departed from his stated purpose of securing adequate troops and funding to wage the Civil War to elaborate on the nation's founding ideals. "The leading object" of the federal government, he said, was "to elevate the condition of men; to lift artificial weights from all shoulders; to clear the paths of laudable pursuit for all; to afford all an unfettered start and a fair chance in the race of life." The following year Lincoln signed legislation that committed federal land to this purpose: the Homestead Act, offering settlers 160 acres of public land to encourage westward migration, and the Morrill Land-Grant Act, which funded the creation of more than 60 colleges including Cornell University and the Massachusetts Institute of Technology.

"The Hamiltonian tradition," historian Michael Lind has observed, "could not have found a better spokesman than Lincoln."

UNFINISHED WORK

At Gettysburg, Lincoln tasked the American people with the "unfinished work" of safeguarding and improving the American experiment. In the century after his death, the federal government advanced an economic agenda to support it. The United States built a modern industrial economy that supported national security, economic independence, and widely shared prosperity, becoming the envy and leader of the world. The tradition of the American System and its School played a central role.

To foster and guide economic development, the U.S. government supported strategic industries through protection and investment and established the foundations for a functioning labor market that could serve American workers and businesses alike. Through World War II, the federal government maintained a robust set of tariffs designed not only to generate revenue, but to buttress American industries. It also created a comprehensive structure for union representation and collective bargaining. As reciprocal trade expanded, policymakers intervened with Farm Bills to support the agricultural sector, preserving sectoral diversification critical for economic self-sufficiency and the vitality of many communities. Taxpayers funded ambitious research and development projects through dedicated agencies, such as DARPA and NASA, that laid the groundwork for the computer revolution of the late twentieth century.

Buttressing this development was a financial system that used public credit and regulatory oversight to ensure that capital was not only efficiently and productively deployed, but safe from corruption and complete destruction by the business cycle. With the creation of the Federal Reserve in 1913, the United States had a central bank for the first time since the dissolution of the Second Bank of the United States in 1836. The New Deal brought a suite of reforms, including the Glass-Steagall Act, that transformed the nation's financial system from a speculative market into something more akin to a public utility. New institutions like the FDIC and SEC provided greater security for Americans' financial assets and necessary oversight of financial markets while institutions like Fannie Mae, Freddie Mac, and the Small Business Administration provided targeted, subsidized financing to American home and small business owners.

The tradition of "internal improvements" lived on as well, as American policymakers recognized that the nation's size was one of its great advantages and that prosperity ought to reach every corner rather than concentrating in a few cities. The United States invested in ambitious infrastructure programs to provide transportation, energy, and communications to the public. With the creation and maintenance of postal, telegraph, and radio networks as well as railroads and eventually interstate highways, the federal government enabled the spread of the population and its economic dynamism across the continent. Projects like the Hoover Dam and agencies like the Tennessee Valley Authority brought electricity to underdeveloped regions.

From every angle available, the United States invested in the prosperity and opportunity of American citizens, recognizing that both a healthy democratic republic and a vibrant economy depended upon prosperity that was widely shared and available to all. The nation assumed an obligation to create opportunity and draw people to it, rather than lecture those who could not find it themselves. The Homestead Acts expanded the availability of land, first opened by President Lincoln, to once-excluded populations and made property ownership available to most Americans. Investments in the American education system—first universal public high school, and then universities—fostered skills to the benefit of both workers and their employers. Land-grant colleges formed a geographically dispersed network of institutions designed for underserved populations, and programs like the G.I. Bill made traditional institutions more accessible.

RESTORING ECONOMIC POLICY

Economic history is filled with policy successes and policy failures, and the American System is no exception. A tradition is not worthy of celebration based solely on its lineage. Nor do its occasional failures invalidate its overarching successes—much less justify a disavowal of the entire project. As Daniel Raymond observed, "The question, therefore, is not, and never will be, between law and no law, regulation and no regulation, but it must always be between the wisdom of different laws and different regulations."

Yet the modern American right-of-center, rather than balance a worthy skepticism of government overreach with respect for an inherited approach to public policy, has forsaken that tradition—indeed, written it out of existence—in favor of free-market fundamentalism. That is neither conservative nor wise.

Leading "conservatives" now label any departure from *laissez-faire* as socialism or, at the very least, as a "hyphenated capitalism" that leads down the "road to socialism." They misunderstand not only the proper role of government in a functioning capitalist system, but the very traditions of American statecraft. If today's critics are right about the role of government in a capitalist economy, then many of America's greatest statesmen—even the nation's and the Republican Party's very founders—were "hyphenated capitalists" themselves. How, with such a heritage, did the United States get anywhere?

Conservative policymakers ought to study the American history of political economy. They should rediscover principles of public policy that are well-suited to contemporary challenges: that effective government is not only achievable with limited, constitutional powers, but can work alongside private industry to achieve national goals.

Economic stability, national security, widely shared prosperity, strong families, a pluralistic society—in short, the American way of life—are achievements plainly worth conserving. So is the only approach to economic policy that has ever proved capable of producing them.

REMOVING THE BLINDERS FROM ECONOMIC POLICY

by Oren Cass

Adapted from an essay first published by American Compass on May 4, 2020.

In unwitting homage to Congressman Barney Frank's line that "government is simply the name we give to the things we choose to do together," Senator Pat Toomey defined "the market" as "just the name that we assign to the sum total of all the voluntary exchanges that occur every day by free men and women participating in a marketplace."

These equal and opposite platitudes share more than a formulation and a woeful inadequacy. Each represents, for the ideologues who adopt it, a comfortably absolute view of the world. If government is nothing more than voluntary collaboration, who could object? What challenge couldn't benefit from choosing to do more together? Meanwhile, if the market is nothing more than the sum of voluntary exchanges, what cause might there be for concern? How could public policy improve upon choices freely made? Frank's statist utopianism has its adherents, and may even be resurgent, but it has long been contested within the American left-of-center—at least since President Bill Clinton's declaration that "the era of big government is over." The same cannot be said, unfortunately, for Toomey's market reductivism.

The blinders that narrow his perception of the market are worn proudly across the American right-of-center, obscuring a proper view in one direction of *what the market is,* and in the other of *what the market is for.* Analysis of the market's voluntary exchanges begins and ends with the personal, immediate, and question-begging formulation that they occur always because each participant believes it will be beneficial. Assessment of the market's effect on society considers only the material living standards that it delivers.

This tunnel vision produces a truncated conception of economic policy's scope and goals—in the same way that seeing baseball as just people throwing and catching a ball, while often technically accurate, would preclude appreciation of the game and render pointless concepts like a team, league, or commissioner. With "the market" reduced to voluntary exchanges between individuals on a quest to maximize consumption, the role for policymakers shrivels to the task of avoiding interference.

In reality, the market is supported, shaped, and constrained by a variety of essential rules for intellectual property, employment relationships, monopolization, and so on. Its participants are guided in their behavior by vital institutions like schools, labor unions, and the military. Its exchanges, particularly when they operate as investment, proceed to support, shape, and constrain future exchanges. With blinders on, one might eagerly profess what Friedrich Hayek called "faith in the spontaneous forces of adjustment." Take them off, and it is impossible not to see the social, legal, historical, and institutional scaffolding that buttresses a growing economy, and the role that public policy must play in its construction and maintenance. A protective instinct, and gratitude, for such structures should come naturally to conservatives.

Instead, guided by free-market dogma, policymakers have spent recent decades forsaking their obligations and celebrating a theoretical and oversimplified ideal. In parallel with an erosion of global leadership, declining productivity growth and dynamism, stagnating wages, and rising social dysfunction, the vital practice of economic policymaking has been lost. If we want the market to serve well the needs of the American people, we must first recover the tools necessary to shape it.

WHAT THE MARKET IS

Begin with a simple economic transaction: a farmer offers a laborer a wage to perform a day's work and the laborer accepts; both believe the transaction will benefit them. This appears nearly the Platonic ideal of a "voluntary exchange" and so the sum total of all such exchanges should define the market. But which market? Is it the market in which the laborer is paid $40 per hour to operate laser-guided machinery, or the one where he earns $40 for an entire day spent picking by hand? The laborer may or may not have union representation. He may or may not even have legal permission to work in the country. He may be the only qualified laborer available, or he may be one of twenty loitering in a parking lot, hoping to find work that day. The farmer may be a sole proprietor, or the employee of a global conglomerate. He may hope to retain the laborer for permanent employment, or to find a better or cheaper option tomorrow. What year is this and what country are we in?

The contents of the market's transactions are contingent on the conditions in which they occur. Each exchange occurs against the substantive backdrop of law, institutions, accumulated capital, culture, technology, and is subject also to transitory conditions like the weather. Each exchange may be freely chosen, but none is inevitable, because under different conditions the parties might choose differently—or be different parties entirely. The farmer may not hire any laborers if a storm is passing through. But the rain does not deprive him of liberty, nor does it make his choice not to hire anyone less efficient than his choice on a sunny day to employ a team. The substantive backdrop shifts more gradually, but far more consequentially, leading for instance to new configurations of the entire agricultural sector—what farms exist where in America, how do they harvest, who does that work and why. No true result exists against which all others can be measured for distortion, because no one set of "free market" conditions exists to provide a baseline.

This is not an indictment of the market. To the contrary, its capacity to mediate between so many forces while deferring to countless individual preferences in a way that generates prosperity is precisely what makes it invaluable—both in principle and in practice. By allowing individuals to exercise choice, it protects liberty and limits the scope of government. By creating and transmitting information about people's preferences in the face of extant conditions, and providing rewards for meeting people's needs, it spurs productive activity and allocates resources efficiently.

For public policy, however, the implications of this broader perspective are immense. With blinders on, so that only the market's exchanges are visible, economic policy might logically entail only tax policy that adds to or subtracts from those exchanges and regulation that constrains them. "As we are dealing with changes in our economy," says Ambassador Nikki Haley, "tax cuts are always a good idea." Conservatives looking beyond those bounds confuse her—they "seem embarrassed by the free market," and she sees their "hyphenated capitalism" as entailing "more tax credits here, more subsidies there, more mandates for this, more regulations for that." Only those sites of policymaking seem relevant and, if an exchange is either free or unfree, policymakers can only impinge.

If markets encompass both voluntary exchanges and the conditions that influence those exchanges, and if a market's outcomes are dictated by interaction between the two, then the scope of economic policy expands and an unwavering preference for non-intervention becomes arbitrary. Consider the law, institutions, accumulated capital, culture, and technology that might influence market transactions. Are markets more or less free when communities operate public schools? Are markets more or less efficient when NASA works on sending a man to the moon? These questions are almost nonsensical.

The narrow perspective fosters a conviction that minimal economic policy yields maximum output. Holding the market's underlying conditions constant, it may generally be the case that interventions by policymakers in the market's exchanges will reduce efficiency and growth. The claim that government action could be constructive might rightly seem suspect.

With blinders off, the picture changes. Because market outcomes are contingent on impermanent conditions, the most efficient outcome under one set may not be the best result available. Raising taxes to fund basic research, for instance, might simultaneously reduce the market's efficiency and improve its conditions such that the end result is higher growth. Requiring firms to manufacture domestically would obviously interfere with international transactions, but the policy would also influence domestic institutions, capital investments, the culture, and the trajectory of innovation. Whether the more constrained market operating under these new conditions would generate more growth than a less constrained one in the status quo has no easy answer.

Policymakers most directly write the law, but their decisions also shape institutions, alter the flow of investments in both physical and human capital, and influence the directions in which culture and technology evolve. In all these ways, they affect the market's exchanges and thus its outcomes and its benefits to the nation. Committing such acts of economic policy is not a crime against capitalism. It was a prerequisite to the emergence of capitalist systems; it is unavoidable to the task of governing them; and it will be vital to their continued success.

WHAT THE MARKET IS FOR

At what should a capitalist system succeed? The standard logic holds that the one true goal for economic policy is to maximize material living standards, which is accomplished by maximizing economic growth, which is accomplished by minimizing the interference of policymakers in the market. Living standards are important, and economic policy should strive to improve them. But only with blinders snapped firmly in place do they appear the only, or primary, concern for policymakers. In a 2019 survey by the American Enterprise Institute, four-in-five Americans deemed having "freedom of choice in how to live one's life" and "a good family life" as essential to "the American Dream." Fewer than half said the same of "a successful career" or "a better quality of life than your parents"; fewer than one-in-five saw "become wealthy" as essential. Pew Research reports that Americans asked to choose between "financial stability" and "moving up the income ladder" prefer the former by more than ten to one.

There is no end to the range of concerns for which one might assert a national interest and require the market's support. But just as the concept of a high and rising standard of living encapsulates countless specifics, other broad categories can help to summarize features of an economy that is serving the nation well, and thus establish the goals for economic policy. Defining and prioritizing among such categories is a critical task of the political process, though one that American politics regrettably has abdicated.

The list of top priorities should be among the axes that most starkly divide liberals and conservatives, explaining many of the differences in their respective agendas. For the conservative who sees established institutions and their practices as critical foundations for prosperity, prefers the private ordering of self-sufficient families and communities to the dependence of individuals on the state and its dictates, and perceives great risk in efforts to defy or reprogram human nature, these four outcomes would likely be important:

1. Security. A well-functioning economy supports the nation with the resources and capacity necessary to assert and defend its interests. This requires the tools for both the outward projection of force and the inward insulation from foreign coercion. To take a recent example, the country with perhaps the world's highest living standard can still find itself with insufficient medical supplies and no ability to produce needed pharmaceuticals in a public health emergency. More generally, national security requires domestic capacity for a wide variety of materials and components if foreign supplies may be corrupted or subject to disruption in the event of a conflict. "Why can't the greatest economy in the history of the world produce swabs, face masks and ventilators in adequate supply?" asked Larry Summers, former director of President Obama's National Economic Council. The answer comes in part from his former colleague Christina Romer, who chaired Obama's Council of Economic Advisers and dismissed the idea of a "manufacturing policy" as a relic of "sentiment and history." Romer argued that "American consumers value health care and haircuts as much as washing machines and hair dryers. And our earnings from exporting architectural plans for a building in Shanghai are as real as those from exporting cars to Canada." Whether piles of money can be stitched into effective personal protective equipment is another matter.

2. Resilience. A well-functioning economy maintains buffers like spare capacity, reserves, and stabilizers so that unpredictable events and temporary trends do not transform into unmanageable crises or trigger the collapse of entire industries or regions. It enables families to do the same, so that their savings allow them to make long-term plans, smooth rough patches for the household budget, launch a new venture, and prepare their children for success. Capitalism anticipates total failure for individual firms and makes owners accountable for their fates—indeed the process of "creative destruction" requires such failure. But for that process to be one that accrues to the nation's benefit, it must operate alongside others that preserve stability and opportunity in the market so that disruption for customers, suppliers, and especially workers is temporary. Innovation always disrupts economically, but in a well-functioning economy it also yields tools and systems that insulate communities and protect people's livelihoods.

3. Pluralism. A well-functioning economy generates broad-based and widespread prosperity that allows people of varied abilities in varied locations to both preserve their ways of life and pursue new opportunities, and to raise children able to do the same. Many people are deeply rooted and value living in the communities where they grew up, often close to extended family. But the market's preference for agglomeration tends to concentrate economic activity in narrow geographies, while its preference for scale and specialization favors the distant conglomerate over the local provider. Fewer than one-in-five mothers with children under four say that full-time work is their preference. But the market's commodification of relationships places enormous economic pressure on households to outsource care of children and the elderly. If the market is to serve the nation's citizens and not the other way around, its quest for efficiency must be balanced by the assertion of more humane values.

4. Justice. The market's performance at its core task of resource allocation must also be evaluated for its accordance with justice. While acknowledging that "the term has been hijacked by the left," Senator Josh Hawley once observed in *National Affairs*:

> *The West's greatest thinkers, no less than its major religious traditions, have insisted again and again on the centrality of justice. "Justice is the end of government," James Madison wrote in Federalist No. 51. "It is the end of civil society." Madison was echoing Aristotle, who argued that justice is the purpose of political community. Though today we often think of justice only in reference to crime and punishment, Aristotle understood that there is far more to justice than that: He contended that justice means arranging society in the right way, in accord with how humans are made and meant to live.*

This requires a labor market in which workers can find good jobs. People enjoy consumption, but they also place great importance on their roles as providers for their families and productive contributors to their communities. A key mechanism for ensuring rising material living standards has been the aggressive expansion of government transfer programs that send more than $1 trillion annually in cash and benefits to lower-income households. But a government check is not a replacement for a paycheck.

Likewise, while people do care about the size of their own houses, they care also about their status relative to others and whether all have received their just desserts. This is not only true as a description of human nature, but also eminently rational and reasonable as a set of concerns. Why shouldn't we want our markets to produce a social order perceived as legitimate, to give people confidence in an expectation of equitable treatment, and thus to reinforce the social fabric?

These categories are not mutually exclusive. Resilience contributes to security and justice, pluralism to resilience, and so on. Often they are compatible with, or even reinforced by, rising material living standards. But in other cases they are not, and it is in managing the tensions and trade-offs that politics and policymakers are indispensable. No evidence or theory suggests that the market will attempt to do this on its own, let alone arrive at a result we should want.

MAKING MARKETS WORK

When the market fails to deliver on the nation's goals, and especially when it undermines them, policymakers ought to examine how their choices influence the conditions in which the market is operating and to ask what different choices might be better. To do otherwise, and to deem any market outcome happening at any moment as sacrosanct and inevitable, is a dereliction of duty.

Historically, as Wells King observes in "Rediscovering a Genuine American System," American policymakers understood this. With blinders on, the "economic policy" of the past can look backward and bizarre: aggressive tariffs and immigration restrictions, an income tax with punishingly high marginal rates, regulation ensuring that industries would serve unprofitable regions and prohibiting banks from operating multiple branches—surely a recipe for stagnation. But the nation's major economic policies included the Louisiana Purchase and westward expansion, the American System with its protection of domestic industries and its investments in internal improvements, the land-grant colleges and the Homestead Act, trust-busting and electrification, the New Deal's social insurance and the Wagner Act's organizing rights, the G.I. Bill, the Interstate Highway System, and the Space Race. Leaders asked and answered the question of what *could* be, and used economic policy to pursue their vision, creating the conditions for a market that produced unprecedented prosperity, material and otherwise.

Today, we "Nudge." Instead of pouring new foundations, we add new trim. The exception that proves the rule is the "Green New Deal," a vague Democratic proposal so obscenely impractical and misaligned with American priorities that Nancy Pelosi, the Democratic Speaker of the House, dismissed it as "the green dream, or whatever they call it, nobody knows what it is." The Senate voted it down 57-0 with 43 Democrats voting "Present." More commonly, the left-of-center seeks expansions of the safety net to cover more of what the market already offers, while the right-of-center pounds the table for "occupational licensing reform." But most of the time, we tweak the tax code.

Reflecting on America's inability to respond effectively to the 2020 coronavirus pandemic, entrepreneur and investor Marc Andreessen declared, "It's Time to Build."

> *We could have these things but we chose not to—specifically we chose not to have the mechanisms, the factories, the systems to make these things. We chose not to build. You don't just see this smug complacency, this satisfaction with the status quo and the unwillingness to build, in the pandemic, or in healthcare generally. You see it throughout Western life, and specifically throughout American life. . . . We need to demand more of our political leaders, of our*

CEOs, our entrepreneurs, our investors. We need to demand more of our culture, of our society. And we need to demand more from one another.

Perhaps Andreessen's vision is not the right one. But as he concludes, "Here's a modest proposal to my critics. Instead of attacking my ideas of what to build, conceive your own!" At least the American people should have visions like his to choose from.

Whatever the vision, the tools for the job will not be yet more rounds of tax reform. The future of American economic policy lies in the creation of a modern American System, establishing the market conditions for an economy that supports our shared national goals. That system will require economic policy operating through four channels:

1. Institutions. Economic policy can shape the structure and foster the growth of institutions critical to the market's operation. These include systems of public education and organized labor, the military, the safety net, and the family. Policy plays more central a role in some than in others, but all represent locations where public action has the potential to move the nation toward conditions in which the market will generate better outcomes. For example, an education system with the primary mission of connecting young people at the outset of adulthood to productive employment would make college just one of several pathways—and neither the most popular nor best funded among them.

2. Investments. Economic policy can direct public resources toward socially valuable ends and induce private actors to dedicate their resources to the same. Important targets for public spending include infrastructure, public health, and basic research. Direct subsidies, prizes, and commitments to purchase can all make private investment more attractive. Public-private partnerships represent a hybrid approach that presents private actors with the opportunity to collaborate on public projects. As Julius Krein observes in "Planning for When the Market Cannot," when private actors lack the information or incentive to invest wisely on behalf of the nation's interests, policymakers complement rather than impede the market's operation by stepping forward.

3. Rules. Government regulations can strengthen the market by altering its conditions and directly mitigating socially harmful effects. Beyond basic legal structures like property and contract rights, patent law creates new rights that induce investment in innovation. Standard regulatory fields like environmental and employment law address externalities where the market outcome is not the efficient one and also intervene where economically efficient activities may have consequences that frustrate equally valid but non-economic goals. Network and utility regulation enable natural monopolies to operate well, while antitrust enforcement disables counterproductive market concentration. Trade restrictions prevent foreign markets from transmitting their distortions and abuses into our own.

4. Public Finances. Fiscal and monetary policy affect the context in which consumers and investors make their decisions and policymakers must approach them with blinders off and proper objectives in focus. The design of any tax system entails choices that affect the relative attractiveness of different economic activities. Likewise, setting monetary policy, and managing its trade-offs, is unavoidable. And government spending, wherever it occurs, by definition diverts resources from where the market might otherwise allocate them. What policymakers must *not* do is obsess over these questions to the exclusion of all others, or perceive every economic challenge as a nail awaiting the hammer of taxing and spending.

A question remains whether policymakers are capable of drawing on these robust fields to pursue ambitious goals. They may not be capable of setting useful goals, identifying appropriate policies, or implementing them. The political process might frustrate the translation of even the best ideas into tangible action. Unintended consequences abound.

Unfortunately, these concerns are often raised as an obstruction tactic. Without question, the concerns themselves are real, and a policymaker should always proceed with caution and humility. But many of the voices loudest in raising the alarm fall silent when focus turns to their preferred topic of tax reform. It would be hard to conceive of a policy initiative more perfectly vulnerable to political manipulation, industry capture, simple error, unintended consequences, and all the rest than rewriting the tax code. Yet those most certain that any government action is doomed to failure tend also to be the most eager to tolerate the risk if a tax cut may be in the offing.

In weighing concerns of policy misfire, the critical question is: *Compared to what?* If the status quo were an idyllic, well-functioning system, the risks of tampering would indeed be high. But the baseline against which any new policy must be judged is an environment that emerged under these same constraints, except that it did so with the wrong understanding of the market, using the wrong tools, and aiming for the wrong target. Even in areas where government is purportedly not acting already, the non-action was itself chosen by policymakers and is often beset with exceptions; it, too, triggers unintended consequences. When an opportunity exists to apply better assumptions to better goals, we should take it.

CHAPTER THREE

Labor

Of the many public debates in which I've participated, none was more clarifying than my conversation with the Heritage Foundation's Stephen Moore. Oddly, for an event titled "Immigration & Wages," Moore failed to mention wages even once in his opening remarks. But the kicker came later in the conversation, when I lamented, "We've had the stock market repeatedly surge as we made incredibly cheap labor available to corporations generating corporate profits." Moore responded, "Cheap labor leads to a booming stock market? That benefits everyone." This, in a nutshell, has been the consensus position for economists concerned only with maximizing consumption and especially among those on the right-of-center inclined to believe that whatever benefits investors will eventually benefit everyone. Like many things in nutshells, it is nuts.

An economy benefits from cheap energy and cheap lumber. But the price of labor is an output as much as an input—or, more colloquially, the creation of family-supporting jobs is a key goal, not an inconvenient obstacle. This theme recurs throughout the volume: The pressure to pay workers well and, in turn, the incentive to invest in boosting productivity is key to capitalism's success, not a "labor shortage" to be relieved. No phrase better captures the backward framework that has dominated policymaking than the toxic "jobs Americans won't do." And so this essay is titled, "Jobs Americans Would Do."

JOBS AMERICANS WOULD DO

by Oren Cass

First published by American Compass on May 4, 2023.

The labor shortage afflicting American employers nationwide is nothing new in the San Joaquin Basin of California's Central Valley, which produces 40% of the nation's fruits and nuts. For Alex, who asked that we use only his first name, the trouble started eight years ago, with an epiphany that came while driving down the I-5 from his office in San Francisco to a conference in Los Angeles. "Our team of programmers was expensive, and demanding," he explained, "our lease costs were spiking. As I looked out my window at the toiling farmhands, I thought maybe I saw an answer."

Alex relocated his app development firm to a small patch of farmland outside Fresno, setting up crates on which workers could rest their laptops in the dusty field, and lowered pay to $16 per hour. Not a single member of the team joined him. Ever since, getting apps developed has proved nigh impossible. "Occasionally someone will apply," he explains, "but they never know Java. It's what I call the 'skills gap.'"

Alex is not alone. Short-staffed coffee shops and machine tools without operators have prompted economists and business groups to raise the alarm. An "imbalance in labor supply and demand" is dragging down the nation's economic prospects and fueling inflation, according to the *Wall Street Journal*. "We hear from businesses every day that the worker shortage is their top challenge," explains Neil Bradley, chief policy officer at the U.S. Chamber of Commerce. The labor market is "overheated" and "much too tight," says Michael Strain, director of economic studies at the pro-business American Enterprise Institute. In his view, we need "a pretty big increase in the unemployment rate."

What exactly is an "overheated" labor market or a "worker shortage," how would we know if one existed, and what would be an appropriate response? Colloquially, a shortage refers simply to having less than a desired amount of something. But in a market mediated by price signals, that concept falls flat and an "imbalance in supply and demand" is incoherent. Supply and demand are not levels; they are relationships that describe the various quantities of a good supplied and demanded across a range of prices. These quantities are, by definition, imbalanced at all prices except the equilibrium point, and a key function of markets is to find that point. Most people experience a private-jet shortage, insofar as they would like one and have none, but this "imbalance in supply and demand" means only that they are not willing and able to pay the market-clearing price.

As with the masses glumly flying commercial, Alex's claimed programmer shortage seems easy to dismiss. The problem comes in distinguishing his complaint from that of his neighbor, Bernie, who operates a more conventional Central Valley farm. Like Alex, Bernie also wishes to pay $16 per hour to workers who would labor all day in a hot field, and he, too, reports that hiring is a major challenge. Unlike Alex, Bernie finds his complaint taken quite seriously by economists and policymakers. The government has expanded the H-2A temporary visa program from fewer than 50,000 agricultural guest workers in 2005 to more than 250,000 in 2021, in an effort to fill, in Bernie's words, "jobs Americans won't do."

If Alex's claim is outlandish, why isn't Bernie's? Markets do experience shortages in response to shocks, before time has allowed for adjustment, but in such situations prices go haywire. The most salient fact about the current labor market is that real wages are slowly falling: down 0.7% in March 2023, compared to a year prior, when wages were down 2.4% compared to the year before that. Median weekly earnings were no higher at the end of 2022 than at the end of 2019. The Chamber's Bradley made his comment in May 2022, in the midst of a two-month period when real wages were falling at an annualized rate of nearly 8%. Employers claiming to be in dire straits are *reducing* the real compensation they offer. In aggregate, the prices *they* charge are rising at the level of inflation, and yet they are not willing even to raise the wages they offer at that same rate. They are all Alex.

The outlandish, panicked response of economists and business leaders to a labor market in which workers are not readily available at the price employers wish to pay illuminates the problem of wage stagnation that has now bedeviled America's economy for 50 years. From 1972 to 2022, real corporate profits per capita rose 185%. GDP per capita rose 141%. Productivity rose 135%. The average hourly wage for production and nonsupervisory workers rose 1%. How is that even possible?

It is possible because employers will tend to raise wages under one, and only one, condition: when they cannot hire the workers they need at the existing wage. All of labor economics turns on that simple fact. If you are happy with the workers you have at $16 per hour, you will not offer $17 per hour. If open positions at $16 per hour go unfilled, or workers earning that wage start to leave or threaten to strike, $17 per hour will be on the table. The average wage went from $28 in 1972 (in 2022 dollars) to ... $28 in 2022, because employers did not have to offer $29. They *could* offer $29—after all, the corporate sector had roughly tripled its profit even after accounting for population growth. But they did not have to, and so they did not.

Rather than follow recommendations from pro-business groups to raise the unemployment rate, policymakers should row hard in the opposite direction, increase the pressure, and make clear that no relief from a tight labor market will come. What tools are at their disposal to make employers offer real wage increases to lower wage workers now and continue doing so for, say, the next 50 years? We have a lot of catching up to do. A wide range of policy options hold promise, but any discussion should start with the straightforward one: limiting the supply of workers available. Of course, this may not be as easy as it sounds. The goal is to ensure good jobs for American workers, so excluding some such workers for the sake of boosting the wages of others would be a pyrrhic victory. But there is another set of workers, not Americans, whose access to the labor market American policymakers could limit.

IMMIGRATION POLICY AS ACTIVE LABOR MARKET POLICY

A few statistics are helpful in illustrating the magnitude of the effect that immigration has on the American labor market. Immigrants accounted for more than half of the increase in the labor force from 2008 to 2023—a total of 7.0 million additional workers. By comparison, the total shortfall in workers caused by a depressed labor-force participation rate at the end of 2021 was 2.9 million. In 2019, immigrants accounted for 19% of workers overall, but 32% of those in occupations with median earnings below $30,000 per year (compared with 16% in occupations paying more than $60,000 per year). Such government figures also presumably underreport the total impact of illegal immigration in the labor market's lower-wage segments. Immigration has provided the margin between a labor market in which employers would feel constant pressure to find and retain workers—especially lower-wage ones—and the labor market as it has operated, in which they can offer the same low wages and poor conditions for decades on end.

Both libertarians and progressives, with their different ideological commitments to open borders, offer a peculiar counterargument to the commonsense case for restricting immigration to boost worker power and wages. Workers are also consumers, they note, and thus immigrants increase both the supply of labor and the demand for it. Make any effort to reduce the flow of immigrants, and employers will need fewer workers to serve them as customers.

This argument fails as theory, because immigrants adding their labor to some segment of the labor market prompts a concentrated increase in supply within that segment but a diffuse increase in demand across all segments. Guest workers picking lettuce do not spend their wages primarily on lettuce. The evidence for the argument's failure in practice is that, quite obviously, no one believes it. The business groups and economists who have been vocally and pretextually advocating immigration to relieve labor shortages or reduce inflation rather give the game away. If an increase in immigration expanded demand by as much as supply, the "shortage" would remain acute. If it didn't suppress wages, inflation would not abate.

In (limited) defense of progressives, they are less inclined to make the pretextual economic argument for their preferred policy than simply to remain silent. A classic example is the Roosevelt Institute's 2022 whitepaper on "A Whole-of-Government Approach to Increasing Worker Power," which mentions immigration only once, in a footnote explaining that the issue will go unaddressed due to "space constraints." So much for whole-of-government. One might make a range of cases, on humanitarian or other grounds, for admitting large numbers of immigrant workers to the labor market's low-wage segments. But it is hard to take seriously anyone who professes a commitment to enhancing worker power and dignity while refusing even to discuss the most direct tool for enhancing them. There is no complicated trilemma here, only a simple dilemma. As I have written, "Worker Power, Loose Borders: Pick One."

The kernel of truth in the case that supply will not affect wages is that immigration generally, with skills composition similar to that of the existing population, need not distort labor-market conditions. When immigrants enter all segments of the labor market simultaneously, their cumulative effect on broadly distributed demand will offset their various smaller and more concentrated effects on supply. Another way to see this is to recognize that, economically speaking, immigration is a form of population growth. The American labor force's expansion as the next generation enters it has little implication for worker power because the economic characteristics of that cohort will generally mirror the characteristics of the market's existing participants. The same would hold true for a cohort of immigrants whose skills mirrored those of the population it was entering.

For policymakers, then, the skills composition rather than level of immigration is the main economic issue. The problem with American immigration policy has not been that it generously welcomes newcomers to our nation but that, as the statistics show, it has concentrated the increases in labor supply at the market's low-wage end. Conversely, immigration could *increase* worker power for lower-wage workers if that immigration were predominantly into other (i.e., higher-wage) segments. Thus, the need for a skills-based immigration system. Maintaining the current immigration level, but skewing its composition toward workers who will compete in the labor market's high-wage segments, will tend to strengthen worker power in the market's low-wage segments even more quickly than would a policy of restricting immigration broadly. It will increase demand for what is today low-wage labor, create strong incentives to invest in improving the quality of those jobs, and have distributional effects that shift income back toward the lower and middle classes.

Corporations and their spokespeople understandably dislike any constraint on their supply of labor, which would put them in the position of having to raise wages. So it is important to remember that capitalism does not succeed when profits are highest, but rather when those activities that will yield the highest profits are also those most in the public interest. As Adam Smith warned in *The Wealth of Nations*:

> [T]he rate of profit does not, like... wages, rise with the prosperity, and fall with the declension, of the society. On the contrary, it is naturally low in rich, and high in poor countries, and it is always highest in the countries which are going fastest to ruin. The interest of [employers], therefore, has not the same connexion with the general interest of the society.

Capitalism works when capital in pursuit of profit must find ways to expand output with the labor present, and when it must share the rising proceeds of that joint project. These conditions are more likely to hold, and will hold more strongly, when workers act as the limiting reagent in the production process. Business leaders will always chafe at this constraint and insist they need more labor, emphasizing the additional production they could unleash. The pleas must fall on deaf ears.

Flooding the low end of the domestic labor market with foreign workers may boost production but it erases the incentives to produce in ways beneficial to the lower-wage workers already here, or to share the proceeds of rising output with them. Total output may increase, but output per person will not. The nation might simultaneously become "wealthier" in aggregate and place itself on a lower trajectory for economic progress—for instance, with 50 years of declining construction-sector productivity. Owners of capital and managers of firms might see their profits and wages rise, even as the typical worker's wage stagnates or falls. In many respects, the impact of reliance on foreign labor entering the United States mirrors the impact of offshoring American production to foreign labor abroad. Capitalism will not deliver on its promise so long as American capital can choose workers in those markets over the workers in its own.

By contrast, when employing the nation's workers is a competitive imperative, and increasing productivity is the key to growth, that is what firms will do. This principle is so obvious to capitalism's proponents in other contexts, as they celebrate the power of competition in free markets to solve any problem, overcome any scarcity, innovate around any obstacle. Yet when labor is the problem to solve, scarcity to overcome, or obstacle inviting innovation, all is suddenly lost. If complaints about "jobs Americans won't do" elicited only laughter, and creating jobs that Americans *would* do were a non-negotiable prerequisite to generating profit, imagine what capitalism's awesome power might achieve.

Rather than set their hair ablaze and run circles around Washington screaming for help, how might firms respond when their best-laid plans are dashed by a labor market that does not offer the desired workers with the desired skills at the desired price? They might make investments in automation or training, allowing them to meet their needs with the workers they have and allowing them to offer better wages, both to those workers and others they might need to hire. They might alter working conditions or reengineer processes to make the jobs they offer a better fit for the workers they can find. They might reduce pay for higher-wage workers, at least in real terms, by no longer raising their wages to keep ahead of inflation. They might revisit their business models, changing the goods and services they provide or the customers they serve, thereby reallocating capital to uses better aligned with labor.

Prices would adjust, consumption would adjust, low wages would rise. Markets can work for workers if policymakers don't step in with the "solution" of bypassing the existing labor force with new and more pliable options.

AN UNPRODUCTIVE CONVERSATION

Pose such scenarios to Alex and Bernie, other CEOs, their lobbyists, or the "free market" economists they sponsor, and the objections are a muddled mix of superficial references to competition, productivity, and consumer welfare that belie a willful ignorance of what markets are for and how capitalism generates prosperity.

The superficially coherent argument underpinning the labor-shortage lament begins with a simplistic claim about productivity. A core tenet of the market fundamentalism that has shaped so much economic thinking in recent decades is the idea that all workers are paid a wage reflective of their individual output (the "marginal revenue product," to be precise). If this productivity does not rise, then wages will not rise—and if productivity appears to be rising while the median wage stagnates, this must mean that all the productivity gains are being achieved by higher-wage workers, justifying their more rapidly rising wages. If workers do not accept jobs at the wages and in the conditions that their productivity will bear, then a "shortage" exists. From this perspective, the question of how to find more workers willing to accept lower pay is an entirely reasonable one.

The fundamental problem with this view is its conflation of two different concepts of productivity. In the hypothetical market of Economics 101, where individuals produce and exchange various goods, measuring each person's productivity is easy enough and showing that his income will reflect that productivity is trivial. The problem emerges when the yeoman farmer takes a job installing windshields at a multinational car company. The company's labor productivity is still objectively measurable: value of cars coming off the assembly line less value of inputs purchased divided by employees. But how can the marginal productivity of various workers be disaggregated, especially seeing as many are not involved directly in any production process? Consider the windshield installer and the industrial engineer. If the engineer is developing new processes that allow the installer to secure windshields more quickly, whose productivity is rising? Who should be paid more? And what wage should the HR executive claim, for overseeing the benefits program used by them all? If one of their cars is a hit and moves off the lot with fewer discounts and thus higher prices, their marginal revenue product will be higher. But which of them has become more productive?

Such questions may seem tendentious, but they are inevitable in a model that pretends an objective measure of productivity validates the wage paid to each worker. The questions vanish painlessly with acknowledgment that, while a firm's productivity determines how much income it has to allocate amongst its workers and as profit, the allocation therein is a function of supply and demand in relevant labor markets and the power exercised by the various claimants. Windshield installers are paid what they are because that is what must be offered to employ the required number. The same is true of marketing executives. The total cost of producing the car is a function (in part) of how much all these workers must be paid, and the costs that manufacturers incur to produce their vehicles in turn affect vehicle prices, and thus manufacturer revenue, and thus the measure of a worker's value. An assessment of how many cars consumers will buy at a given price in turn informs how many cars to produce and thus how many windshield installers to hire. A central function of markets is to find equilibrium amongst these many variables.

The questions become even more interesting across industries. How do we compare Alex's programmers and Bernie's lettuce pickers? The price of a head of lettuce or a downloadable app determines the productivity of the firm growing or publishing it. But the relationship between those prices is itself a function of the relationship between the wages paid to workers in those industries, which depends upon supply and demand in labor markets. Which firm is more productive, the publisher of *Candy Crush*, or the grower of half the lettuce consumed on the Eastern Seaboard? Who should be paid more, a *Candy Crush* programmer or a lettuce picker? This depends upon how much lettuce to exchange for a download, which might change dramatically if food became scarce—*or if farmworkers did*.

Farmer Bernie seems to need the government's help addressing his labor shortage because his competitors are all relying on the lowest-wage labor, too, yielding low prices in the store, thus creating an economic rationale for the jobs to be low-paying ones. The circular logic of productivity measurement makes the status quo view of jobs self-fulfilling.

But if none of the growers had access to low-wage labor, paying higher wages would suddenly appear viable for them all. Picking lettuce for an hour might then appear more productive than spending an hour debugging a new loot box, and worthy of a higher wage. The relevant factors are the number of people available to do each type of work, the wages they demand, and the prices that customers will pay. Isn't this what markets are for?

MARKETS FOR ME, BUT NOT FOR THEE
Bernie, and his lobbyists at the U.S. Chamber, have only two answers available: one commonly deployed but backward in its economic reasoning, the other clearly implied but for good reason rarely said aloud. The first answer is all about consumption. If low-wage workers gain substantial raises, lettuce will get more expensive; so will eating out, completing a home renovation, and so on. Lower-income households and those on fixed incomes will suffer. Consumer welfare will decline, and that is the yardstick by which economic progress is measured.

As a preliminary matter, the scale of the prospective price increase requires consideration. For instance, down on the farm, labor costs are typically less than 20% or for specialty crops close to 40% of total operating costs, and the price from the farm is about one-third the price on the shelf. People colloquially worry about strawberries costing $50 per quart, but the reality is that even if wages quadrupled, farms made no investments to increase output per picker, and the full cost were passed on to consumers, prices might rise 40%. A $3.00 quart of strawberries might cost $4.50, a $1.70 head of lettuce might cost $2.50. Nor are farm products a significant share of the American family's budget. The U.S. Department of Agriculture estimates that 7.4% of American food spending goes to farm production, while the Bureau of Labor Statistics estimates that the typical household spends roughly $1,000 on fruits and vegetables consumed at home, suggesting only about $100 attributable to farm labor. Quadrupling those wages might cost the typical family $300 in a year.

The agricultural example is illustrative, but not the best lens for considering the economy-wide implications of rapidly rising wages at the labor market's low end. A $300 increase in food costs could be quite painful for many families, while only a very narrow category of farmworkers would receive the very substantial benefit. The broader lesson is that low-wage labor is only a small share of the total cost embedded in most products. Especially with an adjustment period, no systemic shocks occur, which is good news for everyone.

The news for the low-wage workers themselves is even better. Because low-wage labor is only one part of what low-income households consume, a broad-based increase in low-end wages raises the earnings for low-income households faster than it can raise their costs. When low wages increase but other costs do not, the total cost increase and thus the final price increase is relatively lower. Wage increases may fuel some inflation, but those receiving the wage increases see real gains. Indeed, a peculiar feature of the present alarm about wages driving inflation is that this is not happening. With real wages falling, they represent a drag on the overall rate at which prices are rising—one wonders why free-market economists do not see fit to focus more attention on, say, the decision of firms to raise prices faster than they apparently need to. Imagine the screaming to come, if and when low-wage workers find themselves with sufficient power to achieve real gains at the expense of higher-wage workers and profits.

If higher wages prompted no investments to increase output per worker (a poor assumption, but a worst case worth considering), real gains for lower-income workers would mean real losses for higher-income ones, who would experience the price increases without the higher wages—in real terms, their own wages would fall. That shift would be an entirely natural one in a well-functioning market. The engineer is as worthless without the windshield installer as the windshield installer is without the engineer, perhaps more so. When forces of supply and demand led to higher-wage workers earning a rising share of firm output, and capital earning a handsome return, while the median worker shared little of the gain, this was "the market working." Economists developed elaborate theories of "skill-biased technological change" to justify the result. If the market now begins to work in the other direction, as HR executives find themselves rather dependent on workers to make products and provide services, surely that deserves at least as much celebration. And how wonderful an illustration of the market's power if, as prices adjust, HR executives find themselves heading down to jobs on the shop floor.

The celebration is not forthcoming. For all its talk about productivity, the business community's enthusiasm for price signals and efficient market outcomes turns out to be rather selective. The implication of Bernie's thinking is a second answer: that some jobs are *better* than others and *should* pay more. The programmer could pick lettuce if he wanted, but the farmworker cannot code. Past market outcomes were so readily celebrated because they reinforced this worldview. The phrase "jobs Americans won't do" is so potent because, in setting out certain classes of work as beneath the dignity of the people issuing the judgment, it makes clear exactly what they really think. The irony is that, to maintain his faith that wages fairly reflect productivity, and advance his preference for a supply of low-wage labor that eases his own life and elevates his own status, the "free market" enthusiast must embrace the role of central planner overriding price signals with his own judgment of what prices should be.

Substantively, though, classifying which jobs Americans will do makes no sense. It wrongly assumes that jobs have fixed characteristics—picking crops or cleaning rooms or shingling roofs is a job Americans won't do because it pays poorly, makes difficult demands, and must be performed under harsh conditions; programming apps or suing for patent infringement is a job Americans will do because it pays well and comes with great perks. But the only fixed element of the job is the function performed—the picking or cleaning or building; the programming or document review—and even that can be mediated in many ways by technology. Described in the abstract, harvesting fruit outdoors or repairing a house is not an inherently inferior task to sitting in a cubicle (or, perish the thought, an open floorplan) staring at a rectangle of glowing pixels while moving fingers up and down on a piece of plastic. Described as a vocation, feeding the nation or providing it with shelter is rather more edifying than targeting it with underwear ads.

Bernie could solve his problem quickly if he and his competitors all had to offer a starting wage of $30 per hour, an engaging experience, flexible scheduling, career paths to management, and 30 minutes in a catered, air-conditioned tent after each 30 minutes in the field. Trucking would be more popular if hauls were shorter, weeks away were followed by weeks off, and pay were more like that of investment banking. Conversely, no one will work for Alex.

For 280 of the first 282 months in the Federal Reserve Bank of Atlanta's "Wage Growth Tracker" dataset, workers in "high-skill" occupations saw their nominal wages grow as fast or faster than workers in "low-skill" ones. In June 2021 the picture flipped and, for the nearly two years thereafter, every month saw higher (nominal) growth for low-skill wages. The near-perfect overlap of that period with the one in which experts have proclaimed the labor market in crisis is, perhaps, not a coincidence.

The choice to treat these types of jobs and workers so differently, and the power that choice holds over public policy, is cultural. Certainly, it has no moral basis. It has no economic basis, either, beyond the circular logic now breaking down at the first sign of labor's insufficient pliability to capital's demands. Good riddance.

HIGH-WAGE IMMIGRATION POLICY

A major benefit of immigration policy is that it acts directly on the relevant variable: the supply of workers. Other tools, from education and training to trade and industrial policy to tax reform and public spending, all have the potential to improve labor market conditions as well, but they require a chain reaction to reach the wages offered to workers, and greater demand for workers accomplishes little if swamped by constant increases in supply. One way to understand the labor market's outcomes in recent decades is that these policies did work, demand did rise significantly, productivity did rise significantly... and the supply of workers was allowed to rise at the rate needed to counteract it all. As a result, the benefits accrued primarily to a narrow set of high-wage workers and to businesses whose profits surged. That certainly seems to be the story that the data tell.

If policymakers want to slow the growth in labor supply through changes to immigration policy, they can do so. The catastrophic failure to enforce immigration law in recent years has led to skepticism that enforcement is possible—indeed, efforts have been so inept that one might reasonably conclude the promotion of such skepticism was the goal. Piled atop these failures comes the rhetoric that setting and enforcing an immigration policy for the benefit of Americans—of all races and ethnicities, including the millions of legal immigrants already in the country and the millions more that we will welcome—is somehow immoral or inconsistent with the nation's values. But setting the terms of entry into the community is the right and obligation of every nation, and applying the law firmly and fairly is the non-negotiable prerequisite to a functioning democratic republic. What we have lacked is the will. What is unbefitting our nation and inconsistent with our values is the lawlessness that we have tolerated.

ENFORCING THE LAW

In isolation, support might be quite broad for a skills-based system, which welcomes large numbers of immigrants and skews the group's composition heavily toward highly skilled newcomers who are likely to compete in the labor market's high-wage segments. But implementation requires a robust system of enforcement that limits labor supply to legally authorized workers. On a prospective basis, the nation must be able to control border crossings, ensure that temporary residents depart when their visas expire, and hold employers accountable for hiring only legal workers. And any effort to prevent future illegal entry into the labor market must grapple with the more than 10 million illegal immigrants living in the country and often participating in the labor market already.

The best chance of making progress is to recognize that putting future immigration policy on sound footing is more important for the economy than dealing with past illegal immigration in one way or another. A compromise on the past, where there are no good answers, coupled with a strong policy for the future, where the right answer is clear, is a far superior outcome than the current impasse. The one caveat for any bargain is that the promise of future enforcement must be credible. If the world believes, based on how the United States deals with its existing population of illegal immigrants, that future illegal entry will be rewarded as well, the nation will never have control of its labor market. Policy reform is impossible without secure borders and effective laws.

Mandatory E-Verify should be the cornerstone of labor market enforcement. U.S. policymakers already have a system, called "E-Verify," that validates the legal status of American workers. What's lacking is the political will to ensure its consistent use. Employers should have no choice, they should face penalties for employing illegal workers even inadvertently, and penalties for intentional and repeated offenses should be catastrophic and include criminal prosecution. The law should recognize that the employer who opts for illegal and exploitable labor and undermines the power of American workers is committing a far more serious and less excusable offense against the community than the illegal immigrant pursuing a better life. Aggressive deterrence of employer malfeasance constrains the labor supply directly and, by eliminating the job opportunities and thus much of the incentive for illegal immigration, offers an efficient means of addressing that challenge as well.

For immigrants already in the country illegally, policymakers need a solution that will neither send sudden shocks through the labor market and millions of lives nor signal lackluster commitment to enforcing the law. They should pursue an approach that has received little consideration from either side of the immigration debate: last in, first out (LIFO). Under LIFO, the more recently an illegal immigrant has arrived in the country, the sooner he must leave. Those who have only just arrived, migrate frequently across the border, or have a criminal record would be barred from the labor market immediately. Those who have already resided in the country for up to five years would be issued a work permit that lasts for the same number of future years as the number of past years for which residence can be established. And those the United States has allowed to settle in the country over five years or more would be granted a five-year work permit that could lead to permanent legal status after payment of a substantial fine, on condition that the more transient groups have left as scheduled and the nation has demonstrated firm control over its borders and its labor market.

ELIMINATING GUEST-WORKER PROGRAMS

Perhaps most obviously—and easily, with robust enforcement in place—temporary visa programs for low-wage work should be immediately capped at current levels and then phased down to zero over a decade. Both the H-2A and H-2B programs, for temporary agricultural and other seasonal work, respectively, provide employers with an alternative to offering jobs to Americans at good wages in decent conditions. The only economic rationale for doing so is to artificially suppress wages and prices below levels where the market would otherwise settle, benefiting consumers and employers at the expense of American workers, and disproportionately benefiting higher-income households that enjoy the lower prices without seeing their own labor undercut.

The H-1B program, designed for high-skilled workers unavailable in the domestic market, would be a more difficult case if it operated as designed. At least hypothetically, employers could seek skill sets that no American workers possess—jobs Americans *can't*, not *won't*, do—and expanding the supply of such specialized and high-wage labor would redound to the benefit of lower-income households whose workers would not be in competition. In practice, the program is a boondoggle. Roughly 40% of the nearly 100,000 H-1B visas issued each year are for employment at 30 companies, more than half of which are top outsourcing providers like Infosys, Tata Consultancy Services, and Cognizant, which use the visas to replace incumbent American workers with temporary foreign workers paid less than market wages, unable to change jobs, and subject to abuse. Roughly 85% of visas are awarded to entry-level and junior workers.

In the short run, rather than assign H-1B visas via lottery, the federal government should award them based on wage level, with all visas going to those positions for which employers are offering the highest wages. Ironically, those highest paying and most attractive seeming jobs, not the typical programming roles, and certainly not the farm work, are truly the jobs Americans won't do; the ones where employers might credibly claim an inability to fill the role and policymakers might serve the common good by providing assistance. But one benefit of shifting permanent immigration toward highly skilled workers is that H-1B visas can be phased down like other temporary programs. If just an additional 10% of the roughly 1,000,000 green cards issued each year went to the most highly skilled workers, the influx would exceed the total number of H-1B visas issued annually.

POLICYMAKING WITH PURPOSE
A temporary visa program may still make sense for the United States, if it operates explicitly as an element of industrial policy aimed at building capabilities and capacity in strategically important sectors. The CHIPS and Science Act's subsidies for domestic semiconductor producers provide a case in point. The issue has arisen that firms hoping to participate are struggling to find the engineers and construction specialists necessary to develop a multi-billion-dollar fabrication plant.

At first glance, this appears to be another lame complaint of "labor shortage," to which the answer should be that the real failure is in the business plan. But note what's different: policymakers have chosen a specific need that the market was not meeting, chip capacity, and they are seeking to override price signals and private capital allocations. The unavailability of labor to support the objective should be neither surprising nor discouraging. The projects are ones that private actors did not consider economical and were not pursuing. That's what the industrial policy is for.

Unlike at Facebook, whose prowess in targeting ads and immiserating teens does little to advance national imperatives or the common good, using temporary workers makes sense to support the rebuilding of domestic semiconductor capacity. That project's immediate purpose is not a jobs program—though in the long run, the industry and the ecosystem supporting it could provide vast numbers of good jobs far from already-booming regions. Clearly identifying other priorities and shaping policy to meet them is necessary and proper. Further, a well-designed policy should not only pair such temporary visas to specific initiatives, but also establish predictable time limits, creating the incentive for employers to invest in building domestic labor capacity for the future.

The question of purpose should always be central for economic policy. Policymakers and business leaders who have viewed the economy's purpose as providing cheap stuff and investor returns have understandably favored an immigration policy that kept wages low. But rising wages, especially for lower-wage workers, are not a threat to broad-based prosperity; they are its source. The "supply-side" theory that prioritizing the conditions for capital's success will eventually redound to the benefit of all is a bastardization of capitalism rightly understood and, as an empirical matter, a failure. Good and dignified jobs that allow workers to support their families and communities are not a hoped-for byproduct of a healthy economy; they are its purpose. Gains in consumption and material living standards are desirable as well, but cheaper prices through lower wages is a losing proposition for affected families and the nation as a whole.

The American economy has not failed in recent decades with respect to the material standard of living. The failure has been the creation of insecure jobs that do not meet workers' needs, a shift in the economy-wide distribution of income that has left working families struggling, and a decay in social solidarity as the economy's winners declare themselves most valuable and the losers expendable. Only the power for workers that comes from being *needed* will reverse those trends.

CHAPTER FOUR

Capital

R obust financial markets are vital to a productive economy, but they are not an end unto themselves. Their task is to facilitate investment by connecting capital to its most productive uses at the lowest possible cost. In recent decades, American finance has metastasized, claiming a disproportionate share of the nation's top business talent and the economy's profits, even as actual investment has declined. This "financialization" of the American economy weakens the nation and threatens our future prosperity.

In "Planning for When the Market Cannot," Julius Krein unravels the baseless assumptions that pursuit of profit will lead to productive investment and that policymakers cannot improve upon what the market might deliver. In "The Rise of Wall Street and the Fall of American Investment," I provide the empirical support for Krein's theoretical case, distinguishing between the different kinds of actual-investment and non-investment occurring in the American economy and suggesting how we might begin to get financial markets back on track.

PLANNING FOR WHEN THE MARKET CANNOT

by Julius Krein

Mr. Krein was the editor of American Affairs
and a member of American Compass's board of directors.

First published by American Compass on May 4, 2020.

The ardent anticommunist intellectual Raymond Aron, when asked to describe the excesses of "liberal [libertarian] economic orthodoxy," pointed to its reflexive hostility toward any kind of government planning. In this worldview, observed Aron, planning is seen as "the beginning of servitude, if not misery. Planning becomes inherently evil, just like Marxists view capitalism as evil."

Indeed, for Friedrich Hayek and his followers, government planning was the root of all tyranny. Twentieth-century fascism, for instance, was not the contingent result of economic collapse, war, historical circumstances, or specific ideological developments—it was the inevitable outcome of government planning. And those who advocate for government planning, said Hayek, "can think of nothing better than to imitate Hitler." Not only is the quality of any particular plan irrelevant, in this vision, but the planning of Hitler or Stalin differed from the planning of the Roosevelt administration only in degree.

Since the end of the Cold War, this anti-planning orthodoxy has in some ways hardened further. Not only Soviet-style efforts to ration resources and micromanage firms by centralized diktat, but also the traditional efforts of liberal democracies to ensure investment in long-term economic and social priorities are now gathered under the "planning" heading and treated as indistinguishably awful. At least savvier neoliberals such as Milton Friedman were once able to admit that the U.S. government's direction of the economy during World War II was beneficial (and that government planning for such an overriding strategic purpose generally could be). Hayek himself famously allowed for basic social insurance and specifically defended "planning for competition"—using the state to create or reinforce market mechanisms. Today's market fundamentalists, however, brook no such concessions. In 2020, Ambassador Nikki Haley argued in the *Wall Street Journal* that policies like "more tax credits here, more subsidies there, more mandates for this, more regulations for that" represent a "watered-down or hyphenated capitalism, which is the slow path to socialism."

The critics do not understand their critique. The theoretical basis for their objections is Hayek's "knowledge problem," which has become widely accepted, even by many who do not share Hayek's or Haley's politics. But the knowledge problem is not generically applicable to all forms of planning, and its indiscriminate use reduces the complex issues surrounding planning to a misleading binary of planning versus liberty that sets every policy discussion on the slippery slope toward tyranny.

The essence of Hayek's argument is that no central planner could possibly aggregate, process, or act upon information as efficiently as decentralized participants respond to the information and incentives conveyed by the price system in competitive markets. Not only will a central planner allocate resources poorly, but the mere attempt to do so will impede the progress and utilization of social knowledge. Government planning, seen in this light, is not simply inefficient but inherently arbitrary and oppressive.

On the surface, the argument that government cannot plan effectively because it cannot possess all the knowledge dispersed across society seems at once philosophically elegant and a matter of common sense. But this argument is based upon a non sequitur, and the categorical rejection of planning that results from it is ideological overreach. The fact that government planners are not omniscient is obvious, but it does not automatically follow that planning is always ineffective. Perfect information is simply not a precondition of successful planning in either the private or the public sectors.

The information that is conveyed by market prices is also severely limited. Price signals, even when perfectly undistorted, are not sufficient for either businesses or government to allocate resources effectively, much less do they engender a "spontaneous order" that is the best of all possible worlds. The fact that government is not subject to market competition does introduce unique perils, but it also creates unique opportunities and even duties. Unfortunately, metaphysical speculation about the "knowledge problem" cannot help us to understand either. A more practical approach is needed for navigating the problems and limitations of government planning, as well as the circumstances in which it is necessary and beneficial.

THE PROBLEM WITH THE KNOWLEDGE PROBLEM

The most common modern objection to government planning begins from the premise that, in Hayek's own words, "the 'data' from which the economic calculus start are never for the whole society 'given' to a single mind which could work out the implications and can never be so given." The assertion that no central planner can possess all available knowledge is hardly controversial. What too often escapes scrutiny, however, is the assumption that such knowledge is necessary to plan effectively in the first place. The historical record makes clear that it is not.

Nonetheless, several generations of libertarian writers have continued to repeat derivative "knowledge problem" arguments. Consider, for example, a 2020 essay by Richard Reinsch in *National Affairs*:

> *In a 2006 paper, economists Howard Pack and Kamal Saggi laid out a list of suggested questions that federal bureaucrats would have to be able to answer in order to successfully implement the sort of industrial policy many economic nationalists now seek. For example, they would have to identify which sectors have a long-term comparative advantage, which benefit from dynamic scale economies, which firms and industries generate knowledge spillovers, and what the magnitude and direction of inter-industry spillovers would be.*
>
> *This is just a tiny sampling of the types of questions federal agencies would need to confront, the answer to each of which is time-sensitive, detailed, and discoverable only in pieces by certain actors with*

deep and regular experience in very particular sectors. Uniting all the answers into some coherent, communicable whole is virtually impossible. This leaves us with the question of how best to approach such questions: via individuals and firms working for their own self-interest, who are heavily dependent on prices and the desire for profits to guide their decisions; or via state actors imposing blunt general directives on industry?

All this may be part of the catechism in the cloisters of libertarian nonprofits, but it is completely at odds with practical experience. Indeed, it is possible to argue that these very questions have been ignored by every successful implementation of industrial policy, which is surely planning insofar as it requires the setting of goals and the development of policy in their pursuit, but which includes no Party functionaries deciding how many pounds of screws to send where.

It certainly would not have been possible to identify any "comparative advantage" in Taiwan's semiconductor industry before the Taiwanese government essentially created it, nor in South Korea's semiconductor, shipbuilding, or auto industries before its government undertook ambitious industrial policies. Likewise, it is possible that the Chinese Communist Party perfectly calculated "inter-industry spillovers" before directing billions of dollars in state subsidies to Huawei, but even if it did, that calculation probably has little to do with the company's present dominance of 5G components. And the same is true for Israel's defense technology sector, America's biotech sector, and countless other examples past and present. Whatever knowledge is necessary to conduct an effective industrial policy, "uniting all the answers into some coherent, communicable whole" is simply not part of it.

If anything, government intervention—and thus planning—becomes more necessary when less market and industry knowledge is available. If a project's commercial prospects (dependent on factors such as comparative advantage and potential commercialization across different or new industries) are easily known, then risk is low and investor capital is cheaper and easier to raise. But if a project's commercial prospects are only dimly perceivable, then it may simply be impossible to raise capital from economically motivated investors, no matter how important the effort. Thus governments typically must take a leading role in critical areas like basic research and the development of infant industries, among many others.

Perhaps, as Reinsch implies, any enterprise unable to raise profit-driven investor capital should not exist. But then it is hard to imagine how thriving U.S. industries built on everything from radar to the space program to the internet would have materialized, or how so many of the companies built via the Asian development model have come to be world leaders. The reality is that many technologies and even entire industries now recognized as foundational or world-leading—including ones that ultimately generated massive commercial profits—required government support at some stage. Had the vast profit opportunities of all these technologies and industries been known prior to their creation, then no government involvement would likely have been needed to produce them. It is precisely because indicators like the potential for commercialization across industries are often unknown and unknowable, however, that government funding and planning can sometimes prove valuable.

Planning also plays a vital role when knowledge, even if available, is of no interest to the private sector. Nations have a wide range of goals beyond the maximization of profit, which the most perfectly free and efficient market will make no effort to achieve. In such situations, it is absurd to reject the planner's imperfect efforts for lack of knowledge and opt instead to rely upon private actors behaving like perfect imbeciles.

None of this is to say that government intervention is always necessary or desirable—only that the extent of "knowledge" possessed by the planner is not a helpful guide in deciding whether it is or not. What differentiates governments (at least those that borrow in their own currency) from the private sector is that they are not constrained by internal profits or external market forces. They can, therefore, take on much greater economic risk than any private-sector actor, which allows them to fund important but highly prospective endeavors. Of course, the danger inherent in such freedom from market discipline is that governments may fund counterproductive activities—maintaining corrupt patronage networks, attempting to realize ideological fantasies, and so on—indefinitely. That danger is real, but it has very little to do with a lack of market knowledge among the planners. One might raise precisely the same concerns of corrupt patronage networks and ideological fanaticism, and indeed find them realized right here in America, among a governing cadre that has forsworn planning entirely. The availability of "knowledge" is simply not a useful metric for evaluating the soundness or unsoundness of any particular government plan.

THE PRICE IS WRONG

In fairness to Hayek, his own critiques of government planning were more subtle than those of his epigones today. Hayek's principal argument was not that central planners would fail to achieve their goals because they could not properly identify comparative advantage or calculate the magnitude and direction of inter-industry spillovers. He largely rejected the pretensions and presuppositions of neoclassical and marginalist economics and recognized that a lack of perfect knowledge did not make planning impossible in either the public or private sectors. Instead, the main problem with government planning, he argued, was that it prevented the spontaneous coordination of individual plans via market competition.

The crucial function of the price system, as imagined by Hayek, is that it enables the unconscious coordination of many decentralized individual plans, despite the imperfect knowledge and intentions of each actor. Thus, market competition allows for the maximum utilization of knowledge and best allocation of resources for society as a whole. Government planning, regardless of whether any particular project succeeds or fails, undermines this unconscious coordination.

But do market prices actually accomplish what Hayek claims they do? Tellingly, abstract theoretical discussions occupy much more of Hayek's attention than any actual, practical commercial activity. Consider one of the few practical examples given in his canonical work, "The Use of Knowledge in Society":

Assume that somewhere in the world a new opportunity for the use of some raw material, say, tin, has arisen, or that one of the sources of supply of tin has been eliminated. It does not matter for our purpose—and it is very significant that it does not matter—which of these two causes has made tin more scarce. All that the users of tin need to know is that some of the tin they used to consume is now more profitably employed elsewhere and that, in consequence, they must economize tin. There is no need for the great majority of them even to know where the more urgent need has arisen, or in favor of what other needs they ought to husband the supply. If only some of them know directly of the new demand, and switch resources over to it, and if the people who are aware of the new gap thus created in turn fill it from still other sources, the effect will rapidly spread throughout the whole economic system. . . . The whole acts as one market, not because any of its members survey the whole field, but because their limited individual fields of vision sufficiently overlap so that through many intermediaries the relevant information is communicated to all.

Central to Hayek's theory of the price system is his claim that the users of any given commodity do not need to know why its price has changed. They simply need to observe the price change in order to adjust, allowing the entire system to maintain its harmony without any conscious design. All the information necessary for the system to function, in other words, is communicated by the price change itself.

Only a lifelong academic like Hayek could possibly believe this. In fact, all but the most trivial buyers of a material need to know the reasons behind price fluctuations to allocate capital effectively in response. If, for instance, the price of tin in Hayek's example changed because of some temporary and random phenomenon, the buyer might simply seek to mitigate the effects of large price fluctuations by purchasing hedges from a financial institution. If, on the other hand, the price change was related to the buyer's transport and warehousing costs, he might look for other distributors. If the cause was the exhaustion of the mineral resource, he might invest in switching to another input material. If it was due to the formation of a monopoly or cartel, he might lobby for antitrust action or attempt to develop another source of supply. Other tin producers, likewise, will need to know the causes of price movements and ascertain how long a new price level is likely to last before investing substantial capital in the development of new resources or curtailing existing production. Price signals alone simply do not communicate sufficient knowledge upon which to base the most important economic decisions. Even the arbitrageur—a figure who occupies a prominent place in both Hayek's writings and today's financialized economy—requires information about the reasons behind price differences to know whether an opportunity will persist long enough to execute the arbitrage.

Hayek's notion of knowledge discovery and market competition fundamentally confuses rationing and investing, but there is a difference between the two. Price competition often (though not always) works well for rationing, or deciding who gets what in the present, which need not require a view of the future. The same is not true of investing capital, which requires taking (more or less) risk on a (more or less contrarian) view of the future. Long-term investment capital (and thus productive capacity) simply cannot be prudently allocated on the basis of price signals alone. Hayek's spontaneous order, in more than one sense, has no future.

Hayek also fails to consider the possibility that the price of tin may have changed because a foreign government banned exports. Or, to make the example timely, what if a foreign government begins subsidizing a strategic industry, resulting in lower returns on domestic investment in that industry? Following price signals and market incentives alone will ensure that domestic investment evaporates and leadership in the industry shifts to the foreign competitor. Perhaps this doesn't matter—consumers should just take advantage of these subsidies, according to one argument. But what if the foreign government subsequently threatens to cut off medical supplies in the midst of a global pandemic, supplies which can no longer be produced in one's own country as a result of the failure to counter the foreign subsidies?

In short, the price system offers no guarantee of optimal—or even adequate—social knowledge coordination or capital allocation. Market prices are just as likely to transmit the interventions of hostile foreign governments as the workings of some benevolent spontaneous order. Indeed, it is an act of blind faith to imagine that any such order exists at all.

Because slavishly following market signals does not always produce the best of all possible worlds, government planning does not always represent the first step on the road to serfdom. Indeed, a healthy market economy often depends upon sound government planning, and sound government planning often intentionally strengthens the private sector—from Hamilton's National Bank to the *Homestead Act* to various New Deal programs to Defense Department research funding. Contra Hayek, government planning does not automatically lead to tyranny; if it did, the American experiment would have failed long ago. But any political community that cannot plan for its own collective future is neither free nor self-governing in any meaningful sense—and probably cannot remain wealthy for long.

OVERCOMING SECULAR DOGMA
Ultimately, Hayekian critiques of government planning are compelling only insofar as one is willing to ignore practical reality. His theories may have been adequate as anti-Soviet propaganda, but they are completely useless as a guide for policy. To be sure, attempting to maintain Gosplan-like control over the economy or to eliminate all market competition would be utterly foolish and in practice impossible. One does not need Hayekian theory to recognize that. The ideological antipathy toward all government planning that such theories inspire, however, has been devastating to America's political economy and strategic position during the last few decades.

Yet no matter how many strategic industries are lost, or how obvious the deterioration of broad swaths of the country has become, another market theodicy is always being written. In this sense, as Aron suggested, Hayekian libertarianism—and much of the economic thinking dominant on the right for decades—is best understood as an ideological project akin to Communism. As political movements, both rely more on secularized theology than any serious reading of history or intelligent analysis of policy. Both are, in the words of Karl Löwith, "essentially, though secretly, a history of fulfillment and salvation in terms of social economy. What seems to be a scientific discovery ... is, on the contrary, from the first to the last sentence inspired by an eschatological faith, which, in its turn, 'determines' the whole sweep and range of all particular statements."

Thirty years after the Cold War, it is time to stop performing Hayekian morality plays. Instead of pretending to dwell in the spontaneous order imagined in theory, we should give ourselves permission to start planning and building a healthier political-economic order in reality.

THE RISE OF WALL STREET AND THE FALL OF AMERICAN INVESTMENT

by Oren Cass

Adapted from an essay first published by American Compass on March 25, 2021.

Confusion over the nature of investment is pervasive among economic policymakers and commentators, has bled into the popular culture, and threatens the nation's future prosperity. Actual-investment, by which I mean the allocation of capital toward the development of new productive capacity—the building of structures, the installment of machines, the creation of intellectual property—has been weakening in America for decades now. By contrast, what we often call investment, and what seems constantly to expand as a share of our economic activity, is merely the trading of assets for profit and power.

The distinguishing feature of non-investment is that it deploys no resources. Take the $100 million purchase of a rare painting. At first glance, this might appear a tragic waste of money. How many malaria nets could this dilettante have bought for the same price? But the outrage is misplaced; no resources have been consumed. One day, Party A has the painting and Party B has $100 million. The next day their positions have switched. Party A may go battle malaria with the $100 million just as surely as Party B could have.

The same phenomenon is at work when someone purchases $100 million in shares of Intel Corporation. First he had $100 million and someone else had the Intel shares; now the reverse is true. But no "investment in Intel" has occurred; indeed, for Intel, little has changed. It has no more resources at its disposal. It will build no new chip foundry as a result. When we call the exchanger of assets an "investor," we imply that he has somehow contributed to the profit he realizes if Intel's stock rises or it pays a generous dividend. But this is not true. He is a non-investor, cheering on Intel from the bleachers like a Dallas Cowboys fan who places a bet on his team in the big game.

Non-investors take three forms. One is the saver, who converts his cash into other assets that he expects will generate income and appreciate in value as the economy grows. Saving is an entirely sensible and responsible activity, but it does not represent actual-investment in the economy. Savers merely use various assets as vessels for their savings and grow richer as those assets increase in value, despite having done nothing to effect that increase. Indeed, the typical "investor" likely has no idea how to make an actual-investment and would struggle to find an opportunity to do so. Anyway, a financial advisor would likely counsel against it: far too much concentrated risk, putting so many eggs in one little firm's basket, and all the worse if that firm is a local one.

Another non-investor, the speculator, is in the business of gambling on particular assets, attempting to outguess the market and thus generate a profit from buying low and selling high. This is what stock pickers do, as do many hedge funds. Thus, the *Wall Street Journal* properly headlined a report on Warren Buffett's recent investments, "Berkshire Hathaway Bets Billions on Verizon and Chevron." This game is worse than zero-sum. For someone to be outperforming the market, someone else must by definition be underperforming it. But in the process, managers extract fees for placing the bets and other intermediaries take their own share for processing the transactions. For them there is no gamble at all, merely a guaranteed profit at someone else's expense.

At least Buffett was buying the actual equity of real corporations. Increasingly, speculators like hedge funds prefer to speculate on mere derivatives that dispense with the fiction of any connection to the creation of wealth in the real economy, while (non-)investment banks specialize in creating such instruments for others to play with. The same day it reported on Buffett's bet, the *Journal* also informed readers that an "Online-Trading Platform Will Let Investors Bet on Yes-or-No Questions." The inspiration, according to the platform's founder, came from working at Goldman Sachs, where he realized that much trading amounted to such betting anyway. In some cases, bets ride on legal rather than economic outcomes, as when hedge funds finance lawsuits in return for a share of any proceeds or acquire distressed debt in hopes of outmaneuvering other parties in bankruptcy negotiations.

The third non-investor is the controller, who acquires an entire enterprise and takes responsibility for its operation but, rather than investing in and improving it, extracts available resources at the expense of its sustainability and those who rely on it. Private equity firms fit this description when they load companies with debt, collect dividends and fees, cut costs, outsource operations, and then resell what's left—often to other private equity firms or even to themselves. They are less non-investors than dis-investors, actively eroding the economy's capital base and converting productive assets and organizations into cash.

Wall Street's descent into an economic sideshow would be mostly amusing if not for the havoc it wreaks in the real economy on which the nation's prosperity depends. As non-investors have overrun the banks and markets and taken control of corporations, actual-investment has slowed. The nation's capital base is smaller by literally trillions of dollars as a result, representing untold enterprises never built, innovations never pursued, and workers never given opportunity. The companies that need to deploy actual-investment have lost the capacity and mandate to do so, and instead hand cash back to non-investors at the expense of their own health. The top business talent that once filled the entrepreneurial and managerial ranks has followed suit, relocating to Wall Street and dedicating itself to collecting the lucrative fees that non-investors command for their performance. The circus tent is propped up by the Federal Reserve, whose bankers seem to have decided that asset prices must always go up, and have the money-printing power to make it so.

The result should be unsurprising: Productivity growth stalled, down from 2.1% annually during 1980–2009 to 1.2% during 2010–19, and *negative* in the manufacturing sector in recent years. Wages stagnated, lower for production and non-supervisory workers in 2019 than 50 years earlier. The trade balance collapsed, falling from equilibrium in the 1970s to below -3% of GDP in 1999 and staying there. A pattern of wealth accumulation emerged in which nearly all gains go to the already-wealthy who hold capital. From 1989 to 2019, the liquid financial assets of households in the bottom 50% of wealth rose by $172 billion (+39%) while the top 10% gained $29 trillion (+291%). Factor in consumer credit, and the gains for the top 10% remain virtually unchanged while the bottom 50% find themselves with $1.5 trillion *less* liquid net worth than 30 years ago.

Markets are not self-regulating, and these problems will not solve themselves. For capitalism to deliver on its promise, policymakers will have to do their jobs and reestablish the conditions in which it will function well.

THE SOFTENING OF THE FIRM

Responsibility for domestic investment lies ultimately in the non-financial business sector, which the capitalist system relies on to deploy the nation's resources productively. The assumption that this will happen undergirds much of neoclassical economics and, especially, the obsession in right-of-center supply-side economics with cutting taxes—lower tax rates should mean more capital available for businesses to invest and the prospect of greater profits should strengthen the incentive for them to do so.

Financial firms and markets play a vital role in this process, moving capital to those who need it and can use it most productively. Operating companies pay for access to that capital, both delivering a return to those who provide it and a fee to those who facilitate its transfer. But typically, an operating company's use of such services would be limited to its start-up, when it must invest before it is profitable, and to situations where an infusion of capital is needed to finance a major new initiative or overcome a crisis. A sustainably profitable firm is, by definition, generating sufficient cash from operations to (1) fund the investment necessary to maintain or grow its capital stock, and (2) return a profit to the shareholders who are the owners of the capital that the business uses.

That was historically the case, and many assume that it remains true. "Profits are what keep a business going and allow it to thrive," says former UN Ambassador Nikki Haley. "They generate the funds needed for more job creation. You don't need an advanced economics degree to understand this." But that's not how the economy works today. "Since the 1980s, in aggregate, corporations have funded the stock market rather than vice versa (as is conventionally assumed)," explains economist William Lazonick. "Over the decade 2005–14 net equity issues of nonfinancial corporations averaged minus $399 billion per year." Whereas corporations used to retain and reinvest roughly half of their earnings, a 2019 report from Senator Marco Rubio notes that share has fallen below 10%, with the rest paid out to shareholders. From 2008 to 2017, corporations paid out 100% of their earnings.

This change in our system of capitalism is more starkly apparent at the firm level. Take firms headquartered in the United States and traded publicly on the New York Stock Exchange or the NASDAQ, and place them into three buckets:

- First are the *Sustainers*, which fit our standard model for a successful company. *Sustainers* are profitable, and that profit is sufficient both to make investments that grow their capital bases and to return money to shareholders. Put another way, they can and do invest in new assets faster than they use up existing ones. Most companies in a well-functioning capitalist economy should be *Sustainers* and, historically, most were.
- Second are the *Growers*, which fit our standard model for a company that requires access to capital from financial markets. *Growers* are investing to expand their capital base and investing more than they can finance through their own profits. They tap the financial markets to make up the difference by issuing equity or debt, generating investable cash.
- Third are the *Eroders*, which do not comport with our intuition. *Eroders* have enough profit to grow their capital bases like *Sustainers* and still return cash to shareholders, but they choose not to. Instead, they actively disinvest from themselves, allowing their capital bases to erode even while paying to shareholders the resources they would have needed if they wanted to maintain their health.

Not all companies fit these profiles, but the vast majority do—90% of market capitalization fell into one of these three categories during 1971–2017.

A healthy market economy should have a meaningful set of *Growers* and the vast majority of firms operating as *Sustainers*. A small group would be *Eroders*, either for miscellaneous one-time reasons or because their businesses were no longer viable and returning cash to shareholders while winding them down was the best course of action. This was indeed the picture in the past. From 1971 to 1985, *Sustainers* accounted for 82% of market capitalization on average, *Growers* for 9%, and *Eroders* for 6%. During this period, these publicly traded companies tapped financial markets for 3.1% of GDP by issuing stock and debt, and they returned 4.6% of GDP to financial markets in the form of dividends, stock buybacks, interest, and debt repayment, producing a net outflow from the real economy equal to 1.5% of GDP.

Then, as described in aggregate terms by Lazonick and Rubio, firms changed their behavior. In the 1990s, *Eroders* accounted for 16% of market capitalization; in the 2000s, 34%; in the 2010s, 42%. In 2017, *Eroders* accounted for 49% of market capitalization while *Sustainers* accounted for 40%. The prevalence of *Growers* had fallen to 3%. The net outflow of cash from the real economy had more than doubled as a share of GDP, to 3.5%.

These trends progressed steadily over time but saw a particular inflection point around the year 2000. For manufacturers, the *Eroder* share of market capitalization climbed from an average of 16% during 1998–2000 to 45% during 2003–05. In the information sector, which includes media, communications, internet, and software companies, the *Grower* share fell from an average of 14% during 1998–2000 to less than 1% during 2003–05, while the *Eroder* share rose from 20% to 60%.

The standard defense of firms returning so much capital rather than investing it is that this allows the resources to reach their best use. If managers believe they can "maximize shareholder value" by disgorging cash, they should do so. The recipients, in pursuit of higher returns, will then invest it elsewhere. "The investor either buys some other stock or invests in some other business that actually needs the money," explained Kevin

Hassett, chairman of President Trump's Council of Economic Advisers. "The money is reinvested and is increasing the efficiency of the economy by moving cash to the firms that need it the most."

This fails in both principle and practice. As *American Affairs* editor Julius Krein has observed, if $1 trillion in annual buybacks indicates that "there are in fact no better investments to be made, and the corporate sector simply has no use for this vast sum," then this "calls into question the viability of the free market capitalist system itself. After all, the entire social justification of free enterprise is that the private sector is the most capable of finding productive investments and deploying capital effectively." It is a dereliction of duty for the managers of a profitable firm to claim they have no productive uses for their profits and so must hand them over for someone else to invest, *especially* when they do so as their own firm loses its competitive advantage or consumes its capital stock.

The maneuver also initiates a sordid game of hot potato—*I* don't want to invest this; here, you do it. In Hassett's imagination, the shareholders to whom the profits return are themselves investors who can deploy the capital productively. That's not reality. When a public company hands back capital to the financial markets, it throws the resources over an invisible wall, from the land of investors who might deploy it productively to the land of non-investors who are unlikely to do so. The non-investor may choose to convert the capital into personal investment or consumption, buying that bigger boat, say, or else turn around and non-invest in some other asset. Perhaps with the cash they receive when Intel buys back its own shares, they purchase shares of Boeing. But they have not invested in Boeing, merely given the cash to someone else who once held the shares. *I* don't want to invest this; here, you do it.

How and when does the capital thrown from the productive economy into the financial markets and the hands of non-investors ever make its way back to productive use, especially in a world where the cash flowing out of *Eroders* exceeds by a factor of 12 the cash flowing into *Growers*? Generally speaking, it doesn't. This is apparent both from the top-down view of macroeconomic data, which shows the long-running investment declines, and from the bottom-up view of firm-level data, which shows the outflow of cash from the operating economy to financial markets overwhelming the inflow of actual-investment. The mystery, then, is: *Where does the capital go?* The best answer would appear to be: Treasury bonds.

As we have seen, the cumulative gross investment shortfall during 2009–17 as compared to 1970–99 amounted to $3.4 trillion. Similarly, the excess outflow of cash from publicly traded companies in the real economy (4.0% of GDP during 2009–17 versus 1.8% during 1971–99) amounted to $3.1 trillion. Over that same period, private domestic holdings of U.S. Treasury debt by individuals, mutual funds, banking institutions, insurance companies, and pension funds rose by $3.5 trillion.

The game of hot potato proceeds until the cash reaches people who do not find attractive any of the non-investment opportunities available, at which point they lend it to the federal government directly or via low-yield savings instruments. If the federal government were issuing bonds to finance important long-term investments in infrastructure, basic research, and so forth, this might still be a happy ending. We are not so lucky. Instead the resources are used to shore up underfunded entitlement programs. The net effect is fewer people developing innovative new products and services and creating the enterprises, facilities, and equipment to provide them.

FROM BUILDING TO BUYING

Our story thus far has focused on the managers of operating companies who fail to reinvest their profits or embark upon projects that require new investment. That story is incomplete, and in some respects unfair. After all, at least the corporate managers are in the corporate sector, trying to run real businesses. At least they *could* invest.

The root cause of the economy's affliction is better located among the many talented business leaders who might once have joined or built businesses and deployed investment, but today choose instead to become non-investors. In the Harvard Business School's Class of 2020, 34% of graduates entered finance and another 24% entered consulting. By comparison, 4% entered manufacturing and 3% entered consumer products. Whereas financial sector wages were comparable to those of other industries in 1980, by 2006 they were 70% higher. At the profession's highest levels the gap was far larger: Graduates of Stanford's MBA program earned three times more in finance than in other industries during the 1990s.

In conjunction, the financial sector exploded in size and changed in character. Value-add attributed to banking and trading rose from 2.5% of GDP in 1970 to 4.8% in 2017, driven by the emergence of a category called "securities, commodity contracts, and investments" that rose from 0.2% of GDP to 1.6%. Whether the "value-add" of all those securities, commodities contracts, and investments added value is another matter. In parallel with financial activities claiming an additional 2.3 percentage points of GDP, net investment was falling by 1.7 percentage points. Capital was becoming no more affordable to firms, and they were choosing to use less of it.

The damage from overdevelopment of the financial sector is twofold, both depriving the real economy of much-needed enterprise-building talent and then using that talent instead to manipulate and cannibalize what enterprises are built. The hedge-fund industry is the most obvious manifestation of this problem. Many just speculate in the secondary market, using shares of stock like poker chips. The "activists," who amass sizable holdings in specific companies, typically do so with the intention of forcing the target to disassemble itself and disgorge more money to shareholders faster.

What's most remarkable about the hedge fund managers is that they no longer succeed even on their own terms. Hedge funds in recent years have consistently and badly lagged the performance of both a simple S&P 500 Index Fund and a balanced portfolio of stocks and bonds that a more risk-averse saver might adopt. The typical hedge fund delivered a 70% return over the past decade, as compared to a balanced portfolio's 160% return and the S&P 500's 270% return. The volatility induced by the pandemic's onset in March 2020 should have been the industry's moment to shine, but funds still managed to lose 11% in the first quarter and then draw just back to even in the second, leaving those who entrusted hedge funds with their savings barely ahead of the index fund and once again trailing a simple mix of 60% stocks and 40% bonds. Hedge fund managers collect their fees regardless.

Private equity firms take full ownership of the companies they purchase, offering the potential for actual-investment, but the strategy tends to be financial manipulation. "As an industry," explains private equity veteran Dan Rasmussen in *American Affairs*, "PE firms take control of businesses to increase debt and redirect spending from capital expenditures and other forms of investment toward paying down that debt. As a result, or in tandem, the growth of the business slows." By using debt to acquire a company and then using its profits to retire that debt, a private equity firm can earn a handsome return even if the company's economic value declines. Being acquired by a private equity firm makes a company ten times more likely to go bankrupt.

As with hedge fund speculation, this strategy is no longer generating strong returns (though, again, the fees it generates to the managers are *quite* strong). Study after study now finds that private equity performs similarly to a simple index fund, yielding "negative average risk-adjusted profits," according to one new working paper from professors at the NYU and Columbia business schools. American Compass's *Returns Counter* likewise finds the industry battling a simple, low-cost index fund to a draw. The "wealth transfer" of $230 billion in management fees over the past decade "from several hundred million pension scheme members to a few thousand people working in private equity might be one of the largest in the history of modern finance," Oxford University professor Ludovic Phallipou told the *Financial Times*.

The exception that proves the rule is venture capital, which does make actual-investments in growing firms that need it. But it accounts for less than 20% of private-equity deal volume and concentrates heavily in a narrow segment of the economy: 77% of 2019 venture-capital investment went to software and the life sciences; 85% went to the West Coast and the Northeast. One must scroll down more than 20 entries in a list of the largest venture capital exits in recent years to find one that is not an internet company. It was a biotech company called Stemcentrx that was acquired for $6 billion in 2016 and imploded three years later.

The venture capital model relies on placing long-odds bets on start-ups whose business models can scale very quickly with as few assets as possible. The goal is to back the next Facebook or Google that hits the jackpot, compensating for the vast sums lost on the majority of companies that go nowhere. The approach disqualifies most businesses and industries from attention and precludes the slow, steady accumulation of productive assets that supports a thriving economy over time.

A surprising number of analysts survey the desolate landscape for American investment and ask, "What's the problem?" Stock markets continue closing at new highs, after all, indicating that these supposedly "eroding" companies have never been more valuable. If capitalists were in fact engaged in systemically destructive behavior, this thinking goes, their strategies wouldn't pay, and they would stop.

But strategies that will not pay for the nation's prosperity in the long run can still pay their practitioners quite handsomely upfront. Especially after decades in which the economy amassed extraordinary stockpiles of valuable assets, the party can go on for quite some time before the keg runs dry. Signs indicate that reckoning may be approaching.

Private equity firms, which rely on someone else to build valuable businesses that they can then load with debt and squeeze for profits, are running out of targets. They are raising non-investment capital much faster than they can use it, and as more such funds chase a dwindling set of potential deals, the valuations are rising, making it that much harder to deliver an above-market return, which of course they are not. As Bain & Company observed dryly in its Global Private Equity Report 2020, "Looking ahead, fund managers will continue to face a broad challenge: how to put record amounts of dry powder to work productively amid stiff competition for assets and worsening macro conditions."

The S&P 500 has thus far managed to defy gravity, but already its returns are unprecedentedly concentrated in a narrow set of massive technology companies. The nation's industrial crown jewels, like Intel and Boeing, have suffered engineering meltdowns and are falling behind foreign competitors who invest like it's their job, which it is. The nation's savers look at their brokerage accounts and trust that the dollar amounts listed represent real wealth that they can someday consume, but that will work only if a robust capital base is ready to produce. Pension administrators who have allowed their funds to become critically underfunded, in part by assuming they could sit passively and reap profits that are not materializing, now count on "alternative [non-]investments" to make up the difference with Herculean returns, but no one can deliver them. Reversing this trajectory will require actual-investment, and people prepared to make it.

THE INVESTOR RETURNS

To help our capitalist system regain its balance, public policy will need to reform market rules in ways that both push entrepreneurial energy away from the destructive allure of non-investment in the financial sector and pull it toward the necessary actual-investment in the real economy. From one perspective, these objectives may appear at cross purposes. A vibrant financial sector, the thinking goes, creates deeper and more efficient capital markets that improve liquidity, distribute risk, and thus allow more capital to flow more cheaply to its best uses. Constrain the sector, and the cost of capital will rise, discouraging the very actual-investment we hope to encourage.

This is absurd. As the financial sector has become more muscular, actual-investment has fallen, not risen. Nor has access to capital corresponded to appetite for investment. J.P. Morgan estimates that the cost of capital for S&P 500 firms in 2013 was 8.5%, slightly higher than the historical median. Yet the median hurdle rate for a sample of these firms—that is, the expected return they would require before proceeding with a project—was 18%. It could be that businesses have become irrational. More likely, they feel incapable of investing effectively and pressure to return cash to shareholders instead. Either way, we can reject the idea that an unfettered financial market, generating massive profits for itself through non-investment, most effectively delivers plentiful capital to its best uses in the real economy.

Dispensing with the financial sector's fictions is a good place to start. We should stop awarding the title of "investor" to people who don't invest.

The millions of Americans placing their savings into the market are *savers*. To be clear, saving is good and important. But savers still leave the investing to others. Those who make their money using those savings to buy and sell assets are traders. Those who try to turn a profit betting on the right assets are speculators. Those who buy firms and try then to engineer greater profits through financial maneuvers are manipulators. We will know an actual investor when we see one: He will be spending money in the real economy on labor and materials that expand an enterprise's capacity and future potential.

Once we understand that the financial sector's glut of non-investment is not just failing to facilitate actual-investment but in fact preventing it, the case for a regulatory response becomes clear. Many economists and policymakers have urged a hands-off approach on the assumption that any interference would reduce capital's availability and prevent it from reaching its best uses, but if the sector's behavior is itself having those effects, then public policy has a clear role to play in establishing guardrails within which the market can function well.

Policymakers should consider options such as imposing a financial transactions tax on asset exchanges in the secondary market, making private equity firms liable for the debt that they load on the companies they acquire, and mandating extensive disclosure from non-investment firms that hold assets for public pensions and nonprofit endowments. Disclosures should include the details of all transactions, the flows of funds to and from operating companies in which they hold stakes, the calculations of returns, and the fees and profits distributed to managers. Steps like these are complements to, not replacements for, a robust national economic policy that makes actual-investment more attractive and channels it toward productive uses: the labor market and education reforms, trade and industrial policy, and so on discussed throughout this volume.

Finally, policymakers will need to accept the disappointing reality that a nation's resources are limited and borrowing or printing more money does not change this. If the government diverts resources from actual-investment toward itself but then fails to use those resources for public investment, the nation's economic trajectory will suffer. Further, monetary policy can only have its desired effect if the market economy is operating as expected—with lower interest rates inducing actual-investment that boosts both demand and productivity. If extra money released into the economy merely inflates asset prices and then gets thrown right back at the government, a vital policy weapon is lost.

Without capital, capitalism is merely an *ism*—a belief set untethered from what is happening in the real economy. A well-functioning financial sector is vital to channeling capital toward its best uses, but so, too, is a public policy that sets the rules and constraints within which that sector operates. Such guardrails are not just consistent with capitalism; they are necessary to its success.

PART TWO
PRODUCTION

CHAPTER FIVE

Globalization

Globalization has produced a radically different result from the widely shared prosperity that its advocates promised. Production shifted from the United States to other countries, taking labor demand with it and leaving behind a weakened industrial base, collapsed communities, and poor employment prospects. These shifts result not from genuine comparative advantage, but rather in response to aggressive government subsidies and the availability of exploitable labor in countries like China.

In "Searching for Capitalism in the Wreckage of Globalization," I argue that the "free trade" practiced by the United States is not the epitome of free-market capitalism but its antithesis. Capitalism relies upon the mutual dependence of a nation's capital and labor to produce good outcomes for both, and for consumers, too. Globalization has severed those bonds, urging the owners of mobile capital to forsake the interests of their fellow citizens and pursue higher profits through labor arbitrage abroad. American workers, their families, and their communities paid the price. In "The Need for Tariffs," Robert Lighthizer explains why trade deficits matter and protectionist measures including tariffs are an appropriate response. As the U.S. Trade Representative in President Trump's first term, Lighthizer achieved a dramatic reorientation of the nation's trade policy based on the principles he describes here.

SEARCHING FOR CAPITALISM IN THE WRECKAGE OF GLOBALIZATION

by Oren Cass

Adapted from an essay first published by American Compass on March 9, 2022.

Globalization is not the logical endpoint of capitalism; it is the antithesis. Capitalism does not work because people with capital, left to their own devices to maximize profits, will behave in ways that deliver widespread prosperity. That's nonsensical and has not a shred of evidence to support it. Nor is "capitalism" a synonym for "economic freedom," notwithstanding the canon of market fundamentalism. Capitalism works because, under a specific set of conditions in a well-governed market, capitalists need increasingly productive workers to achieve increasing profits, and workers need access to capital to achieve increasing wages, and in their mutual dependence both find it in their interest to act in ways that deliver good outcomes for themselves and for consumers as well. Capitalism locks everyone in a room together and encourages them to find a way out.

This system of mutual dependence between capital and labor, not mere "economic freedom," is what Adam Smith so ably described. Globalization destroys it, instead urging the owners of mobile capital to forsake the interests of their fellow citizens and search for higher profits through labor arbitrage abroad. A democratic republic's vast working and middle classes will rightly reject such an arrangement, forcing elites to choose between restoring capitalism by constraining capital or entrenching their own economic prerogatives by subordinating the democratic process. That's as good a description as any of the precipice at which America now stands.

THE INVISIBLE HAND DISAPPEARS

Given the extraordinary degree of confidence that economists and policymakers express about the wisdom of globalization, one might expect to encounter a compelling and well-theorized case in its favor. "The economist's case for free trade is essentially a unilateral case," wrote Paul Krugman in 1997. "A country serves its own interests by pursuing free trade regardless of what other countries may do." Unfortunately, that case relies upon a collective, jingoistic misunderstanding of the 200-year-old writings of Adam Smith and David Ricardo. Of course, those great political economists had many insights that remain relevant today. But their theories were being applied out of context, in ways they never could have imagined, and without concern for the specific warnings they did provide. The case for globalization wallowed in market fundamentalism because no better work had been done.

A 2007 report from *The Economist* summarized well the state of its eponymous profession:

> *Globalisation is a big word but an old idea, most economists will say, with a jaded air. The phenomenon has kept the profession's number-crunchers busy, counting the spoils and how they are divided. But it has left the blackboard theorists with relatively little to do. They are confident their traditional models of trade can handle it, even in its latest manifestations.*

To illustrate the point, the magazine quoted the conclusion of Greg Mankiw, Harvard University economist and recent chairman of President George W. Bush's Council of Economic Advisers (CEA), that "services offshoring fits comfortably within the intellectual framework of comparative advantage built on the insights of Adam Smith and David Ricardo."

This mode of thought was pervasive and bipartisan. "In the last decade of the 20th century," Krugman advised in 1993, "the essential things to teach students are still the insights of Hume [a contemporary of Smith's] and Ricardo. That is, we need to teach them that trade deficits are self-correcting. . . . If we can teach undergraduates to wince when they hear someone talk about 'competitiveness,' we will have done our nation a great service."

The thinking persists. Javier Solana, once the European Union's foreign policy chief and now a distinguished fellow at the Brookings Institution, defended globalization in 2020 with the observation that, "Adam Smith's axioms about specialization, and David Ricardo's regarding comparative advantage, are as true today as they were 200 years ago." In 2022, Glenn Hubbard, dean emeritus at Columbia Business School and Mankiw's predecessor at CEA, published a book marketed by Yale University Press as "taking Adam Smith's logic to Youngstown, Ohio" to "promote the benefits of an open economy." *National Review* published an essay adapted from the book under the title, "The Enduring Logic of *The Wealth of Nations*."

While Smith and Ricardo might be flattered that their work has attained the status of scripture—never modernized, always obeyed—they would certainly be aghast. Both were brilliant analysts who understood that economic principles were contingent on social conditions, and who carefully enumerated the conditions relevant to their analysis. Indeed, seeing as they were not writing about and could not possibly have comprehended 21st-century globalization, it is a particular testament to their intellect that they nonetheless anticipated and disclaimed a feature of our modern economy: the free flow of capital. Their theories applied, they both insisted, only so long as a nation's capitalists invested within its own borders.

Start with Smith and his famous "invisible hand," Exhibit A in the classic account of capitalism. The metaphor stands today for the idea that market forces ensure people pursuing their own profit behave in ways that benefit society broadly. It is "the hand of free commerce that brings magic order and harmony to our lives," in the words of libertarian author Amity Shlaes.

That's not what Smith meant. For all its quotation, the phrase appears only once in the two volumes of *The Wealth of Nations* (1776), in a sentence that begins, "By preferring the support of domestic to that of foreign industry..."

> *By preferring the support of domestic to that of foreign industry, he intends only his own security; and by directing that industry in such a manner as its produce may be of the greatest value, he intends only his*

own gain, and he is in this, as in many other cases, led by an invisible hand to promote an end which was no part of his intention.

They don't teach all that in Economics 101. To the contrary, as Jonathan Schlefer, longtime editor of MIT's *Technology Review* once exposed, the leading economics textbook of the 20th century edited most of it out. In *Economics*, Nobel laureates Paul Samuelson and William Nordhaus reprinted the quote as, "He intends only his own security, only his own gain. And he is in this led by an invisible hand to promote an end which was no part of his intention." Students are not even given an ellipse.

Smith's actual theory assigned enormous caveats to the idea that capitalists pursuing their own interests will behave in ways beneficial to the broader society. Building to his description of an invisible hand, he observed that "every individual endeavours to employ his capital as near home as possible as he can, and consequently *as much as he can in the support of domestic industry*," in part because "he can know better the character and situation of the persons whom he trusts, and if he should happen to be deceived, he knows better the laws of the country from which he must seek redress." Smith continued, "Upon equal, or only nearly equal profits, therefore, every individual naturally inclines to employ his capital in the manner in which it is likely to afford *the greatest support to domestic industry*, and to give revenue and *employment to the greatest number of people of his own country*." Immediately following the hand's debut, he specifies that the businessman can best determine "the *species of domestic industry* which his capital can employ" (all emphasis added).

Neither "magic" nor inevitable, Smith's argument for an alignment of self-interest with the public interest is a logical deduction built upon clearly stated preconditions. If a capitalist wishes to deploy his capital domestically, and if the domestic investment that will generate the most profit for him is also the one that will create the most value and employ the most people in his country, *then* we will have a well-functioning capitalist system.

David Ricardo managed to be even more explicit. Modern economists cite fondly the seminal example in his *Principles of Political Economy and*

Taxation (1817), which described England trading cloth to Portugal for wine. The trade will be beneficial to both sides, Ricardo showed, even if Portugal can produce both cloth and wine more cheaply. This idea of "comparative advantage," suggested Paul Samuelson (he of the mangled Smith quotation), is the only principle of the social sciences that is both true and nontrivial.

But like Smith, Ricardo saw that his model required capital to be constrained. His example only works, he emphasized in the very next paragraph, because of "the difficulty with which capital moves from one country to another." Where Portugal is the low-cost producer of both, "it would undoubtedly be advantageous to the capitalists of England and to the consumers in both countries, that under such circumstances, the wine and the cloth should both be made in Portugal, and therefore that the capital and labour of England employed in making cloth, should be removed to Portugal for that purpose." Echoing Smith, he noted that this does not happen in practice because "the fancied or real insecurity of capital, when not under the immediate control of its owner, together with the natural disinclination which every man has to quit the country of his birth and connexions, and intrust himself with all his habits fixed, to a strange government and new laws, checks the immigration of capital."

Ricardo then went further than Smith, from positive statements about how the world does work to a normative one about how it should: "These feelings [of allegiance to a nation], *which I should be sorry to see weakened*, induce most men of property to be satisfied with a low rate of profits in their own country, rather than seek a more advantageous employment of their wealth in foreign nations" (emphasis added).

In short, Smith and Ricardo stated their propositions in terms incompatible with modern globalization. Both assumed that capital would remain in the domestic market. And as a corollary, both conceived of trade as occurring only on the basis of goods for goods. In Ricardo's telling, England "purchase[s wine] by the exportation of cloth." Smith posited that "if a foreign country can supply us with a commodity cheaper than we ourselves can make it, better buy it of them with some part of the produce of our own industry."

To march confidently forward with modern globalization on the basis of Smith and Ricardo is an act of spectacular hubris, equivalent to consulting a treatise on flight that describes how objects can defy gravity if an engine delivers sufficient thrust and an airfoil delivers sufficient lift, then wantonly shoving passengers off a cliff in metal boxes. At least, in that case, most people would stop after the first few bodies piled up. Our economists wave their manuals and shout, "Congratulations, you're flying!"

A TRADE THEORY IN MOTION

The enormity of the intellectual failure invites speculation of global conspiracy. *The textbook literally rewrote Adam Smith's theory.* That the errors invariably compounded to the benefit of the wealthy, powerful, and cosmopolitan, at the expense of the typical American family and community, is enough to send one searching for the meeting minutes from whichever Illuminati subcommittee had jurisdiction.

But we should probably hesitate to attribute intention to something more easily explained by inertia and ideology. Expanding trade had proved beneficial for many generations, as economic theory had predicted. At the moment of transition, as ships and railcars laden with natural resources and agricultural products gave way to the post–World War II economy of multinational corporations, integrated supply chains, and international finance, the classical model appeared to hold for globalization generally. Its strict assumptions about immobile capital, and goods exchanged for goods, seemed unnecessary. "Until the 1970s," observes Hubbard, "both industry and labor in the United States prospered, with little foreign competition. This success made it easier for the United States to play a leading global role in championing openness to globalization and trade."

Rather than recognize that a particular set of conditions had supported the desirable outcomes, economists concluded that markets delivered such outcomes automatically—that with greater globalization would always come greater benefits. In *The Constitution of Liberty* (1960), Friedrich Hayek criticized those who "lack the faith in the spontaneous forces of adjustment" and he promoted instead the "attitude to assume that, especially in the economic field, the self-regulating forces of the market will somehow bring about the required adjustments to new conditions." As a prime example, he assured readers that "some necessary balance . . . between exports and imports, or the like, will be brought about without deliberate control." How sensible this must have seemed, midway through two decades in which U.S. exports and imports were indeed closely balanced. Why force all those economics students to suffer through Smith's overly verbose asides about "preferring the support of domestic to that of foreign industry"?

The result is that the modern economist often plays the role of Wile E. Coyote, pressing confidently forward with plans that, unbeknownst to him, have no actual support. Except it is not his own well-being but that of countless American workers, families, and communities that risks a plunge into the canyon below. Still, the effect of forcing the economist to look down can be striking.

Press a proponent on why capitalism will deliver prosperity under globalization, and the account drifts gently off into the void. In the domestic economic context, so-called "supply-siders" have developed a theory whereby whatever policies are most beneficial to investors, who are presumed to be employers, will inevitably benefit workers as well. At least the myth that a "rising tide lifts all boats" can assume that the boats are all moored on the same side of the ocean. What is the story of how the Ohio worker benefits when the local investor moves his capital to Shenzhen in search of a higher return?

One approach might focus on the Chinese worker. Additional investment in Shenzhen boosts employment and wages there, and those workers will consume more American goods and services, boosting employment and wages here. But even stipulating that some Chinese consumer demand might eventually reach back to America, it will not match the demand spurred by a domestic enterprise. Smith and Ricardo never suggest that this pursuit of profit abroad will align with the public interest at home; no other theory gives a reason that it should, and empirically it has not.

A second approach might focus on the American investor. By maximizing his profit in Shenzhen, he will himself have more income, which he can then spend on a larger sofa in Ohio. Of course, the sofa itself will probably be made in Shenzhen as well, but perhaps the Ohio salesman can receive a larger commission. This story has not misapplied Smith; it has ignored him completely. The rationale for capitalism has never been that by maximizing the profits paid to investors, society will prosper. Its rationale is that in *trying to maximize their profits* under certain conditions, investors will behave in ways that do generate prosperity.

Smith saw high profits as inversely correlated with the public interest, warning that "the rate of profit does not, like rent and wages, rise with the prosperity, and fall with the declension, of the society. On the contrary, it is naturally low in rich, and high in poor countries, and it is always highest in the countries which are going fastest to ruin." Unlike "the proprietors of land" and "those who live by wages," he observed, the interest of "those who live by profit has not the same connexion with the general interest of the society."

We can as easily tell this alternative story about our Ohio investor: He invests in Shenzhen instead of Ohio, reinvests his profits into other foreign operations or uses various legal mechanisms to avoid the taxation that would accompany a realization of his capital gains, and ultimately hands his money over to a hedge fund that speculates in options markets. He never consumes or invests a dime more in Ohio than he would have as owner of a local factory—though he may finance a foreign factory that bankrupts a local one. He signs the "Giving Pledge" and, dying a wealthy man, leaves enormous sums to reputable foundations that provide addiction treatment and housing assistance to the underemployed residents of his home city. He also leaves a tidy sum to a prominent think tank, endowing a chair in international capitalism, whose holder delivers an annual speech on the ways open markets help Americans economically.

Does this alternative story about our Ohio investor seem more or less likely than the one where he becomes an avid sofa connoisseur, boosting local employment for furniture salesmen? Economic theory cannot answer the question definitively. The political economist must make assumptions about the opportunities available and how someone would weigh the economic and social costs and benefits of each. Ricardo cited "the fancied or real insecurity of capital, when not under the immediate control of its owner," but does that hold today, after decades in which guaranteeing the security of investments abroad has been an explicit policy goal? In his *Theory of Moral Sentiments* (1759), Smith argued that nature had endowed mankind "not only with a desire of being approved of, but with a desire of being what ought to be approved of; or of being what he himself approves of in other men." Of what does the modern financier approve, after decades of enthusiasm for Milton Friedman's declaration that "The Social Responsibility of Business Is to Increase Its Profits"?

What economic theory *can* tell us is that, insofar as the Ohio investor does reallocate his capital to Shenzhen, America is worse off than had he chosen the best option available in Ohio. That the investor might earn a lower return domestically is simply not of much concern to the people of his community, who would have a local employer offering well-paying jobs and supporting a broader ecosystem of suppliers and customers. Let all of them buy sofas.

At this juncture, many economists will attempt to conflate globalization's corrosion with useful features of economic dynamism like automation and competition. With such skepticism of the "free" market, the argument goes, the people of Ohio would all still be living and working on farms. Not so.

The process innovations by which capitalists find ways to produce more output with less labor are the *sine qua non* of economic progress and a great force for good in the domestic economy. They differ from globalization's substitution of foreign labor for domestic in two vital respects. First, they tend to occur gradually and to boost output more rapidly than they reduce labor. In the manufacturing sector, for instance, productivity growth from 1947 to 2000 averaged more than 3% annually—that is, producers halved the labor needed for the same level of output every 20 years or so. Yet manufacturing employment grew by millions. Only since 2000, when similar or slower productivity growth was accompanied by stagnant or declining output, has employment collapsed. Second, even when process innovation does reduce employment, the result is a still-healthy and typically growing local enterprise, offering higher-paying jobs for some that can in turn help to support other enterprises and employment in the community. That's hardly comparable to shuttering a business, or failing to start one in the first place.

Domestic competition moves employment opportunities to a new firm, or perhaps even a new location or occupation. But in this circumstance, declining labor demand in one place bears a hydraulic relationship to increasing labor demand in another. Typically, some firms in a given region will be winning while others are losing, which buffers the net impact on local economies. Long-term net flows of capital from one region to another will tend to occur on the same timescale as domestic migration. Areas with relatively looser labor markets become more attractive sites for subsequent investment. None of this holds true when regions separated by 7,000 miles of ocean, a century of economic development, and incompatible political systems find themselves in a common market.

The prosperity-creating cycle of creative destruction requires entrepreneurs working in parallel both to render labor less necessary in some places and find new uses for it in others. Only when capital must seek out the labor available—when conditions are such that, per Smith, each businessman "naturally inclines to employ his capital . . . to give revenue and employment to the greatest number of people of his own country"—can we expect this cycle to operate well and to the nation's benefit. In recent years, it has not.

BOUNDING THE MARKET

If we want capitalism to deliver broad-based, rising prosperity in America, then we must have a well-theorized understanding of the conditions under which it will succeed. A model focused on ensuring that wealthy people can earn the greatest possible return on their capital is not capitalism; it's oligarchy, and its track record is quite poor. Capitalism works for capital, labor, and consumers when all are indispensable to each other's goals and each gains from their achievement. Interdependence is what translates the pursuit of private profit into public benefit.

An indispensable element for maintaining this interdependence is the bounding of the market, so that the various economic actors have no alternative to each other. In a bounded market, economic analysis and legal treatment of activity depends on whether it occurs within the boundary, across it, or beyond it. That boundary might hypothetically take any form, but in practice it will be a physical boundary, typically a national one. By contrast, globalization and its underlying theory make the goal a boundless market, in which borders have as little relevance as possible to economic transactions.

A bounded market is not an isolated one; goods and services, capital, and people can enter and exit. But their flows are controlled, and for a well-functioning capitalist system the principle of control is balance. Through restrictions on trade or capital flows, public policy can force imports and exports into balance, so that goods and services are exchanged for each other rather than for financial instruments. Increased fulfillment of domestic demand via foreign labor (imports) would occur only alongside a parallel increase in foreign demand for domestic labor (exports). Inflows and outflows of capital would equalize as well. Balance imposes the necessary interdependence on labor and capital while also allowing for the actual benefits of trade that Smith and Ricardo described.

Choosing a free but bounded domestic market over globalization implies neither "central planning" nor a "closed economy." A great benefit of defining clear boundaries for the market and then deferring to private-sector competition therein is that this strategy requires far *less* state intervention than with the enormous demands placed on bureaucracies to make globalization work. "Free trade" agreements are a case in point: Instead of negotiating endless treaties on "Investor-State Dispute Settlement" to ensure that the American government protects investors when they venture abroad, wouldn't it be simpler just to tell those investors that they'll be on their own?

Similarly, while limits on globalization's cross-border flows are not the only constraints capitalism requires, they can reduce the need for other interventions. Competition policy, investment policy, labor policy, and financial regulation, for example, all play roles as well in creating the conditions in which the invisible hand leads the individual "to employ his capital in the manner in which it is likely to afford the greatest support to domestic industry, and to give revenue and employment to the greatest number of people of his own country." Greater returns must not be available through the pursuit of monopoly rents or financial speculation. Incentives must exist to reward innovation and expansion that generates a high ratio of public to private returns. Workers must possess sufficient power in the labor market to advance their interests. Globalization makes all this much harder, while a bounded market lessens the need for government action on these fronts.

Even beyond the reach of the invisible hand, the bounded market advances the common good. Economic interdependence invariably strengthens the social fabric, as elites who might otherwise look outward for both peers and employees must instead look inward. Entrepreneurs would pay much greater attention to the quality of public education and the rigor of noncollege pathways—as economic imperatives, not subjects of charity—if the failure of those systems meant their own failure rather than an excuse to hire foreigners instead. Corporate executives in coastal cities might understand their fellow citizens in the domestic hinterland better if their supply chains traveled through it and thus so did they.

But where to draw the boundary? The coherent objection to insisting that American capital use American labor is that the "American" modifier is itself arbitrary. Why not draw the border around Ohio, or Cincinnati, or a particular neighborhood? Why not the Midwest, or North America, or, ultimately, the world? Many facets of that debate are beyond the scope of this discussion, but a few points bear noting.

First, nations matter, and they operate as the basic political building blocks of our world. Globalization's boosters prefer not to argue on these terms because doing so requires admitting that they do *not* think nations matter, or at least they do not *want* nations to matter. But devaluing the nation-state, weakening its sovereignty, and reducing a citizenry's democratic control are inevitable consequences of constructing a global market. And notwithstanding liberalism's one-world ideals, leaders in many other countries remain firmly committed to operating on behalf of their own national interests. If America pursues global supply chains while China pursues national ones, the result will be Chinese supply chains.

Second, a nation's borders define a market with a common legal and economic regime. This limits variation in economic conditions and cost of living, cultural norms and expectations, and regulatory standards. Competition occurs and investment flows based on innovation and value, not arbitrage. With differences in degree rather than kind, shocks from sudden exposure to unprecedented circumstances are rare and change proceeds at a manageable pace.

Third, the national community is itself defined by the mutual dependence of citizens. Whether between labor and capital, rural and urban, civilian and soldier, members of a nation recognize that they owe something to each other that they do not owe to those outside the group. This is true not only as a moral matter, but also as a function of law and policy. Programs of social insurance, for instance, place a nation's citizens in reliance on one another and their combined productive capacity. The national government takes on debts that burden the taxpaying public to make investments that benefit it. The political unity required to preserve a democratic republic relies upon recognition and reinforcement of these relationships, and the economic order should reflect it.

Fourth, markets tend toward convergence, so their borders should be drawn around areas within which convergence is desirable. Insofar as the nation recognizes itself as a community, it can support convergence that lifts up those least well off. Insofar as citizens face few linguistic, cultural, and legal barriers to internal migration—at least as compared to emigration—their potential mobility more closely matches that of capital and offers a release valve for economic pressure. Historically, America's regional economies experienced strong regional convergence, stitching the nation more closely together.

In the era of globalization, convergence within America has stalled and even reversed, replaced by a convergence between the United States as a whole and the much poorer nations of the developing world. This is exactly what we should have expected, and indeed what many did expect and wish. Perhaps, from the perspective of a benevolent global dictator, this would be desirable. From the perspective of the American people, it is not.

The irony of the relentless push for globalization by the most passionate free-marketeers is that, in the process, they have grievously wounded the free market they prize above all else. The elimination of trade and capital barriers between China and the United States has imported not just cheap Chinese goods but also Chinese distortions and abuses. The investment decisions of American corporations now turn on the machinations of authoritarian communists. Every consumer shops in a market rife with forced labor. As Chinese policies warp investment decisions in ways harmful to the economic trajectory and national security of the United States, American policymakers must forfeit vital industries or respond with more heavy-handed interventions of their own. As the fortunes of a narrow set of "winners" diverge further from the broader base of "losers," more redistribution is required to fulfill the empty promise of a larger economic pie.

Globalization's internal contradictions mean that, far from optimizing capitalism, it has left capitalists with a thorny dilemma: Free trade or a free market, choose one. The correct choice is a free market in which domestic capital must make use of domestic labor to serve domestic consumers. Unlike globalization, that is a formula for broad-based prosperity.

The bounded free market is the economic model I thought I was defending in my confident case for free trade, because it is the model within which capitalism works, and it is the model that economists teach. Unfortunately, it is not the model they have implemented. If they cannot defend globalization as it operates—and now would be rather late to start trying—then the time has come for them to find new work. Damage to their industry will be more than compensated for by advancements elsewhere.

THE NEED FOR TARIFFS

by Robert Lighthizer

Mr. Lighthizer was the U.S. Trade Representative during President Donald Trump's first term and a member of American Compass's board of directors.

First published by *The Economist* on October 5, 2021, under the title, "Robert Lighthizer on the Need for Tariffs to Reduce America's Trade Deficit."

International trade has largely failed America over the past three decades. Indeed, it is slowly bleeding the country to death. This is true not because the basic principle articulated by David Ricardo that there are gains from trade was wrong (it is not) but because a situation has developed that he never could have imagined. One country has become a great, persistent trade debtor. This has come about neither by intention nor by design. America became the world's great consumer and borrower quite by accident.

The scale of the problem is hard to comprehend. America has rung up over $12 trillion in accumulated global deficits since 2001. Thirty years ago the trade deficit was around $80 billion a year: today it is eight times larger and likely to grow even bigger this year—some believe it may exceed $1 trillion. Over the same period, the economy's nominal GDP merely grew by three and a half times.

People tend to think of trade deficits on an annual basis but the reality is that they are cumulative. Deficits in some years and surpluses in others are unimportant because they might even out. But that is not what is happening. The important issue is not America's annual global trade deficit nor its bilateral trade imbalances but the decades-long trend of enormous deficits without any surpluses. The country has literally handed over trillions of dollars of its wealth to other countries, with China getting the lion's share. This was never supposed to be able to happen under the theory of trade espoused by economists. But it has.

None of this is to denigrate the benefits of trade. International trade has clearly helped some parts of the United States. The country is the second-largest exporting nation after China, and overseas markets help to support millions of American jobs. For example, the profitability of the agricultural sector depends in large part on exports. The country's services sectors run substantial surpluses every year and it is a leader in technology, financial-services exports, and other areas. Clearly, America has many competitive advantages and often benefits from them.

The problem is that America is also by far the largest importer in the world—and that has contributed to making it the world's largest debtor. The country has been running trade deficits averaging well over $500 billion a year (or 3% to 5% of GDP) for more than 20 years and the figure is growing. Deficits are bad for a number of reasons. They can be a drag on economic growth, they can negatively affect the composition of the labour force and wages, and they can lead to macroeconomic distortions.

Perhaps more important, with these persistent deficits America has shipped trillions of dollars of its wealth to foreign countries in return for goods, often short-term consumer goods. Those dollars don't just sit in a foreign vault—our trading partners use them to purchase American assets and debt instruments. In a real sense, America is trading ownership of its productive assets and economic future for short-term consumption.

America's net-investment figures—how much it owns in other countries compared to how much they own in the United States—show that America has gone from being the country with the largest net-investment surplus to the one with, by far, the largest net deficit of more than $15 trillion. (For perspective this figure is about one-half the total value of America's 100 biggest corporations.) Ten years ago, the number was less than $5 trillion. There are many reasons for this, including the recent increase in the value of foreign-owned U.S. assets. But undoubtedly the principal driver is the trade deficit.

There is much discussion about the causes of this trade imbalance: an overvalued currency, America's tax policy, unfair foreign trade practices, closed markets abroad, subsidies, and so forth. But whatever the causes, the situation is unsustainable. A country cannot exchange future wealth for short-term consumption indefinitely.

Of course, not all foreign investment in America is bad. Some of it creates jobs and increases productivity. But most of the inflow is not for new factories or manufacturing. Indeed foreign direct investment is a tiny fraction of all capital flows into the country, on the order of 1%. These investments bid up our equity markets but also transfer to the buyer a right to future profits and national wealth.

Some have suggested that the long-standing trade deficit results from a low savings rate among Americans. But this claim simply renames the fundamental problem—it does not offer a solution. Whether the trade deficit results primarily from foreign countries using market distorting policies to put American producers at an unfair disadvantage—as I believe—or whether American policymakers should do more to encourage savings in the country, society still faces the same challenge: how to create a more balanced global economy in which Americans are not giving away their economic future by selling assets to fund their short-term consumption.

A FRESH LOOK AT TRADE DEFICITS

For years economists concluded that trade deficits were unimportant. Goods come in, dollars go out. Ultimately there is balance because the dollars come back in the form of investment. This construct, however, is usually based on a static, one-year analysis. To appreciate the actual impact of these deficits we need to consider the nature of what is exchanged—often short-term consumption for a country's wealth—and the long-term, multi-year, dynamic effect. Specifically, the annual transfers of half a trillion dollars have a compounding effect: they result in progressively more investment, jobs, and innovation for one's trading partners and less for the debtor country. This sort of dynamic analysis provides a more accurate picture of the situation, albeit a darker one. If wealth is the lifeforce of an economy, America's persistent, massive trade deficit means it is being bled to death.

Some people have warned about this for years. Almost 20 years ago the investor Warren Buffett was alarmed by these deficits and wrote an essay about two hypothetical lands, Thriftville and Squanderville. He described what happens when a country consistently runs trade deficits. It sells its assets to pay for short-term consumption and in the end the people of Squanderville are impoverished and working in a country owned by Thriftville. Mr. Buffett often explains that by running huge deficits America is like a farmer who spends more than he makes and sells pieces of the farm and gives mortgages on other parts to pay for the excess consumption. That can't end well. And there is a brutal intergenerational aspect to it: current consumers are impoverishing their children.

In 2003, when Mr. Buffett wrote the article, he warned that "the rest of the world owns a staggering $2.5 trillion more of the U.S. than we own of other countries." As cited above, that figure now exceeds $15 trillion. Even then, Mr. Buffett warned: "We have entered the world of negative compounding—goodbye pleasure, hello pain."

It is interesting that very few countries run large trade deficits. Among the largest are Britain, France, Canada, India, and of course America, whose deficit is eight times larger than the next highest. These numbers must be interpreted relative to the size of the economies but absolute numbers are also informative. On the other side of the coin, only two countries consistently run huge surpluses—China and Germany. Both benefit from what many believe to be an artificially weak currency, varying levels of industrial policy and citizens who are willing to forgo current consumption.

Another negative effect of this huge wealth transfer is that America's biggest single bilateral trade deficit is with China. I am primarily focused here on the dangers of cumulating enormous global trade deficits and I don't believe, generally, that bilateral deficits are a problem absent unfair practices or systemic issues. But the wealth transfer to China is another matter.

China is not only our global adversary but it is in a competition with the Western, free, democratic system to determine if it or their system will endure—whether liberal democracy or autocratic socialism is better. It is not an exaggeration to say that the hundreds of billions of dollars that we send to China every year has made the Chinese Communist Party much richer and helped pay for a great expansion of its military capability. This is neither in the interests of America nor the free world.

Not so long ago the view of classical economists prevailed. It was hard to fathom that one country could run up trillions of dollars in accumulated trade deficits year after year. The assumption was that when a country ran a trade deficit it would see its currency adjust. As one purchased from the surplus country, this bids up its currency; the converse is true of deficit countries. So as the deficit went up, the value of the currency would go down, and imports would be more expensive and exports cheaper overseas. In short, the situation would correct itself. Yet this mechanism has not worked for America. Its reserve currency status, the safe-haven effect of the dollar, and foreign-currency manipulation have kept the dollar higher than it should be. The IMF estimated in 2019 that the dollar was overvalued by as much as 12% and other economists argue it is even higher.

During the period of the gold standard this chronic deficit situation could not have existed because the deficit country would see its gold reserves disappear and it would be left with no means to purchase imported goods. Under the postwar Bretton Woods system of fixed exchange rates, fears that accumulating trade deficits would lead to a draining of the American gold supply prompted the Nixon Administration to take the country off the gold standard and impose across-the-board tariffs on imports in 1971.

This persistent wealth transfer is fairly recent and unprecedented. It is worth noting that Ricardo himself always framed the trade debate in a balanced context. England would sell cloth and Portugal would sell wine. Experts who studied these matters always assumed balance over time. When John Maynard Keynes was outlining his thoughts for the International Trade Organisation after the Second World War, he included a mechanism to allow countries to adjust their tariff rates to bring about balance when necessary. This concept was carried forward in a vaguer form in article 22 of the General Agreement on Tariffs and Trade (GATT) in 1947 and now in the rules of its successor, the World Trade Organisation. Countries facing balance of payment issues can suspend their GATT obligations following certain prescriptions. There was always an assumption that trade would be more or less balanced over time.

Even Friedrich Hayek, Keynes's adversary in debates over the role of the state in the economy, assumed that trade imbalances would be temporary, not perpetual. Hayek would never have approved of any mechanism to bring about balance but, as Oren Cass points out in his essay "Hayek's Broken Promise," the great man always believed a country needed exports and imports and that balance would come from natural forces. After decades of accumulated trade deficits, we are entitled to question Hayek's confidence in natural forces and explore other ways to bring about needed balance.

Furthermore, trade deficits create political problems as well as economic ones. America's trade situation has contributed to a hollowing out of manufacturing capabilities, loss of millions of jobs, wealth inequality in the country, and damage to the cities and towns that have relied on these jobs. There is a strong sense in the American body politic that something is very wrong. This is part of the reason why Donald Trump was elected president and populism is on the rise. Economists can debate the importance of savings rates and productivity but voters have their own instinctive reaction.

President Trump followed through on his campaign promise in 2016 and radically changed the trade agenda. He raised tariffs, renegotiated agreements, and threatened to do much more. The populist, worker-first United States–Mexico–Canada Agreement passed a historically divided Congress a year before the presidential election in 2020 with 90% of lawmakers, both Republicans and Democrats, in favor. The backlash from farmers and others that was predicted by pundits never happened.

In fact, both presidential candidates ran on essentially the same trade platform. Joe Biden abandoned his past support for comprehensive trade deals like TPP. Both emphasized the need to bring back jobs that were outsourced overseas and to reduce dependency on China, even if their tone and preferred tactics differed slightly (though there has been little discernible difference so far). In short, the public demands balanced trade and politicians of both parties are responding.

NEW THINKING FOR NOVEL PROBLEMS

There are a number of possible ways to achieve greater balance. In his article in 2003, Mr. Buffett suggested that America require import certificates. These would be issued to those who export and would be sold by them to importers. This system would be effective because it would penalize imports and subsidize exports. Yet it also might be quite disruptive. It would create a market for these certificates with possibilities for manipulation and speculation.

Others have suggested that America implement a so-called "market-access charge." Essentially, the Federal Reserve would impose a variable tax on capital flows into the country from foreign persons. It would raise or lower the tax to disincentivize foreigners from buying American assets; this drop in demand for the assets would lower the value of the dollar. The idea is that this would "realign" (that is to say, "weaken") the dollar and bring about trade balance. This mechanism also would work but the process is complicated and easily misunderstood. Some might argue that it would discourage investment.

A third approach, more consistent with Keynes's notion, would be for the United States or any country that experiences the emergence of a huge, regular trade deficit to impose a temporary tariff on all imports and gradually increase it or decrease it depending on the level of the deficit. For example, a 10% tariff could be applied to all imports. If the deficit did not go down in a couple of years, the tariff would be increased to 20% for several more years. If this did not have the needed effect it might go up to 30%. (Of course, the program would make exceptions for critical goods.) When the deficit was substantially reduced, the tariffs would also decline and eventually be eliminated.

All three of these approaches would reduce the trade deficit. They all would have costs too. They would raise the price of imported goods (both for personal use and as inputs for companies) and discourage consumption. They would add regulation to the economy and they would be opposed by our trading partners. These downsides, however, would be temporary and surely would be outweighed by the benefits of balanced trade. It would improve economic growth, encourage manufacturing and job creation, and put upward pressure on wages.

Of the three approaches the best one would be that which would have the least interference with markets: yes, tariffs. The mechanism is already in place to collect them. As every ornate custom house in every international port attests, governments have collected tariffs for over a millennium and economists know their effects. None of this is likely to reverse the negative net foreign investment that resulted from trade deficits in the past, but it may reduce or stop the outflow.

Most importantly it represents a vital shift in thinking. America's cumulative deficits hurt the country: the pain is apparent even if the reason is camouflaged. Policymakers, business leaders, economists—and the public, most of all—need to abandon the dogma of trade from 18th-century philosophers of the political economy, and embrace new thinking for novel circumstances.

CHAPTER SIX

China

Globalization's rise coincided with the Cold War's end, in part, because a global free trade system that incorporated the Soviet bloc had been unthinkable. The "holiday from history" of the 1990s created a presumption that liberal market democracy was on the march everywhere, and globalization's proponents argued that incorporating China into a global marketplace would accelerate its own liberalization. They were wrong. Instead, China changed us—corrupting the free market, distorting investment flows, capturing valuable industries, and even exporting its authoritarian politics through campaigns of economic pressure.

"Trading It All Away" is an essay adapted from then-senator Marco Rubio's remarks at American Compass's inaugural Henry Clay Lecture, which happened also to mark the twentieth anniversary of China's ascension to the World Trade Organization. Rubio analyzes both the causes and consequences of that catastrophic mistake. As for recovering from the mistake, Gabriela Rodriguez and I propose an approach in "The Case for a Hard Break with China." While debate rages over "strategic decoupling" and "de-risking" and other euphemisms for tolerating the continued entanglement of the U.S. and Chinese economies, Rodriguez and I argue that market integration between such fundamentally incompatible political and economic systems has never in history succeeded and will inevitably fail here. Then, turning to foreign and national security policy, Elbridge Colby argues in "After Hegemony" that the proper U.S. objective is to prevent China from attaining its own regional hegemony in Asia.

TRADING IT ALL AWAY

by Marco Rubio

Mr. Rubio was a U.S. senator from the state of Florida.

First published by American Compass on December 10, 2021; adapted from a speech delivered at Hillsdale College in Washington, D.C., on December 8, 2021.

Henry Clay is especially appropriate for a lecture series focused on the long-term interests of our country. During his time in public life, he was known for taking the long view on the best interests of a then-infant republic. He had a very specific vision for American economic policy. To summarize: First, he didn't want American prosperity to depend on any other country; and second, he wanted ours to be a diverse industrial economy.

That vision, and the work of those who followed him, steered the course of history. Economic independence helped to preserve the union in the early years of our republic. And, less than 100 years later, industrial capacity and diversity became the war machine that tipped the scales of World War II. Now we stand here a century and a half later, and America once again finds itself at a historic pivot point—not just for America, but for the world.

A WORLD-HISTORICAL MISTAKE

The post–Cold War world is fading from view, and we are being rapidly pulled towards a new era in human history. But in this era, our nation is not being steered by statesmen like Henry Clay. In January, I tweeted, "Biden's cabinet picks went to Ivy League schools, have strong resumes, attend all the right conferences. And they will be polite & orderly caretakers of America's decline." The condemnation was swift and loud.

The permanent bureaucracy that runs our government, the people who run our largest corporations, many of the think tanks that generate our ideas, and the media that cover our politics are all devout worshippers of a late 20th century ideology. This ideology was formed in the elite universities that inculcated in them the economic and political theology of a time much different from the one we are now entering. They are the authors, practitioners, and defenders of a post–Cold War bipartisan consensus that has dominated policymaking for the last three decades. We must either abandon this consensus or be forever defined as the generation that managed the steady decline of a once great nation.

The course of history is generally determined not by individual and dramatic decisions, but by the cumulative effect of incremental choices that people, nations, and governments make over time. But there are some singular moments whose impacts are felt for generations. One of those moments occurred this week 20 years ago.

At least half of the items in any room across America are probably labeled "Made in China." Why? It stems from that decision 20 years ago to allow Communist China to join the World Trade Organization (WTO)—a decision that now shapes how our most powerful corporations behave, what is available for us to buy here in America, and ultimately, the future of our country.

Five years after China became a full member of the WTO, our trade deficit with them had nearly tripled. Before China's ascension, the U.S. was the largest trading partner of 152 countries in the world. Today, we are the largest trading partner for only 57, while China is the largest trading partner of 128. This decision was a pivotal moment in world history—and 20 years later, it is increasingly acknowledged to be a critical mistake.

Why was it a mistake? Because it was rooted in the flawed assumption that global economic integration was more important than anything else: more important than dignified work for Americans, our ability to make things, and even our national security. This assumption was perfectly summarized by President Clinton when he said, "By joining the WTO, China is not simply agreeing to import more of our products, it is agreeing to import one of democracy's most cherished values—economic freedom."

The fact that I do not need to spend any time convincing anyone that this is not how things turned out is a testament to how wrong they were.

The damage that decision has inflicted on our families, communities, and country is almost incalculable. Instead of exporting "economic freedom," we exported our industrial strength, and the result has been an economic, social, and geopolitical disaster.

Tens of thousands of American factories disappeared, and an estimated 2.5 million American manufacturing jobs were lost. This loss has contributed to historic declines in men's labor force participation, wages, and even marriage. We've seen an opioid addiction crisis whose geographic hotspots happen to be the very regions most impacted by the loss of factories and jobs. This loss has led many Americans to believe that the American Dream is no longer in reach. This is the dream my immigrant parents and millions like them achieved here in this country: not a dream of becoming rich, but a dream to have a stable and dignified job that allows you to get married, start a family, own a home in a safe neighborhood, retire with dignity, and leave your children better off than yourself.

And this terrible mistake didn't only hurt America; it empowered the Chinese Communist Party. They now use their new and growing economic strength and influence to turn American companies into their lobbyists, their spokespersons, and their advocates in Washington. They use it to tell our companies what to do with their businesses, coerce Hollywood studios and American sports leagues to self-censor, and intimidate international organizations to serve China's interests at the world's expense.

In Washington there is a greater and growing awareness of this reality. Many are actually very serious about doing something about it, while others just play along because they know it polls well.

But let there be no doubt: There are still very influential and powerful voices who cling to the failed consensus that brought us to this point, hoping the growing awareness of this danger we face is just a short-term movement, a populist fad that will soon fade. For the sake of our country and the world, I hope we prove them wrong. Because if they are proven right, and the attention to this problem is transitory, it will mean that most of us who are alive today will live to see the day when a genocidal communist regime ascends to become the most influential and powerful country in the world, while the greatest beacon of liberty in human history is relegated to a status of a once-great power in decline.

FLAWED ASSUMPTIONS

I think it is impossible to forge a different path forward without first understanding how the failed consensus that produced this current predicament developed. If we address the assumptions that led to this mistake, hopefully we'll abandon them and, in the process, adopt the right assumptions.

The first flawed assumption was the belief that Americans are primarily consumers—that our primary economic identity isn't as a worker, a parent, the head of household, or a member of a community, but as a shopper. If you believe that we derive our identity and happiness from the things we buy, and not from work, children, and family, then it becomes easy to justify opening up to China in exchange for cheaper prices. But we all know that what gives life meaning and purpose isn't how many things we can buy or own—it's the time we spend and things we do with our family and in our communities. That requires the stability that comes from good jobs.

To view Americans solely as consumers ignores the dignity that comes with work, and it ignores how corrosive it is to the individual and ultimately to a community when good jobs are no longer available. It leaves you with an unemployment rate, for example, that drops consistently below 5%, not because more people are working, but because more people have given up looking for dignified work and dropped out of the labor force.

It leaves you at the mercy of any disruption in the supply chains. When shortages make it harder to find what we want to buy and inflation makes everything more expensive, you still don't have the jobs, the dignity, and the industrial capacity—and now you don't even have the cheaper prices. That's the predicament we unfortunately find ourselves in right now. Eventually, if cheaper prices at the store are the result of sending the job you once had to a cheaper worker in another country, you're inevitably going to face widespread anger and despair.

And still, many don't get it, ignore it, or hope we overlook it. When the Chamber of Commerce and the Business Roundtable petition the Biden Administration to lift Trump's tariffs on China, or when 91 senators vote to cut tariffs on Chinese goods, it shows you just how deeply embedded this flawed thinking still is in our country.

The second assumption that underpinned the flawed bipartisan consensus was that the stock market and corporate profits are the same thing as real economic growth and innovation. For 20 years now, presidents from both parties have pointed to the stock market as a scoreboard indicating whether we are winning or losing economically. A thriving stock market is not a bad thing, nor is it unimportant. But our economy is a lot more than just the stock market. And most of the time, whether the market closes up or down has zero correlation with how the economy is working for our country, for our families, and for our communities.

Over the past two decades, the stock market has gone up 120% when adjusted for inflation, but "middle income" Americans have seen only seen marginal growth of about 6% over that same period. And lower income Americans have actually seen no growth at all.

The "Cost of Thriving Index" produced by Oren Cass found that in 1985, when my father was a banquet bartender in Coconut Grove, Florida, it took the median male worker 30 weeks of work to afford a year's worth of the basics that it takes to raise a family. Today, that same index indicates it would take 53 weeks in a 52-week year to do the same thing.

When did this trend take off? It coincides almost perfectly with the collapse of American manufacturing after China entered the WTO. We lost 33% of our manufacturing jobs in just the first decade after that decision was made. It was a collapse so stunning that shortly after the year 2000, finance became a larger share of U.S. corporate profits than manufacturing.

Wall Street and Corporate America could now make the same products, or something new they invented, but at a lower cost, using cheaper workers working in a Chinese factory. The lower cost of manufacturing didn't mean just cheaper consumer prices; it also meant larger corporate profits. Larger profits meant greater returns for shareholders, but it didn't necessarily mean greater prosperity for working Americans.

There is nothing inherently wrong with greater profits for corporations and better returns for shareholders. But on their own, they are not a good way of measuring the strength of our economy and the well-being of our people. Lower prices alone can never make up for the fact that you lost the stability and dignity that comes from a well-paying job. Greater returns on investors' stock portfolios can't make up for the closure of a factory that left behind a hollowed-out community. And record corporate prices can't make up for the insecurity that comes from being a nation that can't make masks during a pandemic or produce the active ingredients in our most basic medicines.

Socialism is a failure. It's a failure because it considers wealth to be immoral. It is possible to have a free market that generates wealth, while also benefiting working families and serving our national interest. But when you have an economy where wealth is being generated in a way that is divorced completely from the well-being of a people or the security of a country, it foments discontent and the resentment that Marxists always seek to exploit. It gives an opening to argue that capitalism is inherently unfair and repressive. And it creates an opportunity to argue that the time has come to abandon free enterprise and empower the government to "Build Back Better."

When wealth is generated by sending our jobs and our manufacturing capacity to a country that seeks to rise at our expense, that views our relationship as a zero-sum game in which either it wins or we do, we are left vulnerable to whatever disruptions that country seeks to create and any coercion they seek to pursue.

The third assumption behind the flawed bipartisan consensus was that if our companies sent our factories and jobs to China, it would give America more influence over China and the world. It is a misguided belief that is rooted in the once popular theory that the end of the Cold War signaled the "end of history." The theory was best expressed by Francis Fukuyama, who argued that after the fall of the Soviet Union, the whole world would become democratic. The economic ties of globalization would reduce conflict, and mass communication would bridge cultural divides.

It may sound silly today, but not long ago there was a catchy talking point that was popular in college economics courses, conferences, and sound bites. To paraphrase, it went something like this: "No two nations with a McDonald's have ever gone to war with each other." Twenty years ago, the world's most powerful companies were American. So, the belief was that this new world centered on global commerce would inevitably lead, not just to more McDonald's, but to greater American influence as well.

But that's not how it turned out. We soon learned that you could eat Big Macs and still view the country that invented them as a rival to be defeated. And we learned that when American companies are forced to choose between what's good for America and bigger profits, they will usually pick bigger profits.

The Chinese Communist Party never wasted any time believing that the "end of history" had arrived. They saw and still see history as thousands of years of greatness interrupted by a century of shame and humiliation at the hands of the West. They viewed it as their destiny to become the world's preeminent power at America's expense. For a time, they chose to "hide their capacity" and "bide their time." But by 2008, they felt strong enough to no longer pretend.

ELITE FAILURE

Our economy is now controlled by people who have more allegiance to the global economic order than to their own nation. Our leading companies have no problem helping China build missiles that may one day kill American soldiers or give China access to American semiconductors if it means they can make bigger profits for the next quarterly reports. Our major corporations say the United States has "human rights" problems while proudly sponsoring Olympic Games hosted by a government responsible for genocide and slavery.

Our culture is now influenced by studios that produce movies about how evil our history is but proactively self-censor anything that would offend the Chinese Communist Party because they want their movies distributed there. Our culture is also influenced by prominent athletes like LeBron James, who has no problem claiming our police departments are overrun by killer cops, and Colin Kaepernick, who has no problem making a documentary about how systemically racist and evil our country is. And yet, they both make millions of dollars endorsing shoes made by the slave labor of Uyghur Muslims in China.

In his first speech in the Senate, Henry Clay warned that some "have been engaged, to overthrow the American System, and to substitute the foreign." He suggested that while they were "long a resident of this country," they have "no feelings, no attachments, no sympathies, no principles, in common with our people." His words spoke to a different time and place, and yet they have taken on new relevance and meaning in our day.

As noted earlier, the people running our country today are acting as caretakers of our decline. These are not foreign agents. They are not supporters *per se* of the genocide being committed by a communist regime. And yet, even as I speak to you now, some of the most powerful people in government and business are working to make sure my *Uyghur Forced Labor Prevention Act* never becomes law. Because they believe that making sure American consumers have access to iPhones and sneakers is so important that not even stopping slave labor should be allowed to stand in the way. They believe they must maximize the profits of their shareholders at any cost, even if it means relying on factories filled with slaves.

Perhaps the most dangerous result of the decision to open up to China is that it left us with people at the highest levels of government and business who consistently advocate for policies that serve the interests of a foreign power and damage the interests of our country. The defenders of this status quo often hide behind capitalism to defend their actions and stances. But an economic relationship in which one side must follow the rules and the other doesn't is not capitalism.

Real capitalism—American capitalism—wouldn't allow China to steal our trade secrets and then produce cheaper imitations to put our companies out of business. It wouldn't let Chinese companies do whatever they want in America, while American companies are either banned in China or forced to partner with a Chinese company (who steal their trade secrets and then put them out of business). This isn't about capitalism—this isn't capitalism. This is about corporations and big investors who are making billions by cooperating with China and simply do not care that it is coming at the expense of their country and their fellow citizens.

Lenin once predicted, "The capitalists will sell us the rope with which we will hang them." For at least a decade now, everyday Americans have been telling us that the trade-offs made two decades ago have not worked out well for them or our country. A fateful decision made on flawed assumptions accelerated the global rise of a communist regime at the expense of American workers, industrial capacity, and national security. And now, the commonsense wisdom of our people is finally beginning to find influence in our politics and government.

FORGING A BETTER PATH

Forging a path towards a pro-American capitalism that protects our nation's interests and serves the common good will not be easy. Some of the most powerful interests in our economy are deeply invested in the status quo, and many of the most powerful people in our government are too deeply committed to the road we are on now. But charting a new path is the only way forward. It will not be the work of one person or one party. To succeed, it must be the work of an entire generation and cross the entire political spectrum. It must become our new consensus. Only the free market can make this century a new American Century. But it must be a capitalism that serves the interests of our country, not the interests of the global economy. The market must serve our people, not the other way around.

What does that kind of future look like? It is a future where private industry, not government spending, creates good jobs for our people while also building the resiliency of our country. It is a future where taking risks can result in both wealth for those willing to take the risk of investment and innovation and prosperity for those willing to work and produce.

We live in a country and in a world that is much different than the one Henry Clay knew. And yet, ironically, a new American Century is in many ways not unlike the vision laid out by Henry Clay almost 200 years ago: an America that does not depend on any other nation for its prosperity, and an America with the industrial capacity to tackle any challenges that comes our way.

THE CASE FOR A HARD BREAK WITH CHINA

by Oren Cass & Gabriela Rodriguez

Ms. Rodriguez was a policy advisor at American Compass.

Adapted by permission of *Foreign Affairs*, July 2023 (online). Copyright 2023 by the Council on Foreign Relations, Inc., www.ForeignAffairs.com.

Never in human history have nations with such radically different economic and political systems as the United States and China attempted economic integration. Before the modern era, neither the markets nor the technology existed to facilitate such a project. During the Cold War, facing similar differences, Washington and Moscow stayed economically far apart. PepsiCo's opening of a Soviet bottling plant was front-page news in 1972, and because rubles were not convertible to dollars, the Soviets paid for the bottling equipment with vodka. No wonder that globalization gained steam only after the Berlin Wall fell.

In the early post–Cold War years, U.S. theorists and policymakers ignored the potential risks of integration with an authoritarian peer. Globalization was predicated on liberal economic standards, democratic values, and U.S. cultural norms, all of which were taken for granted by economists and the foreign policy establishment. The United States set the rules for international institutions and multinational corporations, most of which were either American or heavily reliant upon access to U.S. technology and markets. Under these conditions, economic entanglements were regarded as opportunities for Washington to exert leverage and impose its rules. Incursions in, and distortions of, one market by another were Washington's strategy, not its problem.

When welcomed into the international community in the late 1990s, China was still a developing nation. Its GDP was roughly one-tenth of the United States' GDP, and in 1999, it was still one of the world's poorest countries per capita, ranked between Sri Lanka and Guyana. U.S. leaders across the political spectrum were confident that by encouraging China's integration into the global economy, they could ensure that the country would become a constructive participant in a U.S.-led world order. U.S. President Bill Clinton spoke for many when he declared that China's accession to the World Trade Organization was about "more than our economic interests; it is clearly in our larger national interest."

It has not turned out that way. Instead, China has rapidly become—by some measures—the world's largest economy and a powerful counterweight to U.S. influence. Its state-controlled economy and increasingly authoritarian leadership have subverted U.S. investment, supply chains, and institutions. Beijing's efforts to use global integration to enhance Chinese power and harm U.S. interests have proliferated. The Chinese government has leveraged market access to force technology transfers from U.S. firms including Westinghouse, General Electric, and Microsoft. It has dominated global markets by flooding them with subsidized goods, including solar panels, and it has forced the National Basketball Association and its players into humiliating silence on Chinese human rights abuses.

The fundamental problem is that the United States' free-market economy is incompatible with a Chinese state-controlled one. U.S. liberty and democracy are antithetical to the authoritarianism of the Chinese Communist Party. The United States must break from China or else become irrevocably corrupted by it.

TIME TO WALK

Presumably, had U.S. policymakers known in 2000 what they know now about China's trajectory, they would not have conducted the reckless experiment of tightly coupling the U.S. economy to a larger one controlled by a communist, authoritarian dictatorship. But rather than admit their error, many in Washington seem determined to stay the course under the illusion that they can constructively influence Chinese policy through continual efforts at conciliation, even though Beijing has shown no desire to reciprocate.

U.S. Secretary of the Treasury Janet Yellen said as much in April, envisioning "a growing China that plays by the rules" and fosters "rising demand for U.S. products and services and more dynamic U.S. industries." In June, she told the House Financial Services Committee that "we gain and China gains from trade and investment that is as open as possible." National Security Adviser Jake Sullivan made a similar argument in an economic policy speech in April, describing the Biden administration's strategy as "de-risking and diversifying, not decoupling." Sullivan says that he wants only a "small yard and high fence" to safeguard a narrow set of critical U.S. military technologies. Commerce, otherwise, should continue to flourish.

This posture misunderstands the challenge posed by the integration of the U.S. and Chinese markets, which is not only, or even primarily, one of national security. Although that challenge is immense, even if China were to disarm tomorrow, credibly forswearing any aspirations beyond its borders, its economic influence would remain deeply corrosive to the U.S.-led system of democratic capitalism. That system relies upon the assumption that economic actors in a free market pursuing their self-interest—namely, profit—will also advance the public interest. If everyone plays by the same rules, government constrains unproductive behavior, and a strong social fabric supports workers and their families, this kind of market can generate unparalleled prosperity. But if the free market comes into contact with a powerful state-controlled one, in which foreign policymakers have made serving their nation in word and deed the path to greatest profit, too many companies and investors will do just that.

Asking U.S. firms and workers to compete with their China-based counterparts and operate in the Chinese market grants the Chinese Communist Party the power to shape American capital allocations and labor-market conditions from the far side of the Pacific. If U.S. firms seek to maximize their profits, and the greatest profit can be had by kowtowing to the CCP, that is what U.S. business leaders will do. Distortions that Beijing introduces in the Chinese market become distortions in the U.S. market. Washington is left with little choice but to counter with interference of its own. Free trade ceases to be a logical extension of the free market and instead undermines it.

Rather than seek out so-called market failures and craft tailored interventions that might enhance economic efficiency, Washington must turn to the blunt and the bold. The goal should not be to make an integrated Chinese—U.S. market work better but to obstruct and discourage the operation of such a market altogether. Trade in goods can still occur at arm's length and be subject to tariffs that protect U.S. interests. But investment should not flow in either direction. Joint ventures and research partnerships should end. Perhaps someday China will liberalize and a strong economic relationship can develop. But U.S. policymakers should be under no illusion that such reform is coming soon or that further cajoling or tinkering with the U.S.—Chinese relationship will help. Washington must stop trying to repair this marriage and, citing irreconcilable differences, move toward a prompt divorce.

DANGEROUS ENTANGLEMENTS

Both the United States and China have large-scale investments in each other's economies, which has created serious problems for protecting U.S. interests. U.S. citizens and firms channel capital and technology into China, seeking to advance their financial profits—generally, without consideration of whether it helps or harms the United States. In fact, by doing so, U.S. investors are furthering the goals of an authoritarian government that has shown no compunction manipulating foreign investors and leveraging market access to advance its national interests. The most recent instance of this came in July 2023 when, at Beijing's behest, Tesla signed a letter pledging to curtail its competition on price with rival Chinese manufacturers and enhance "core socialist values" in China.

In the other direction, Chinese investments in the United States are almost always implicitly or explicitly controlled by the CCP. "Part of China's economic strategy relies on acquiring foreign companies and their technology and data through government-supported acquisitions," warned Ambassador Robert Lighthizer in his congressional testimony in May. "As a result, when Chinese firms acquire American assets, they frequently are not making profit-motivated business decisions. Instead, they are acting to advance China's national interest." Yet Washington has done little to constrain how that foreign control is used. On its own, the U.S. model of private actors choosing freely has clear advantages. In contact with the Chinese model, however, it is deeply vulnerable.

U.S. law is not designed to address the problems caused by economic integration with a state-controlled market. Only specified entities, technologies, and transactions are addressed, otherwise leaving commerce free and investment unconstrained. This is the Biden administration's "small yard and high fence," which facilitates further entanglement of financial flows and ownership and thus further subversion of the American market. Even with respect to national security, limiting interference to narrow exceptions does not address China's "Military-Civil Fusion" strategy, which, as the U.S. State Department described it in 2020, aims at "acquiring the intellectual property, key research, and technological advancements of the world's citizens, researchers, scholars, and private industry in order to advance military aims."

U.S. law must, then, address the challenge of preventing CCP control over U.S. investors in China and investments in the United States. Washington should prohibit capital flows, technologies transfers, and economic partnerships between the United States and China by default.

To prevent inbound investment, U.S. law should define a class of "Disqualified Foreign Investors." These should include Chinese nationals who are not permanent U.S. residents, China-based entities, and any other entities that are affiliates of the CCP or subject to CCP control. These investors should be prohibited from conducting transactions, forming corporations or partnerships, participating as limited partners in U.S.-based investment funds, and acquiring real estate. Addressing outbound U.S. investment, the new law should prohibit U.S. citizens and entities from pursuing transactions that entail the acquisition of equity, debt, or real estate in China. Joint ventures between U.S.- and China-based entities should be prohibited, preventing them from conducting business in any jurisdiction and transferring advanced technology to the Chinese.

Washington should also ensure that the Defense, Treasury, and Commerce Departments harmonize their various export and investment restrictions. China-based firms should be denied access to U.S. capital markets and stock exchanges.

NEITHER FREE NOR FAIR

In principle, trade in manufactured goods could be the least concerning element of the U.S.-Chinese economic relationship: the United States puts things on boats, China puts things on boats, the boats pass one another somewhere in the Pacific and get unloaded on the far side. But that form of trade bears little relationship to the imbalanced and distorted exchange occurring between the two countries today. In 2022, the United States imported $537 billion in goods from China and exported $154 billion.

For Beijing, this trade imbalance is part of a deliberate strategy; the Chinese government mostly refuses to open its country's markets to U.S. exports and instead trades its own exports for U.S. assets while implementing an aggressive industrial policy to dominate critical supply chains. Demand from U.S. consumers is met from offshore, hollowing out U.S. industry with no commensurate foreign demand emerging for American products.

The existing U.S.-Chinese trade relationship must be changed to end this situation, and Washington should invest heavily in creating domestic capacity. A sharp reduction in imports from China will have real costs, especially in the short term as the United States redevelops its own industrial muscles, but those costs tend to be wildly overstated. Tariffs imposed by the Trump administration on broad categories of Chinese goods caused dramatic declines in U.S. imports from China in those categories but had little to no perceptible effect on domestic prices. U.S. manufacturing may have a lot of catching up to do, but production moving out of China can go many places—indeed, the break from China presents the United States with a significant opportunity to support the economic development of Asian and Latin American allies.

Currently, China enjoys "most favored nation" status and therefore receives the same trade terms that the United States offers to all World

Trade Organization members. Revoking this status would impose high tariffs on nearly all categories of Chinese imports. Washington should then identify situations where Chinese imports dominate a market and impose rising tariffs on those products until market share of Chinese imports falls to an acceptable level.

Domestically, the United States must embrace a robust industrial policy. In their own pursuit of profit, private investors and multinational corporations give little consideration to the health of the U.S. manufacturing base and industry—a reality vital to the CCP's strategy. The federal government must step in to alter this equation. Washington will need new institutions, including a cabinet-level National Development Council and a development bank that can cooperate to reshore manufacturing and strengthen the defense industrial base with financial and technical assistance. U.S. law should then stimulate demand for domestic production by requiring goods sold in the United States to contain a certain proportion of U.S.-produced components manufactured by U.S. workers. The free market should determine how best to fulfill that demand through investment and innovation.

CALLING OUT BEIJING'S ABETTORS

Action must also be taken to safeguard institutions vital to U.S. democracy—not only formal centers of learning and discourse but also the broader public square. The U.S. culture of free speech and inquiry is built upon an assumption that no one in the system will possess the power to coerce or manipulate individual citizens, and the one that does, the government, will be constrained by law and custom from doing so. China alters that calculus. An open society cannot tolerate the imposition of authoritarian incentives and penalties from afar and must be insulated from them.

China has long targeted U.S. universities, think tanks, and research institutes to extract economic gain and advance its own ideological agenda. These organizations, whether operated by government, within academia, or as tax-exempt nonprofits, rely to some degree on public funding and are expected to operate in the public interest. That means they must accept processes and controls designed to ensure the integrity and security of their work. U.S. law should be changed to prohibit these institutions from entering into any partnerships with China-based and -affiliated entities. Any funding flowing from one nation's institutions to the other's must be stopped. U.S. universities should be prohibited from collecting more in tuition and fees from any Chinese national than the average amount collected from American citizens and permanent residents enrolled in the same program of study.

China also uses the powerful incentive of market access to force American investors into promoting its propaganda. The United States cannot outbid these incentives, nor should it. What Washington can do is lower the economic stakes by foreclosing profits in China. U.S. law should impose cultural export controls that prevent U.S. firms from making profits on the sale of films, musical recordings, broadcasts of sporting events, personalized footwear and apparel lines, and live performances in China. If making money in China is as difficult while complimenting the CCP as while criticizing it, the incentive to curry favor with the Chinese government will vanish.

Washington should also seek to raise the reputational stakes for public figures by calling them as witnesses before the House Select Committee on the Chinese Communist Party to testify about their experiences with the CCP and their operations in China. The CEO of the Walt Disney Company and the commissioner of the National Basketball Association, for instance, would both make excellent witnesses. The financier Stephen Schwarzman has surely learned much that he can share from his experience attempting to launch the "Schwarzman Scholars" program at Tsinghua University. The same is true of former New York mayor and financier Michael Bloomberg, who hosted the Bloomberg New Economy Forum in Beijing.

Ideally, other developed economies would break from China, as well. But collective action is not necessary, and a hard break remains the best course for the United States, regardless. For Washington, preserving democratic capitalism must be the nonnegotiable starting point; other policy priorities are secondary to that imperative. A commitment to free markets has meaning only if it is matched with the actions necessary to ensure that the U.S. market remains free. That objective can still be achieved by going it alone and is preferable to not going at all.

The United States should build a broader partnership of allied countries willing to make similar commitments in their own supply chains and on issues including technology transfer and research funding. Participants in such a trading bloc should have preferential access to the U.S. market. Nations declining to join should face worse terms of trade, and nations committing fully to the Chinese sphere should face the same treatment as China.

For policymakers and analysts committed to globalization and conditioned to fear any inefficient overstepping in the market, a hard break from China may seem implausible. But in response to Russia's invasion of Ukraine, the United States revoked Russia's "most favored nation" status and imposed aggressive sanctions designed to separate Russia from the international economic system. This was the hardest of breaks and was supported most strongly by those who are most vocally enthusiastic about global engagement and a rules-based international order. Whether the United States should take action on a similar scale against China is not a question of legality or capacity but of values and will.

AFTER HEGEMONY

by Elbridge Colby

Mr. Colby was cofounder and principal of the Marathon Initiative.

First published by American Compass on November 19, 2021.

For the last generation, one nation has wielded unmatched military power, bent the international financial system to its will, established almost unilaterally the standards of global communication and infrastructure, and dominated culture and media. For Americans, these seemed good years. And for most others, America's tutelage was easy, its burden light—certainly compared to history's other real or aspiring hegemons.

Those days have come to an end. China is the most formidable state Americans have dealt with certainly since the Soviet Union and in some ways since the 19th century. China's economy is almost as large or perhaps larger than America's already and, with roughly four times our population and an increasingly educated workforce, its overall (if not per capita) productive capacity should eventually exceed ours by a comfortable margin. By contrast, the Soviet Union, Nazi Germany, Imperial Japan, and Imperial Germany were all considerably smaller economies. China has also proved capable of succeeding in the global economy in a way that the Soviets never would or could. As a result, China has *a lot* of power to use on—and against—us and the things we care about.

Indeed, recognition that China is a profound challenge is one of the few matters that draws forth near unanimity in American politics. While the Trump Administration was the first to adopt a more realistic and confrontational response to Beijing's growing power and assertiveness, the Biden Administration has essentially continued its predecessor's basic line, albeit in different form and fashion and with different areas of focus. The view that China poses a very serious challenge may be one of the few areas of genuine and meaningful bipartisan agreement in the Congress, and polls indicate that the American people themselves increasingly recognize China as a serious and primary threat.

But after decades of foreign policy debates centered on dealing with states and actors far weaker than ourselves, the United States has lost the "fingertip feel" and grammar for determining how to respond to a nation that is comparable to us in power. Why China is such a challenge and what we should try to do in counteracting it remain at best vaguely defined. In point of fact, the answers to these questions are far from obvious. After all, China is far away, as is Asia, where most of Beijing's influence is currently felt. Meanwhile, America is physically secure, located behind two great oceans and protected by a large military and survivable nuclear arsenal. The chances of China invading and occupying the United States are therefore remote. Further, America is very rich. While our nation has serious problems, including social alienation and inequality, we are in relative terms doing well and our growth prospects emerging from the pandemic appear relatively good.

So, what, then, do we have to worry about? And what should we be trying to achieve?

OUR INTEREST IN ASIA

In answering these questions in the context of such a powerful challenge, we need to start from first principles. As a republic of free and equal citizens, our interests are: first, our physical security; second, our freedom; and third, our prosperity. The promise of American life, in other words, depends on our being reasonably safe, free, and prosperous. Our interests in confronting China are precisely to protect these, especially our prosperity and, relatedly, our freedom.

It is of critical importance to our prosperity and ultimately our freedom that no state dominate one of the key market areas of the world. This sounds abstract and detached but, if allowed to happen, would be very real in its implications for Americans. A state that could exercise sway over a very large portion of the global economy could and almost certainly *would* use that enormous leverage to shape—really even determine—international economic flows, regulations, and trade to its benefit.

Over time, this would make us increasingly dependent upon a foreign power and weaken our companies, our workers, and our economy.

The most plausible and consequential threat of that coming to pass is China's attainment of hegemony over Asia. Asia comprises roughly half of the global market, and that share is rising. China constitutes roughly half of Asia's GDP. If Beijing exercises control over Asia's huge and growing market area, its influence will ultimately be dominant worldwide as well, giving it the market, scale, and regulatory power to define the world's future. Building upon such economic advantages, it could intrude into and shape our national life, using its position to coerce, bribe, and cajole companies, individuals, and governments to do its will, diminishing our economic vitality and, through that, our freedoms.

We already see this happening around the world, as China brings its immense economic power to bear. The most famous example is the Belt and Road Initiative, a massive network of Chinese investments designed to net China closely with the countries of Eurasia through overland and maritime links, as well as the financial links that accompany those investments. This is giving China more leverage throughout the region, leverage it has increasingly put to use. To take just one example: When Sri Lanka failed to pay its heavy Belt and Road debts, China extracted a 99-year lease to a key port in the island country.

But China is not just picking on the small fry; rather, it is using its growing economic leverage to seek to coerce more advanced economies as well. For instance, it is currently trying to use its status as a major importer from Australia to compel that nation to submit to 14 searching and even humiliating demands, including changes to Australia's domestic legislation and dampening of media coverage that is critical of China. The proximate cause of Beijing's pressure is that Canberra had the audacity to call for an independent investigation of the origins of the COVID-19 virus. Beijing has also sought to its economic heft to coerce South Korea over missile defense deployments and Japan over territorial disputes in the East China Sea.

There is little reason to think that the United States would be spared such manipulation if China had the power to effect it. Indeed, we have already seen Chinese economic leverage marshalled against major American brands like Disney, the NBA, and Marriott—sadly, with some success. Even cage fighter John Cena, concerned for his movie's success in China, was reduced to apologizing for inadequately toeing Beijing's line on Taiwan.

This is just a taste of what China will do if it attains a hegemonic position over Asia. First and foremost, such a China would reshape international economic flows, regulation, and trade in its favor and to its preferences. This is a natural instinct of dominant states, as it provides great benefits on multiple levels. It allows the dominant state to ensure that the most lucrative and beneficial forms of economic activity cluster within and for itself rather than for others and somewhere else. It generates scale, enabling firms to gain advantages and compete more efficiently, thereby becoming more productive and dominant and making their investors, officers, and employees wealthier and more secure.

Think how the American-born internet supported Silicon Valley, and vice versa, leading to a World Wide Web governed by formal laws and informal norms almost entirely of American design. Think how the desire for access to American capital markets gives American regulators de facto control over global accounting standards, or how the need to transact with American institutions allows U.S. Treasury officials to freeze the assets of designated targets anywhere in the world. Think how Americans take for granted that English is the universal language and that everyone accepts dollars. Think how the American university degree has become the preeminent global academic credential, with searching implications for everything from global educational standards to measures of professional success.

Now think instead of the yuan as the reserve currency of the globe and the dollar supplanted, with China rather than the United States enjoying that "exorbitant privilege." China's central bank, not America's, would set the global economy's tempo. Think of China's sanctions power equaling America's today. Think of China dominating fractious and economically anemic Europe as well, with Beijing acting as gatekeeper and term-setter for access to the enormous market of Asian consumers. Standing alone in comparison to such a dominant China, America would no longer be the decision-maker; it would have to conform to China's preferences.

And forget lobbying Congress to change how social media companies are regulated; Americans would have to petition Chinese officials and regulators, with far less chance of accountability, let alone hope of success. Today's internet has been decisively shaped by the United States, with its strong preference for open and broadly "liberal" ideas. Europe, meanwhile, focuses on privacy protections. Yet the People's Republic of China values neither. Beijing represses speech on its own internet and allows little if any privacy protection. If China set the rules of the internet, Beijing would naturally tend to shape them in such directions. The same would go for everything from surveillance to speech controls to banking. It already uses technology, including facial recognition, big data, and artificial intelligence, to impose and police so-called "social capital" scores for its own citizens. Why would famously nationalistic China treat foreigners more leniently?

Instead of being the world's great large economy, the pinnacle of mass prosperity, and the master of its own fate, America would become something much less. We would likely remain more prosperous than many countries, but we would live under China's economic shadow. Chinese companies would gobble up or render dependent American—and European, Japanese, and South Korean—companies, leaving America's economic fortunes to be decided upon in China. China could insist on labor, information, regulatory, environmental, and legal changes that decisively shaped Americans' lives. The professional and probably much of the personal lives of Americans would be shaped—if not determined—by Chinese leaders.

Importantly, China need not create a great territorial empire to achieve this position of hegemony over Asia and, from there, a predominant global position. Rather, it simply needs to exert enough influence over the countries of the region with respect to their important economic and strategic decisions. A hegemonic China would not directly rule over countries within its sphere, but those countries would follow Beijing's line on key economic, political, and military matters—or else. In practice, such subordinated states would orient their trade, economic, and regulatory policies to China's demands, and avoid provoking Beijing by making or sustaining alliances or independent trading relationships with rivaling states—above all the United States.

A STRATEGY OF DENIAL

How do we head off this outcome? Let's first be clear about what we *don't* need. We don't need China to fundamentally change its internal system. We don't need to dismember it. We don't need it to bend the knee to us. We don't need to establish *our own* hegemony over Asia. Such delusions led us to the sorry impasse in which we now find ourselves. What we do need is disciplined focus on what our enlightened interests specifically require.

Our goal should be a favorable, stable, and enduring balance of power with China. We want—in coalition with other states that share our interests—to agglomerate enough power that we can prevent China from undermining our prosperity and the liberty it enables. We want to reach a point at which we—along with our allies and partners in this balancing coalition—are strong enough that China, recognizing the futility of attempting serious coercion or violence against us, must respect our interests. Once we have attained such a position of strength, we can pursue *détente* with Beijing, but not before.

As a basic yardstick, we need a balancing coalition that is larger in GDP terms than China and its allies, probably by a decent measure given that China is a unitary giant of a state and thus can act more cohesively than a large coalition. That standard is a bit crude, but it captures the core idea: An effective balancing coalition needs to be a group of states whose "hard" economic and military power is greater with respect to the theater of focus than that of China's own group. Think primarily of the United States, Japan, India, Australia, South Korea, Taiwan, some South and Southeast Asian states, and, less directly, some states from outside Asia. Europe can help, primarily by contributing economic scale and by taking care of its own security and that of its immediate neighborhood. But the core of this coalition will be in Asia.

If we can assemble and sustain such a group, we can blunt China's aspirations to dominance. If Beijing tries economic coercion, our coalition will be able to make up losses by deeper economic connections amongst ourselves. If Beijing tries military force, our combined military power will be able to effectively defend the states China targets.

This standard achieved, Beijing will have to respect our interests, but it will still have immense power and a leading place in the international system, something in which the Chinese can take enormous pride. The downside is that China will remain a formidable threat. But the upside of drawing the limits of our strategy here outweigh this downside.

First, we can live with that China. We don't need anything else *from* China for our security, freedom, and prosperity. We will retain plenty of market scale within our coalition and in the wide swath of countries likely to avoid affiliating with either us or Beijing.

Second, this standard will not require that we do anything *to* China. We won't have to transform its government, dismember its territory, or establish our hegemony over it. This is critical because it will give China a compelling incentive for restraint—in other words, for Beijing to accept a stable balance, sufficiently content that the arrangement provides it enough security, dignity, and prosperity. We will need to confront China and push it hard to uphold the balancing coalition, but China will in any plausible future be hugely powerful, with a range of ways of gravely hurting us, from economic leverage through conventional military force all the way to a growing nuclear arsenal. We don't want to push China so far into a corner that it judges lashing out too much with these instruments to be the best course.

By contrast, alternative strategies that insist we must democratize China or fundamentally weaken or collapse it would provoke far more cost and risk for Americans than is worthwhile. We might be better off with a democratic China—although that is not a given—just as we might be better off if we remained the only superpower. But thoroughgoing pursuit of those goals would trigger China to take drastic measures, with consequences far graver than the stakes are worth for us.

This doesn't mean we should oppose a democratic China or swear off undermining the People's Republic. To the contrary, we can and should support democratic government in China. Indeed, it already exists among the Chinese on Taiwan. And we will need to take steps to weaken China's economic and military power to secure ourselves and our coalition partners. But we should only insist on these measures as needed to attain that favorable, stable, and enduring balance of power in Asia. We may hope for beyond that—for a free mainland China, for instance—but we should not force the issue.

TAKING ACTION

It is important to underline, though, that the situation is urgent, because the key to preventing China's attainment of regional hegemony over Asia is acting now. We need to blunt Beijing's ambitions presently *in* Asia, rather than deferring the problem. The Pacific Ocean is huge, but consulting the map reminds us that most of it is empty. Outside the United States itself, the vast majority of the Pacific's economic activity clusters on its western shores—Japan, South Korea, China itself, Southeast Asia. If we wait to meet China halfway it will already have subordinated this huge economic area, essentially winning before the struggle has even started.

The problem this creates is that we must muster resolve to stand up—and, if necessary, fight—for very distant stakes, 10,000 miles from our homeland. And it is even more acute because Beijing's incentive is to pursue a classic "divide and conquer" strategy. Rather than precipitate a large struggle or war with a consolidated coalition, Beijing's incentive is to pick any such balancing coalition apart, selectively pressuring or attacking vulnerable members, positioning each effort as not justifying a robust enough American response. The most pressing threat is to Taiwan, on which China has focused its military efforts for a generation while we have been distracted in the Middle East. This is the very real and painful quandary we face.

Part of the solution is preparing the right kind of defense: economic resilience so countries can resist Beijing's economic coercion, and military defenses that defeat China's ability to subordinate targeted countries, including Taiwan, while minimizing the costs and risks to ourselves. But equally crucial is for Americans to *understand* why this is worthwhile, which in turn will harden our resolve for such a contest. And this, in turn, will be the best deterrent to Beijing precipitating such a conflict, as it will see that we and our partners in this balancing coalition have both the way and the will to defeat any such attempt.

It's one thing to *say* we are in serious, long-term competition with China. It's quite another to follow through on such a policy. Americans must wrestle with why we are confronting China and what our goal in doing so is. Too much of our national discussion now about competing with China is disconnected, abstract, and hortatory. It needs to be much more concrete and connected to Americans' interests, and in any event focused and candid. Failing here risks a fundamental breakdown in the event we are put to the test with China. And that moment may arrive, and may arrive soon.

CHAPTER SEVEN

Industrial Policy

A hallmark of the neoliberalism that dominated economic thinking across the political spectrum since the end of the Cold War was that industrial policy is unnecessary and unwise. It did not matter what a country made, or whether a country made anything at all. So long as free markets were growing the economic pie, everyone would prosper. And anyway, policymakers could not do better if they tried. This logic has proved a catastrophic miscalculation, quickly exploited by nations that did understand the strategic value of certain vital industries to seize leadership from those that did not. An essay published early in 2020 by Samuel Gregg, Fredrich Hayek Chair at the American Institute for Economic Research, made a quintessential presentation of the neoliberal case. The first essay in this chapter, "Comparative Disadvantage," is my effort to address the basic conceptual error in response.

But seeing is believing, and American Compass has undertaken a long-term research project to present examples of industrial policy done well. This chapter includes three. "The American Camry," by Wells King and Dan Vaughn Jr., describes how the Reagan administration's negotiation of a quota on Japanese auto imports gave birth to the hugely successful auto manufacturing industry in the American South. King's "Myth-Busting Silicon Valley" supplements the narrative of American technological leadership borne of entrepreneurs toiling in garages with the reality that every step of the digital revolution was driven by policy choices and taxpayer dollars. In "How Airbus Took Flight," Gabriela Rodriguez looks across the Atlantic at how a consortium of European governments built the dominant commercial aerospace company that trounced the free-market American model.

Finally, in "Rebuilding the Supply-Side Platform," Chris Griswold updates the conservative conception of "supply-side economics" to modern circumstances. Creating favorable conditions for productive investment is indeed among the most important goals for economic policy. And when tax rates were at their 1970s level, cutting them may indeed have been the ideal supply-side policy. But that does not mean cutting taxes will always be the answer. The experience of the past twenty-five years suggests that a very different set of policies would better encourage the investments that the nation now needs.

COMPARATIVE DISADVANTAGE
by Oren Cass

First published by *Law & Liberty* on January 15, 2020.

The heart of Samuel Gregg's case against economic nationalism is an abiding faith in the theory of comparative advantage. So well does this theory guide national economic development on behalf of the national interest that interventions by policymakers can only make matters worse. His faith is misplaced.

"In the first place," writes Gregg, "economic nationalism makes it harder for individuals, regions, and nations to discover their comparative advantage." As an example, he suggests that "Israel may be able to produce more manufacturing goods and technology than Australia. It's still, however, the case that Israel can obtain more manufactured goods from Australia by specializing in technology and trading some of that output for imported manufactured goods."

This description is the "A" answer on an introductory economics exam. Comparative advantage allows trading partners, whether individuals or nations, to specialize where each has the lower opportunity cost, increasing total output and, through mutually beneficial exchange, leaving both with more to consume. The sooner that each side "discovers" its advantage and specializes accordingly, the sooner benefits can flow. By contrast, Gregg argues, a protectionist policy that interferes with trade in a free-market international economy "gradually dulls a nation's awareness of its comparative advantages."

But the description bears no resemblance to how the international economy operates. Even the stylized example raises more questions than it answers. Israel is indeed an international technology powerhouse. But why? Is it simply in the nature of small, socialist agricultural communities founded by refugees and beset constantly by war and terrorism to become centers of innovation? Is it something about the Mediterranean winds, perhaps? Or, as the World Bank suggests, has it "been the Israeli government's explicit goal to position Israel at the core of the knowledge economy.... There is broad agreement as to the significant role played by the government in the emergence and development of Israel's vibrant and dynamic high-tech sector."

Australia, for its part, might appear sensible to specialize in manufactured goods. The example conveniently provides only the desirable-seeming technology and manufacturing industries as candidates for specialization. What about kangaroo meat? Would Australia be wise to outsource all its technological needs to Israel so that it can focus on its own comparative advantage in marsupial herding? The theory assures us that, in year one, the Aussies will enjoy a greater bounty of software and 'Roo-ribs than if it tried to develop software itself. But what sort of economic trajectory would the nation then travel?

The idyllic conception of an international economy in which countries all benefit from specializing in their discovered comparative advantages fails both because comparative advantage is not discovered and because specialization can backfire.

COMPARATIVE ADVANTAGE IS CREATED, NOT "DISCOVERED"

The conventional concept of comparative advantage emerged in the early 19th century when trade consisted primarily of agricultural commodities and natural resources, sometimes between nations with wildly different economic conditions and productivity levels. Comparative advantage, typically a function of geography, was *exogenous* to the economic activity—it was a fact of life to be discovered and pursued. That specialization made sense and could benefit both parties was an important insight.

Economists have long understood that the basic model describes poorly the modern international economy. For example, one crucial driver of comparative advantage is scale. The things which one makes a lot of, one is likely to make more efficiently. Thus, rather than a nation focusing where it has comparative advantage, it has comparative advantage where it focuses. In technical terms, the advantage is *endogenous*—it emerges from the behavior of the participants. Paul Krugman won his Nobel Prize in part for advancing this theory.

Likewise, a nation's public policies exert a strong influence on its place in the global marketplace. Does its legal system provide for the predictable rule of law and enforceable contract and property rights? Does its education system produce a large supply of high-quality engineers? Does its labor regulation allow workers to exert power or leave them ripe for exploitation? Does its trade policy make domestic production a condition of access to its consumer market? Does it offer generous subsidies to producers? Answers to these questions—not any traditional, discovered comparative advantage—best explain the decisions of the international financiers and multinational corporations whose very visible hands move capital around the globe.

Analysts casually assert that some countries make more sense as manufacturing centers because they have "cheap labor." But hourly wages say nothing about a market's attractiveness. If workers are paid the marginal product of their labor, then employing someone at $1 per hour to produce $1 per hour of value is no more or less attractive than employing someone at $40 per hour to produce $40 per hour of value. A "cheap labor" country is not attractive because the wage is $1 per hour, but rather because the worker is generating far more than the $1 per hour of value that he is able to capture for himself. While much closer to the truth, "it is efficient for corporations to move operations to developing countries because the legal and cultural regimes there allow for more profitable exploitation of labor," rather softens the narrative's appeal.

If comparative advantage is created rather than discovered, and if nations understand this and develop their economic strategies accordingly, then a nation refusing to participate in the game will find itself left with the comparative advantage that no one else wants. Gregg contrasts the possibility that American industries have suffered from "unfair foreign competition" with what he sees as the "far more likely" explanation of "shifts in comparative advantage." Those are two ways of saying the same thing.

In 2017, the United States ran a $100 billion deficit in trade of Advanced Technology Products. We were, however, the world's leading exporter of garbage. A nation indifferent to what it produces might be untroubled by such a development. If other nations are willing to trade us their advanced technology for our trash, perhaps they are the suckers. As Michael Boskin, chairman of George H.W. Bush's Council of Economic Advisers, supposedly said, "computer chips, potato chips, what's the difference?"

That may be true if we concern ourselves with only a single point in time. But economic development is the ultimate repeated game. Our levels of investment in advanced technology and trash in 2017 have serious consequences for our opportunities in 2018, which in turn will influence investment throughout the 2020s. A nation heads down a dangerous path by specializing contentedly in sectors that are neither economically nor strategically important, that face declining demand and weak productivity growth, and that fail to provide opportunities for workers of widely varying aptitudes in widely varying places to support themselves and their families.

SPECIALIZATION CAN BACKFIRE

For an individual in a modern society, specialization is unavoidable. No one person can possibly develop the skills to produce more than a miniscule fraction of the goods and services he wishes to consume. For a small nation, the same logic might hold. It may grow most of its own food, provide its own financial services, even build its own infrastructure; it cannot design and produce all of its own pharmaceuticals, electronics, and airplanes.

But where possible, diversification has real benefits. "The products a country makes today," explains *The Economist*, describing the work of Harvard professor Ricardo Hausmann and MIT professor César Hidalgo, "determine which products they will be able and likely to make tomorrow, through the evolution of their capabilities." Whereas traditional economic theory suggests that specialization is key to prosperity, their research has shown the opposite to be true. The more diverse is the array of knowledge and capabilities within an economy, the stronger is its long-term health.

Especially in the most complex, technologically advanced industries—where productivity is often highest, and future growth likely to be strong—sophisticated supply-chains and engineering know-how are critical to the economy's vitality. Writing in *Businessweek* in 2010, long-time Intel CEO Andy Grove explained Intel's decision to invest heavily in chip fabrication and lamented that American firms no longer make such choices:

> [Intel] was founded at a time when it was easier to scale domestically. For one thing, China wasn't yet open for business. More importantly, the U.S. had not yet forgotten that scaling was crucial to its economic future. How could the U.S. have forgotten?... Consider this passage by Princeton University economist Alan S. Blinder: "The TV manufacturing industry really started here, and at one point employed many workers. But as TV sets became 'just a commodity,' their production moved offshore to locations with much lower wages. And nowadays the number of television sets manufactured in the U.S. is zero. A failure? No, a success." I disagree. Not only did we lose an untold number of jobs, we broke the chain of experience that is so important in technological evolution. As happened with batteries, abandoning today's "commodity" manufacturing can lock you out of tomorrow's emerging industry.

Unlike in the nation of five million, the U.S. economy is large enough to support any and all domestic industries. Its failure to do so is not a result of having "discovered" a comparative advantage in soybeans (or having "discovered" that it can trade U.S. Treasury bonds for foreign goods rather than make anything at all), but its choice to abandon once-held advantages in infrastructure, engineering, and manufacturing.

The failure has become so grave as to now pose a substantial national security threat. In opposing economic nationalism, Gregg acknowledges an exception for "making the necessary provisions for national defense." On the modern battlefield, those provisions can be quite extensive. Presumably they must extend to the domestic manufacturing capabilities necessary to smelt aluminum and steel, fabricate all manner of semiconductor, and maintain secure communications networks. If such activities are to be conducted efficiently and at the cutting edge, they will require scale.

THE DRUNK DONKEY PROBLEM

To observe that comparative advantage is created, and that a nation should care greatly about its economy's industrial composition, is not to prove the validity of any particular policy. Indeed, one might use these arguments to advance any number of bad policies, from efforts by federal agencies at playing venture capitalist to wholesale nationalization of firms or industries. What these arguments do establish, however, is the *potential* for affirmative policy to improve upon the free market's status quo.

Enamored of the idea that unfettered markets yield efficient and thus optimal outcomes, and the corollary that any political effort to improve upon them must backfire, market fundamentalists slip casually into the claim that the same holds true for the distribution of investment and production across industries. This is wrong—not only in the sense that one might disagree with it, but also in the sense that it lacks any substantive support. The social benefits that we expect from individuals pursuing their self-interest *do not extend to macroeconomic allocations*.

This confusion is evident in Gregg's lament that, "at the heart of industrial policy is the assumption that governments can often better identify which industries are more worthy of investment than others." Note what's missing from the sentence: governments can often better identify... than who? By what mechanism is the identification happening in the absence of an effort by policymakers? Certainly not individual investors or profit-seeking firms. That concern could not be further from their minds.

To the contrary, to quote Grove again, "Each company, ruggedly individualistic, does its best to expand efficiently and improve its own profitability. However, our pursuit of our individual businesses, which often involves transferring manufacturing and a great deal of engineering out of the country, has hindered our ability to bring innovations to scale at home. Without scaling, we don't just lose jobs—we lose our hold on new technologies. Losing the ability to scale will ultimately damage our capacity to innovate."

We face what I call the Drunk Donkey Problem. Markets do some things very well, but when we attribute to them the power to do well things that they don't do at all, we err by privileging a default outcome that deserves no such deference. Suppose that the allocation of investment across American industries were dictated each year by a drunk donkey stumbling across a grid. If that were the default, we would think that policymakers might improve upon it, even as we carefully weighed which tools would be appropriate to the effort and acknowledged the ways in which they would undoubtedly fall far short of anyone's ideal. Gregg's concern that "no one can know what will be the future growth businesses in any given nation. No one knows what technological innovation or entrepreneurial insight will upend the present economic landscape" would rightly seem irrelevant.

In some respects, a drunk donkey would improve upon the performance of our multinational corporations, who are not just oblivious to the national economy's health but actively lured to act against its interest by foreign governments seeking to create their own comparative advantage. Gregg trusts that "accurate information" will allow "entrepreneurs, investors, and businesses to identify the most optimal economic path for each of them to follow—a process which constantly allows millions of piecemeal improvements to the overall economy." Until that accurate information tells them they can create greater shareholder value by downsizing and offshoring, slashing investment and buying back shares. What then?

THE AMERICAN CAMRY

by Wells King & Dan Vaughn Jr.

Mr. King was the research director and Mr. Vaughn was an analyst at American Compass.

First published by *National Review* on September 29, 2022.

Tesla's annual "Impact Report," released in May 2022, surveyed thousands of its "key stakeholders." Most were in China. Tesla's largest plant and export hub is in Shanghai. It has just opened a research-and-development center there as well. Founded in America, dependent on American innovation, nurtured by American subsidies, the world's most valuable car company might best be described as Chinese. When its executives promise "stakeholder engagement," they mean kowtowing.

Faced with such results, policymakers and their economists are belatedly discovering that globalization is not a "no-brainer," an easy "win-win," or even a particularly good idea. Researchers have shown that free trade with China cost America millions of jobs, with consequences ranging from declining family formation to increasing substance abuse and suicide—the so-called deaths of despair. The Covid-19 pandemic's disruptions have exposed the strategic disaster of dependence on China, the costs of moving supply chains overseas, and the ways that the single-minded pursuit of efficiency can make a nation less resilient.

The economic-policy tools that conservatives most comfortably wield—tax reform, deregulation, expanding trade, and so forth—were chosen long ago in response to different challenges. They offer little help here. So policymakers have begun rummaging through the garage to make a bigger toolbox. In the semiconductor industry, for instance, Taiwan and South Korea supplanted U.S. leadership through an aggressive industrial policy of direct public investments and subsidies for their own chip manufacturers. China is now attempting the same. In America, the *Chips and Science Act* of 2022 represents the beginning of a response, with funds aimed at supporting both construction of chip-fabrication plants here and research that could produce future breakthroughs.

But conservatives rightly prize America's market economy and worry that subsidies will fuel cronyism and misallocate capital. Subsidies for particular firms and projects are a double-edged sword: Their narrow targeting might seem to minimize market intervention, but they also leave room for mischief. The *Chips Act* is better than the alternative of simply abandoning technological leadership to Asia, but the conservative toolbox has more to offer. Much blunter instruments can often get more done and, counterintuitively, they can do much less damage to markets in the process.

The best illustration comes from our own shores, during the presidency of Ronald Reagan. When he took office, the domestic auto industry was in a tailspin. Facing a flood of Japanese imports, the "Big Three" automakers—GM, Ford, and Chrysler—had just suffered their first losses in more than two decades and collectively laid off a tenth of their factory workers. While some in his cabinet advised doing nothing, Reagan negotiated an import quota with Japan, sharply constricting the flow of vehicles into the United States. This was not a subtle or fine-tuned policy; it simply prohibited imports from rising above the 1979 level.

And it worked. Detroit turned around, and the Japanese firms invested tens of billions of dollars in a massive new manufacturing base in the South that created hundreds of thousands of American jobs—the single, exceptional example of significant foreign manufacturing capacity relocating to America instead of the other way around. Anyone hoping for more of the same today should take note.

After four decades of aggressive public support from its Ministry of International Trade and Industry (MITI)—direct subsidies, tax breaks, cheap loans, and information-sharing—Japan had built an automotive juggernaut by the 1970s. Economics textbooks predicted that such policies would yield sclerosis and cronyism, but in this case, the results were the world's most efficient production processes and its highest-quality cars. Japan's top automaker, Toyota, had perfected its management of material to the point where its inventory costs were only a tenth of General

Motors'. American automotive engineers awarded many more product-quality honors to Japanese automakers than to American ones. Over the decade, the Japanese industry raised its productivity by 4.3 percent annually—three times the American rate of progress.

From 1970 to 1976, Japanese cars tripled their sales volume in the United States, to more than 1 million units and 8 percent market share. Then came the decade's second oil crisis. In the wake of the Iranian Revolution in the spring of 1979, as oil prices more than doubled, American consumers lost their taste for American-made "gas guzzlers" and switched en masse to smaller, more fuel-efficient cars. In 1980, nearly two out of every three new automobiles sold were small or compact cars, up from fewer than half in 1978.

Such cars were a Japanese specialty, and the American automakers, unable to quickly retool, quickly lost ground. Japanese automakers reached 21 percent market share in 1980, at which point they were exporting nearly 2 million cars annually to the U.S.—more than they were selling in their home market. That year, the Big Three suffered a $6.2 billion loss, as compared with an average of $4.4 billion in annual profits during the previous decade. In the span of two years, Big Three sales had plummeted 30 percent, to their lowest level since 1961. Chrysler was on the verge of bankruptcy. Over 100,000 auto-factory workers had been laid off, and the United Auto Workers (UAW) had lost 40 percent of its membership.

It was far from a fair fight. Whereas American firms competed in a free and open market, Japan had insulated its automakers from foreign competition. On top of the aggressive government support it provided to its own producers, high tariffs kept imports uncompetitive, while onerous standards made it virtually impossible for foreign firms to build operations in Japan. American tolerance for such an imbalanced arrangement was a feature of Cold War–era trade policy and had long been a source of frustration for American auto executives. "In America's determination to establish and hold ties to Japan and maintain it as a Far East buffer against Communism," Chrysler CEO Lee Iacocca complained, "the United States set trade agreements without thought to reciprocity." The UAW urged

Japanese automakers to build assembly plants in the United States and hire American workers, but the requests were flatly denied.

Nor was there any light at the end of the tunnel. According to a later analysis by the U.S. International Trade Commission (ITC), the Big Three's downward trajectory was showing no signs of slowing. Industry analysts argued that American automakers required "breathing room" and an estimated $80 billion to retool their factories and regain their competitive footing in the Japanese-dominated market for cheap, fuel-efficient compacts. But when Ford and the UAW filed for import relief from the ITC, their petitions were rejected by a 3–2 vote. While acknowledging that imports had been "a significant thorn in the industry's side," the ITC concluded that recession was the leading cause of its woes and speculated that import relief might "generate a perverse influence on the ability of the United States to attract foreign producers to establish new domestic facilities."

The Carter White House was similarly unmoved. Foreshadowing the free-trade consensus that would define the 1990s and 2000s, President Carter opposed import restrictions of any kind. He accepted the industry's decline and suggested a program of palliative care, aimed at ameliorating plant closures through government aid to surrounding communities. To address unemployment, he proposed retraining laid-off workers. If only the software industry had been better developed, he could have suggested they "learn to code."

Ronald Reagan knew better. Government, in his view, was partly to blame—not for doing too much, but for failing to do enough. "Government has a role that it has shirked so far," he remarked during a campaign visit to a Chrysler plant in September 1980. "The deluge" of Japanese imports, he insisted, "must be slowed while our industry gets back on its feet." Reagan not only promised import relief but threatened retaliation: "If Japan keeps on doing everything that it's doing, obviously there's going to be what you call 'protectionism.'"

It was an unorthodox stance for a disciple of the free market. Then again, the auto industry's predicament betrayed free-market orthodoxy. Markets were supposed to create the incentives and competitive pressures that would spur productivity and innovation. Interfering in markets was supposed to backfire. The Japanese auto industry, insulated from foreign competition and subsidized by the state, should have been a catastrophic failure; America's open market should have fostered firms that were more resilient and responsive to consumer demand and competition. What was to be done when the opposite occurred?

Economic reality's defiance of economic theory stoked a debate among policymakers seeking remedies. Newly inaugurated, President Reagan formed a cabinet-level task force to address the crisis. It soon divided along ideological lines. A free-market faction, led by the treasury secretary, former Merrill Lynch executive Donald Regan, opposed any action beyond broad supply-side reforms. Import restrictions, as another top Reagan official speculated, might "take the heat off the domestic industry to do other things it should, to take corrective steps." Opposing them was a "pragmatist" faction, composed of seasoned businessmen such as Commerce Secretary Malcolm Baldrige and Labor Secretary Raymond Donovan, who came from the manufacturing and construction industries, respectively. They pushed for import restraints, fearing that the proposed supply-side reforms were inadequate to address the auto industry's challenges. A task-force memo to the president warned, "Even a successful recovery program may not generate sufficient capital to enable the industry to meet changing customer demands, increasingly stringent government regulations, and competition from abroad."

As it debated whether to fulfill the president's campaign promise, the divided task force came under additional pressure from Congress. Senate majority leader Howard Baker (R., Tenn.) feared that "the situation's out of hand," and Senators John C. Danforth (R., Mo.) and Lloyd Bentsen (D., Texas) introduced legislation to impose a three-year import quota on Japanese automobiles. It was a threat—both to the Japanese and to the free-market faction in the White House. A Treasury Department memo admitted, "Congress may take the question out of our hands if we fail to act."

President Reagan chose a diplomatic solution. In addition to seeking supply-side reforms that reduced fuel-economy standards and eased antitrust enforcement, he would restrict Japanese auto imports for three years.

Armed with the threat of an outright import quota, his administration negotiated a "voluntary export restraint" (VER) with the Japanese MITI, which preferred to restrain its own industry rather than face restraints imposed by Congress. MITI limited the number of cars that Japan exported to the United States each year to 1.68 million, the level in 1979.

The predictions of the two factions on the task force would be put to the test: Would such a blunt obstruction of trade insulate Detroit from competition and thereby allow it to decay further, leaving consumers with costlier and lower-quality vehicles, or would the Big Three learn their lesson and become leaner and meaner? Would workers lose out in the long run or, contra the ITC's prediction, would the Japanese invest to make cars in America?

The quota immediately stabilized the American market. According to the ITC's later analysis, American-made cars had been on pace to hold just 68 percent of the market by 1983. Instead, the share recovered to its 1979 level of 77 percent by 1984.

American automakers took advantage of the breathing room to boost their capabilities and compete in the newly fuel-conscious consumer market. Car size and weight declined, while fuel efficiency increased. Improved operations raised quality while cutting costs. Ford reported that defects fell by 78 percent over the decade; J.D. Power found a decline of defects across all domestic automakers of 40 percent. By 1989, American automakers could make cars with 25 percent less labor than in 1979, which equated to a robust 3 percent annual productivity growth.

As important, VER reshaped the American manufacturing landscape by bringing Japanese production onshore. The quota set no limit on the number of vehicles Japanese automakers could sell in America, only on how many they could import into the country; cars built in the U.S. were exempt. As a result, the firms had great incentives to build cars here and hire American workers.

In 1980, there were no Japanese auto-assembly plants in the U.S. Within a decade of Reagan's action, every major Japanese automaker—Toyota, Honda, Nissan, Mazda, Mitsubishi, Isuzu, and Subaru—began assembling cars in America.

And assembly plants were only the beginning of the story. As assembly moved onshore, economic forces pulled suppliers along, too. By 1991, Japanese automakers had built not only eight auto-assembly plants, but also more than 300 other production facilities that employed over 100,000 American workers and represented over $25 billion in capital investment (in 2022 dollars). For a sense of scale: Total foreign direct investment in new domestic capacity, across the entire economy, has averaged $10 billion per year since 2015.

VER's lasting legacy is the millions of "Japanese" cars on American roads that are in fact American cars—Toyotas and Hondas are not only assembled in America but also have consistently ranked among the cars with the highest share of American-made parts. Japanese automakers continued to gain market share, but while that competition forced the Big Three to sharpen their performance, it did not threaten American workers as Japanese imports once did. The share of American-made cars held steady.

Economists were proven right, in a narrow sense, about the costs of restricting trade. According to government estimates, VER raised prices on Japanese cars by about 8 percent, which translated into an additional $5.1 billion for American consumers between 1981 and 1984. But within the decade, the policy had also prompted nearly three times that much foreign direct investment. The cost per new job in the Japanese supply chain was only about $50,000, and that does not even include the jobs saved at American automakers and suppliers. From one perspective, the exchange may seem unfair—a diffuse cost to millions of consumers for the benefit of a smaller number of workers. But Americans had a different perspective: In a 1980 *New York Times* poll, 71 percent favored "protecting jobs at the cost of higher prices on foreign products."

And while the intervention was temporary, the benefits were permanent. VER had been lifted by 1985, and Japanese automakers have not faced any quotas since. But once their American investments had begun, maintaining and expanding them took on an economic logic of its own. No one today suggests that American consumers face higher prices because their Camrys come from Kentucky instead of Tsutsumi; the best place to locate production in a free market is not some immutable truth, but rather a function of previous policies and investments.

President Reagan's approach was not an indictment of free markets or international trade. Both were necessary, after all, to the establishment and growth of the transplanted Japanese industry. Rather, the quota offers a simple lesson in political economy: Blunt constraints that set market boundaries, while encouraging competition within them, can help ensure that capitalism serves the national interest. Neither tax cuts nor deregulation would have given Detroit the chance it needed or incentivized Japanese investment.

What was a fairly unique challenge for the auto industry in 1980 has become a commonplace across the American economy four decades later. The United States ran a $59 billion trade surplus in advanced technology products in the early 1990s; by 2020, that surplus had collapsed to a $189 billion trade deficit (both figures in 2020 dollars). From semiconductors and communications equipment to solar panels and electric-vehicle batteries to pharmaceuticals and personal-protective equipment, the United States has witnessed a systematic hollowing out of its industrial leadership—and with it, of jobs, investment, and innovation—met largely with a shrug by economists and policymakers who saw it as inevitable or perhaps even beneficial. As we finally awake from that stupor, conservatives inclined to ask what Ronald Reagan would do should remember what he did.

Proposals already on offer illustrate the wide variety of tools available. For example, President Trump's U.S. trade representative, Robert Lighthizer, has proposed an across-the-board 10 percent tariff that would increase steadily so long as America continued to run a trade deficit. As with an import quota, the tariff's effect would be to redirect market forces to domestic production and then let them rip. Another approach, proposed by Senator Josh Hawley (R., Mo.) and Representative Claudia Tenney (R., N.Y.), would be a "local-content requirement" for critical goods, requiring that 50 percent of the value in their supply chains be produced domestically. The market would decide which parts of the supply chain made most sense onshore, but it would have to choose something.

As longtime Intel CEO Andy Grove warned just as his successors were sacrificing the firm's manufacturing edge, simple production goes first, but more-complex processes and entire supply chains follow, and then research and innovation go, too. He predicted the same would happen in the advanced-battery industry, and he has already been proven right. Happily, though, this process flows in both directions: Where production returns to American shores, broader supply chains and greater innovation will, too. Just as Tesla released its report of predominantly Chinese stakeholders, Toyota announced a new series of research projects at one of its five American R&D centers, to be conducted in partnership with six American universities.

MYTH-BUSTING SILICON VALLEY

by Wells King

Mr. King was the research director at American Compass.

First published by the *American Conservative* on November 28, 2022.

Every regime has a founding myth—a self-validating account of its origin, propagated by its elites to confer legitimacy upon them. In Silicon Valley, the fabulously wealthy entrepreneurs who regard themselves as the Sun Kings of American prosperity have a story they tell about "founders."

The Valley, in this story, is the cradle of progress because obsessive geniuses congregate in garages to invent new technologies and launch start-ups, taking enormous risk and reaping a small part of the reward they bequeath upon us all. Its pantheon of billionaires—Gates, Jobs, Zuckerberg, *et cetera*—presents the scrappy entrepreneur as the archetype of success.

The "founder" myth begets a culture of superiority among the techno-elite that demands deference from the political system. Beyond mere paeans to entrepreneurship, Silicon Valley expects policymakers to accept without reservation its preferred blend of self-regulating markets and limited government. Theirs is the land of "permissionless innovation" and "failing fast," and any public servant who dares intercede risks killing the golden goose.

Some in the Valley go even further. Venture capitalist Katherine Boyle advocates for tech bros to "tak[e] on important missions of government" because it's "easier to solve critical national problems through startups." Her case in point: the Middle East. "The best comparison is that in the last two decades," she explains, "roughly $1 trillion has gone to venture-backed companies in the U.S., while $6 trillion went to the War on Terror and failed nation-building in Afghanistan. The outcomes are different due to incentives, not investment." What's app-building, after all, but nation-building with a better stock-options plan?

Libertarians and fellow believers in market fundamentalism rely on the myth to advance their own, even bigger myth: that innovation, progress, and growth are the product of government's absence. As Adam Thierer of the libertarian Mercatus Center has argued, "The best role that public policy can play at this time is to clear the way for ... innovation by removing barriers to entry and trade." As in every domain, the recommended innovation policy is no policy—and here, at least, the libertarians claim some empirical evidence on their side.

While all founding myths contain exaggerations and even fictions—that's what makes them myths—good ones reinforce that which is best about a regime and provide a foundation on which a community can build. But Silicon Valley's founder myth has things backward, misunderstanding the source of the regime's power and flattering its worst instincts.

Silicon Valley was the product of aggressive public policy. The key technologies of our digital age were not the happy accidents of "permissionless innovation" in the "self-regulating" market, but of deliberate and prolonged government action. Public officials "picked winners" and decided the trajectory of technological development—from the materials used in chips to the protocols for networked computers. When the Valley was humming, it did so as a symbiosis of capitalist pursuit of profit and government pursuit of the public good. Left to its own devices, it has devolved into a "unicorn" hunting party while subsequent waves of innovation happen elsewhere.

LET THERE BE CAPITAL

A better myth would go something like this: In the beginning, Silicon Valley was a tract of orchards.

At the end of the Second World War, the region had only a nascent technology sector, centered around Stanford University. The venture capital industry did not exist, and the region's few entrepreneurs were former academic researchers like David Packard and William Hewlett, who expanded from their garage by filling military contracts. Packard and

Hewlett received the prestigious Army-Navy "E" Award for excellence in wartime production four years before formally incorporating as the Hewlett Packard Company.

The Cold War transformed the region as the Pentagon's imperatives became the Valley's. Tasked with advancing technological capabilities for advanced espionage and warfare, public officials mobilized America's ever-growing computing power, which was centered initially on the East Coast. Public funding sponsored roughly 25 percent of Bell Laboratories' transistor research and more than half of R&D at IBM through the 1950s and, by the late 1950s, three-quarters of the nation's computers were committed to public purposes.

Uncle Sam employed a set of complementary policy levers to channel the Valley's technological development in the national interest.

First, the federal government created an entirely new agency to fund and coordinate cutting-edge research and development. In the wake of the panic sparked by the USSR's Sputnik launch, President Eisenhower created the Advanced Research Projects Agency (ARPA) in 1958. The independent agency, which would become the engine of the Space Race and Cold War innovation, was designed to spur "blue-sky thinking" beyond the traditional federal R&D and military procurement system.

It became a remarkable success of industrial planning. Rather than build its own laboratories, the program adopted a decentralized structure manned by training engineers and computer scientists. These expert-practitioners-turned-program-officers were granted the autonomy to advise and direct research efforts across firms, universities, and government labs.

Contra Hayek, such work did not require perfect knowledge or information, only a coherent view of the future. With the market's price signals offering little useful information to the researchers and entrepreneurs advancing the technological frontier, bureaucrats were indispensable. Only the federal government had the resources, perspective, and incentives to fund and coordinate academic and private-sector researchers as well as facilitate the initial application and commercialization of their discoveries. As Julius Krein has observed:

> *Price competition often (though not always) works well for rationing, or deciding who gets what in the present, which need not require a view of the future. The same is not true of investing capital, which requires taking (more or less) risk on a (more or less contrarian) view of the future. Long-term investment capital (and thus productive capacity) simply cannot be prudently allocated on the basis of price signals alone. Hayek's spontaneous order, in more than one sense, has no future.*

For a single agency, ARPA's reach was remarkable. In the early 1960s, the agency alone funded 70 percent of all computer research in the U.S. Even those commercial technologies were direct products of government investment and planning. The vision of the personal computer, including monitors, keyboards, and "electronic pointer controllers called 'mice,'" was not first envisioned by Steve Jobs, but by ARPA officials in 1968. The agency would go on to fund research at Stanford University and MIT that would develop the first mouse-and-windows graphic user interface, single-user computer workstations, and Internet protocols.

In addition to shaping innovation across the industry, ARPA's own operations spawned extraordinary breakthroughs. Its computer network known as ARPANET functioned as a proto-Internet. As a vehicle for experimentation rather than a fully developed service, the network was responsible for developing the first communication protocols, spawning network applications like file transfers and e-mail. ARPANET both pioneered and publicized such technological breakthroughs, enabling later developments by NSFNET and the government-backed Project MAC at MIT that developed time-sharing networks and the first Internet protocols.

As a second policy lever, public and military officials acted as a "collaborative first customer" for new technologies. In new fields where no commercial market existed and the capital requirements for scaling up manufacturing processes were prohibitive, federal procurement contracts were vital.

The market for transistors and, later, integrated circuits depended on these government contracts. Fairchild Semiconductor's first contract was with defense contractor IBM, for high-voltage silicon transistors used in B-70 bombers' on-board computers. Later, two procurement decisions by NASA and the Air Force for missile and space-guidance projects pushed chips into large-scale. NASA alone constituted 60 percent of the integrated-circuit market in the 1960s.

The customer is always right—especially when the customer is the Pentagon. Beyond revenue to tech companies, government contracts shaped the trajectory of technological development and key features of early computing technologies to suit the particular needs of military and defense applications. Santa Clara County only earned the name Silicon Valley, not Germanium Valley, because of the Air Force's specific preference for new silicon transistors, rather than standard germanium ones.

In theory, chipmakers and other early technology companies could have ignored the government market and attempted to foster a private one. But in reality, they didn't. There was no one else to sell to, because no customers were building their own businesses reliant on products that did not yet exist. There was nowhere else from which to attract investment because no private institution had adequate resources or appetite for risk. Only government had the scale and incentives to fund and purchase breakthrough technologies.

Third, federal policymakers addressed the shortfall of private investment in technology. As the nascent venture capital industry began to emerge, it was augmented by government funding that matched private investments. Beginning in 1958, the Small Business Administration operated a venture capital fund-matching program, investing two dollars for every venture capital dollar.

Venture capital would remain an important—albeit small—industry boosted by federal subsidies until the late 1970s, when regulatory reforms opened up a massive pool of institutional capital for venture capitalists. But by this point, the government had already funded the core R&D, sponsored advanced manufacturing, and facilitated the commercialization that made tech start-ups attractive to private capital.

The Valley's booming technology sector fared well despite a lack of venture capital. Government funders directed capital to cutting-edge labs and firms commercializing new breakthroughs. Rather than crowd out private investment or distort the incentives of entrepreneurs, government proved an essential partner in the Valley's success. Even after venture capital had boomed, government remained an essential investor in technology. Federal programs like the Small Business Innovation & Research program filled critical funding gaps for early-stage tech firms, investing where even the boldest venture capitalists would not.

THE VALLEY LIES FALLOW

A core tenet of market fundamentalism is the practice of rejecting all evidence of effective government support, suggesting that things might have been even better if policymakers had stayed out of the way. But with Silicon Valley, the counterfactual is also on disastrous display.

By the 1980s, federal policy had narrowed its focus to basic and applied research, leaving commercialization and scaling to the market. Without support and demand for domestic production, new technologies migrated offshore.

The breakthrough LCD technology underlying flat-panel displays was first discovered by military-funded researchers at Westinghouse in the 1970s. But after Westinghouse shut down its LCD research, no major computing companies were willing to fund it without immediate, commercially viable output. Apple, Xerox, IBM, Compaq, and others all denied requests to support the project, citing a lack of manufacturing capability necessary to create flat-panel displays at a competitive price.

ARPA (renamed "Defense Advanced Research Projects Agency" or DARPA in 1972) eventually picked up where private industry failed, funding research that would form the basis of portable electronic displays. But by then the damage had already been done. Japan had taken up the flat-panel technology, and Seiko was selling color pocket televisions in the United States—a direct infringement on Westinghouse's patents. American industry refused to fight, neither challenging Japanese IP theft nor setting up production of its own.

Without adequate government support and left to their own devices, major American computer companies were uninterested in producing their own supplier base of flat-panel displays, and instead continued to rely on cheap imports from East Asia. To this day, all of the world's flat-panel display factories are located in Korea, Taiwan, Japan, and China; none are in the U.S.

Other key critical technologies suffered a similar fate—even in sectors where the U.S. was an undisputed leader. Semiconductors eventually fell prey to the "market-based" policy program and its blithe disregard of its importance to the innovation ecosystem and the information economy. "Potato chips, computer chips, what's the difference?" as Michael Boskin, chairman of George H.W. Bush's Council of Economic Advisers, quipped. As U.S. support for semiconductors waned and rivals emerged in East Asia, the industry turned to offshoring fabrication and eventually major American chipmakers lost the ability to design and produce the most advanced chips.

Second, a free-market wave of new and better technological advances has failed to materialize. The frothy boom of V.C.-backed asset-lite firms in the 1990s yielded little and was built upon the hardware innovations of prior decades. In theory that decade's boom would have enabled the buildout of digital infrastructure led by American hardware companies. But America's would-be champions opted for a different course.

IBM, for example, had replenished and even grown its capital stock for decades. It was a leading innovator in mainframe computers, magnetic stripe cards, and P.C.s but had experienced no real financial boom since its IPO in 1980. That changed after the turn of the millennium, once it sold off Lenovo and acquired PwC consulting. It has essentially transformed into a consulting firm that hasn't sustained its capital stock in nearly two decades.

The telecom company Cisco adopted a similar strategy. It was poised to build the Internet's hardware infrastructure after introducing modems and router during the Nineties Internet heyday.

It was the most valuable company in the world at the height of the dot-com bubble. But it chose to migrate from hardware into software and began to erode its capital stock in 2003; it has yet to recover. While China has boosted Huawei as a national champion, the would-be American telecom leader has executed $101 billion in stock buybacks in the last 15 years but made just $15 billion in capital expenditures over the same period.

Today, Silicon Valley concentrates in capital-light, fast-scaling, derivative app development and "software-as-a-service"—a predictable course in the absence of public investment, demand, vision, and coordination. It's "innovation in bits, but not in atoms" as Peter Thiel complains.

During the heyday of public-private partnership in the twentieth century, America's corporate labs earned three Nobel prizes for their advances in microelectronics. Tech giants such as Google, Apple, and Facebook, deemed the "most important companies on the planet" by AEI's James Pethokoukis, have never earned one—as if they ever aspired to.

The United States once marshaled its best minds to discover scientific breakthroughs and master engineering challenges. Today, under the banner of "market-driven innovation," it has liberated them to more efficiently target ads for subscription underwear services to Instagram users.

LET A THOUSAND SUBSIDIES BLOOM

The passage of the bipartisan *Chips and Science Act* this past summer is a sure sign that policymakers are beginning to realize that the "design here, make there" business model doesn't work for America—especially when the business in question is in a critical sector. Though a necessary measure, its deficiencies underscore just how much more policymakers must do if the United States is to retain technological dominance, retake the lead in key sectors, and spur a new generation of innovation. As a first step, they should suspend whatever deference they have to the purported geniuses of Silicon Valley.

The case of Elon Musk is illustrative. After making his fortune founding PayPal, Musk went on to build his reputation on literal moonshot "hard tech" projects such as Tesla and SpaceX. Both are ambitious, but neither was viable on its own. The market's ruthless demand for profit, rather than innovation, has only been trumped by "f*** you" money—and a little help from Uncle Sam.

The latter, as it turns out, is critical, especially for long-term viability. Market fundamentalists lament that involvement by government will distort incentives and crowd out private investment. But Musk shows that that's exactly what we need.

Tesla is a success because the federal government decided to subsidize electrical vehicles. SpaceX depends on NASA contracts—much as Fairchild once did. Musk is a subsidy farmer, but that phrase does not deserve its negative connotation. The government plants subsidies precisely in the hope that entrepreneurs like Musk will harvest them, thereby aligning the pursuit of profit with the public interest. All of us enjoy the bounty.

HOW AIRBUS TOOK FLIGHT

by Gabriela Rodriguez

Ms. Rodriguez was a policy advisor at American Compass.

First published by the *American Conservative* on April 12, 2023.

One hallmark of any fundamentalism is the habit of refashioning past events into imaginary histories that validate unchallengeable truths, preserving internal coherence in a narrative that drifts ever further from reality. For the high priests of free trade, the strong track record of trade barriers and industrial policy in spurring economic development, both in America and around the world, has long been an awkward subject best unstudied. But as they lose ground in the public debate, that strategic silence is now giving way to embarrassing revisionism.

The latest absurdity comes from Adam Posen, president of the Peterson Institute for International Economics, in his *Foreign Policy* cover story on "America's Zero-Sum Economics." Rejecting a strategy of subsidizing strategic industries, Posen points to "the long-running conflict between Airbus and Boeing." In his telling, foolish government intervention in both the United States and Europe, as "these two giant economies subsidiz[ed] their respective champions," which were "deemed too strategically important to fail," has led to "limited innovation" and "substandard production" that "put both the underlying system and many of their customers at risk of devastation."

The aircraft industry's real lesson for policymakers is nearly the opposite.

After World War II, American firms dominated the aircraft manufacturing sector, propelled by industrial strength, management expertise, and a robust engineering talent pool. Europe trailed behind, with national champions specializing in shorter-range aircraft. By 1970, the U.S. aerospace industry's revenue was almost six times that of Europe. In response, European governments founded Airbus to reduce dependence on American manufacturers and develop their own industrial capacity and workforce.

From the start, Airbus was a state-backed enterprise, receiving government direction in its strategy and financial support in the form of R&D funding, infrastructure expansion, equity infusions, and loans. Total launch aid subsidies eventually exceeded $22 billion. This government assistance kept Airbus afloat until it made its first operating profit in 1990, 20 years after its launch.

As Airbus grew, shareholder-controlled Boeing failed to recognize its European competitor as a legitimate threat. Airbus's initial market-share gains came at the expense of McDonnell Douglas (MCD), which merged with Boeing in 1997. The merger boosted Boeing's global market share to 70 percent, but MCD's financialized corporate culture supplanted Boeing's long-running emphasis on engineering excellence. In his book *Boeing Versus Airbus*, journalist John Newhouse documented that several years after the merger, a longtime Boeing engineer lamented that MCD's "predatory, autocratic culture has displaced Boeing's old problem-solving culture." As a result, Boeing shifted its focus from creating new products to maximizing gains for shareholders.

In contrast, Airbus remained committed to its core purpose: bolstering the European aerospace industry. It invested heavily in aircraft innovation, pioneering composite materials and a digital fly-by-wire system that became the industry standard. Faced with high labor costs and obstacles to layoffs, Airbus adopted automated machinery more quickly and invested in worker training and development. In his book *Flying Blind*, Bloomberg journalist Peter Robison notes that a mid-1990s Boeing analysis found Airbus enjoyed a 12 percent to 15 percent advantage in production costs.

Airbus's triumph culminated in 2003 when it surpassed Boeing's market share and held the top spot for nine consecutive years.

The success of Airbus presents American policymakers with invaluable lessons for future industrial investments. First, the Airbus story demonstrates that policymakers can successfully identify critical industries primed for public investment. European politicians and bureaucrats correctly identified aerospace as a critical sector and executed a long-term strategy for building technical and commercial leadership. Second, government support can foster competitive firms. Airbus's ascent to be the global leader in sales, quality, and innovation stands as a testament to a successful government-led initiative to boost a specific sector.

Finally, the diverging paths of Airbus and Boeing reveal that shareholder primacy does not always yield the most competitive or innovative firms. Boeing, in its quest for short-term shareholder returns, reduced R&D spending and outsourced aggressively. Although this approach generated record profits, it resulted in a loss of market share to Airbus and a struggle with production and safety issues. Airbus, meanwhile, built a European supply chain, kept workers employed, and fostered an entire European aerospace industry—all while catching and passing Boeing from a standing start.

After design flaws led to the tragic crash of two 737 MAX aircraft within five months in 2018–19, Boeing was forced to ground the planes for nearly two years. Repeated quality-control with its 787 Dreamliner, meanwhile, led to multiple FAA-ordered delivery halts from 2021 to 2023. During the pandemic-disrupted years of 2020 and 2021, Airbus continued to average approximately 588 deliveries per year, while Boeing managed barely about 248. When Adam Posen laments that "supply chains in aircraft manufacturing have become highly fragile, as evident in production problems long before the COVID-19 pandemic," this is precisely half true.

In an era where shareholder value often trumps other considerations, the Airbus story serves as a potent reminder that there is more to success than simply chasing short-term profits. By strategically investing in research and development, fostering a skilled workforce, and focusing on the long term, Airbus refutes claims that state-backed enterprises cannot match the performance of private corporations. At the end of 2022, Airbus beat Boeing for the fourth year in a row.

As the United States faces mounting global competition, the need for strategic industrial investment is only growing. Policymakers must identify sectors critical to national security, economic resilience, and technological advancement, and provide targeted support to nurture innovation. This kind of public investment has the potential not only to level the playing field but to create globally competitive domestic industries, just as Airbus did for European aerospace.

REBUILDING THE SUPPLY-SIDE PLATFORM

by Chris Griswold

Mr. Griswold was the policy director at American Compass.

First published by American Compass on November 2, 2023.

Gary Cohn had, it seemed, drawn the easy assignment. In the all-hands-on-deck push for passage of the *Tax Cuts and Jobs Act* in 2017, the Director of the National Economic Council was making the pitch to the *Wall Street Journal*'s annual CEO Council meeting at the Four Seasons in Washington. "We want companies to invest back in the economy, not give money back [to shareholders], or sit on money because they don't think there's anything to do with it," he explained.

But journalist John Bussey turned to the gathered CEOs and asked, "If the tax reform bill goes through, do you plan to increase investment, your companies' investment, capital investment? Just a show of hands, if tax reform goes through, okay?" One or two raised their hands. With the same confusion that afflicts so many policymakers who insist tax cuts hold the key to generating investment and economic growth, even though they keep failing to deliver it, Cohn was left to ask: "Why aren't the other hands up?"

For more than 40 years, GOP orthodoxy has proclaimed that high marginal tax rates are a major barrier to a thriving economy, and that rate reductions are the vital response. This focus is a central feature of what became known as "supply-side economics," so named because it emphasizes the interests of producers (and their ability and willingness to increase supply) rather than stabilizing or increasing demand as the older Keynesian orthodoxy recommended.

The central supply-side insight—that producer incentives matter—is certainly correct. But the market fundamentalist misinterpretation of this truth embraced on the American right-of-center, that, to quote

Ambassador Nikki Haley, "as we are dealing with changes in our economy, tax cuts are always a good idea," does not follow. Perhaps high marginal tax rates were at one time the primary barrier to American investment, but they have not been for quite some time. Instead, tax rates and investment rates have declined together. Economic performance has consistently been as good, or better, when tax rates are higher.

The question for policymakers is why investment has weakened, and what is to be done. A supply-side economics for the 21st century would worry far less about the difference between a 39% and 37% top marginal tax rate and more about how the incentives created by forces like globalization and financialization have made investing in the American economy an unattractive use of talent and capital. If conservatives can put down their 1980s playbook long enough to look at the world around them, they will find their principles are uniquely suited to leading a new supply-side revolution that addresses the challenges of today.

SUPPLYING SOME SUPPLY-SIDE THEORY

The ideological power of supply-side economics resides in its appeal to common sense: remove the impediments to businesses investing and growing, and they will do more of it. As presented by Ronald Reagan, the Great Communicator, this line of thinking entrenched itself deeply in the American psyche and in the messages of politicians across the ideological spectrum. Its ubiquity makes it hard to recall what a significant revolution it once represented.

The insights gleaned by British economist John Maynard Keynes from the Great Depression dominated policymaking in the middle of the 20th century. Prior to the 1930s, classical economics held that economic downturns self-correct. When demand drops, production does, too, leading to declines in prices and wages. Lower costs then create an opportunity for producers to increase investment, thus stimulating renewed growth. But in the Great Depression, Keynes saw that this process had clearly broken down.

Keynes realized that an economic downturn, rather than encouraging new capital investment, can prompt low confidence. As businesses hesitate to invest in production for which they perceive no forthcoming demand, the pessimism becomes a self-fulfilling prophecy. Wages, meanwhile, are "sticky" and slow to change—in practice, workers are reluctant to accept declining wages no matter what the economy is doing, thereby short-circuiting the process by which costs should supposedly fall and investment become more attractive. What matters, in Keynesian economics, is raising aggregate demand to restore confidence and induce investment. Government spending is the way to do it.

The challenges of the 1970s fractured the prevailing Keynesian confidence. Inflation was high, but so was unemployment, in defiance of the expectation that higher prices would induce investment and employment. Neither high deficits nor low interest rates seemed to help. The combination of inflation and stagnation produced a gloomy and restless political mood; "stagflation" entered the national lexicon. The moment was ripe for a new argument.

Economists including Milton Friedman, Friedrich Hayek, and Arthur Laffer championed the idea that supply, not demand, could be the key driver of growth. Like Keynesianism, supply-side theory described a way that an economy could get stuck far below its optimal performance and proposed that policy intervention could unstick it. But instead of boosting demand to prime supply, it focused on increasing supply to employ wage earners and lower prices, and thus induce demand. Policymakers should seek to move the supply curve first, and so need to address the factors that influence decisions to invest and produce.

Reagan took this theory, combined it with Hayek and Friedman's arguments that free markets produce a spontaneous efficiency that government never can, and turned it into a political pitch: get the government out of the way and leave businesses to pursue their own interests. High marginal tax rates and heavy regulation made economic activity more costly and returns less attractive. Cut the rates and the red tape, he argued, and the economy would boom.

His message not only earned the support of the business community, but also persuaded American workers that cutting taxes on business and top earners was good for them, too. In 1980, President Reagan won 44 states. The following year, he signed the *Economic Recovery Tax Act*, which reduced the top income marginal income tax rate from 70% to 50% and the capital gains rate from 28% to 20%. His 1986 tax reform dropped the top income tax rate to 33% and the corporate rate from 46% to 34%. As described by the Reagan Foundation, "reducing tax rates restored the incentive to produce and create jobs, and getting government out of the way allowed people to be entrepreneurs. From there, the free marketplace operated as it was supposed to." This has been the heart of the Republican economic agenda ever since.

WHAT WOULD REAGAN DO?

The basic claim of supply-side theory is that policy should seek to induce greater productive investment. In Reagan's time, high marginal tax rates and sclerotic regulatory regimes were obvious culprits to target. But you only get to reduce tax rates from 70% once. Subsequent efforts at repeating the trick have brought diminishing returns and rising costs.

Unfortunately, the Republican Party confused the principle of supply-side economics for the policy tool of tax cuts, dogmatically embracing a permanent, ossified diagnosis of tax rates as the primary obstacle to investment and growth, and tax cuts as the answer. Supply-side economics does not support this in theory, and repeated rounds of tax cuts have failed in fact. Neither the Bush tax cuts of the early 2000s nor the *Tax Cuts and Jobs Act* yielded the hoped-for gains. In fact, over the past few decades, the economy's performance has been at least as strong in the periods after tax increases as in the periods after tax cuts.

An explanation of America's supply-side problems, and a supply-side policy response, must look beyond tax policy. A good place to start would be the economy's financialization and the increasing tendency of firms to maximize short-term shareholder returns and disgorge profits back to financial markets rather than pursuing investment at all. In the 1970s, publicly traded companies returned roughly 50% of their profits to shareholders each year. From 2008–17 that rate averaged 100%, and in four of those years exceeded 100%.

The Brookings Institution's William Gale and Claire Haldeman provide an illustration of how this trend stymied TCJA. The law's provision permitting U.S. corporations to repatriate profits without a U.S. tax penalty worked, insofar as annual repatriated funds increased by $470 billion in 2018 and 2019 relative to the 2010–17 average. But "rather than boosting investment or wages," the increase "generated a wave of corporate stock repurchases." And what was true of this one-time provision has been true of TCJA in general. In 2018, the S&P 500 bought back about $800 billion of its own stock. Annual stock buybacks reached $950 billion in 2021 and $1.2 trillion in 2022. A lower corporate tax rate will not generate higher investment if its result is merely higher after-tax profits to pay out. A lower cost of capital will not make much difference if firms are already ignoring their cost of capital in setting the internal hurdle rate that any new investments must clear.

Globalization has likewise altered the calculus for business investment. Beginning in the 1990s and accelerating with China's accession to the World Trade Organization in 2001, multinational corporations have shifted their investments in productive capacity outside of the United States. Even in advanced technology products, America's $24 billion trade surplus in 1999 collapsed into a $192 billion deficit by 2020. Growth in manufacturing output stalled and, since 2007, output has declined. Productivity growth turned negative: American factories required more labor in 2022 to produce the same level of output as in 2012.

The modern supply-sider should not begin with a tax cut any more than Reagan began with Wendell Wilkie's 1940 agenda. Smart supply-side policy addresses itself to the specific obstacles facing production at a given time and uses the tools appropriate to overcoming those obstacles. Reagan himself knew this to be true, even if his successors eventually forgot it.

Trade policy is an obvious example, relevant in the modern context. American automakers' struggles in the face of intense competition from Japanese imports during the 1980s could not be relieved with a tax cut. The Reagan administration solved the problem by aggressively protecting the industry from Japanese competition through direct diplomatic intervention that curtailed the level of imported vehicles. In a win-win for American workers, Detroit's Big 3 manufacturers had time to get back on their feet, while Japanese automakers relocated significant production to the U.S., prompting extensive investment and creating hundreds of thousands of jobs in the process.

Creating strong incentives to meet domestic demand with domestic rather than foreign production is quintessentially supply-side policy, and much needed today to reverse the harms wrought by globalization. Policymakers should take a page from Reagan's (other) playbook and seek to boost the relative attractiveness of domestic productive capacity. Import tariffs and local content requirements are tools better suited than tax cuts to the task. Reducing taxes on desirable activity is the right way to alter incentives in some situations, but raising taxes—a tariff is, after all, simply a tax on imports—on the undesirable alternatives can be the better approach in others. Far from a departure from supply-side principles, using tariffs to privilege domestic production over foreign imports is a direct application of those principles to the problem of globalization.

Financialization, too, must be directly confronted with policies that channel capital away from unproductive investments and make productive ones more attractive in comparison. Congress should ban stock buybacks, closing the avenue by which the U.S. corporate sector disgorges so much of its cash rather than investing it. Congress should discourage financial engineering and high-risk leveraged buyout strategies by eliminating the tax deductibility of interest. It should reduce speculation that contributes no real economic value by imposing a financial transaction tax that would disadvantage high-frequency trading and prod Wall Street back towards long-term capital investment.

Investment can also be supported with industrial policy aimed squarely at the goal. Funding for pre-competitive research partnerships can foster industry-strengthening innovation that no tax cut could. A national development bank that can provide financing and expertise to major industrial projects, and activate many times more private capital than the public capital deployed, is a much smarter way to jump-start supply-side focus on urgently needed projects that private markets currently ignore.

Smart tax incentives certainly do matter, too. The tax code should subsidize research and development and privilege long-term capital investment. But taxes are not the reason that cutting-edge semiconductor manufacturing moved abroad, or the reason half of publicly traded firms are eroding their own fixed capital faster than they invest in it.

When Congressman Kevin Brady, a chief architect of the 2017 tax cuts and the top Republican on the House Ways and Means Committee, went on Fox News in July 2022 to argue against the *Chips and Science Act*, he did so by appealing to the same prescription as always: tax incentives:

> *I think we're missing the bigger picture here...China in their "Made in China 2025" economic plan are seeking to dominate ten manufacturing and technologies in the world. It doesn't make sense to me to cede... to China nine of those industries and provide tax breaks to one. Republicans have proposed that we have tax incentives that help all of our industries compete and win against China, and that includes doubling the research and development tax credit. That means guaranteeing 100% expensing so they can write off that expensive equipment, whatever industry they're in. And then, of course, making sure R&D is fully deductible.*

The congressman's mistake was not to recommend incentives for R&D and full expensing for capital investment; those are sensible suggestions. His mistake was to consider this sufficient—as if tax rates were the main reason advanced manufacturing had fled the U.S., and finding just the right tax break would bring it back.

SUPPLY-SIDE ECONOMICS FOR THE 21ST CENTURY

An obsession with tax cuts follows naturally from market fundamentalism's insistence that all economic activity is of equal value, simply because the market places a price on it. A supply-side economics grounded in reality, however, must account for the fact that this view has served America poorly. The American public does not seem to agree that profits generated by offshoring, or the capital gains from trading a millisecond ahead of a competitor by placing a fiber optic cable a bit closer to the stock exchange, are just as valuable as those generated by building productive capacity in the United States and creating secure jobs for American workers. The policymakers who represent that public shouldn't agree either. Some forms of investment are more socially valuable than others; some pursuits of profit are more conducive to the common good and the national interest. Supply-side theory for the 21st century must reflect this judgment as it updates its toolkit.

America faces a range of serious economic challenges that have little to do with tax rates. Just as Reagan looked beyond the orthodox but ineffective policies of the 1970s when confronted with that decade's stagflation, conservative policymakers today need to look beyond the received orthodoxy of tax cuts, observe the actual circumstances in which American business operates, and write a new chapter in the American playbook that addresses the obstacles that currently constrain supply-side growth. A reality-based supply-side economics must seek to expand the set of tools available to the urgent task of expanding domestic investment and capacity, not simply reuse an old tool that has long since worn out.

PART THREE

PEOPLE

CHAPTER EIGHT

Worker Power

The American labor movement's slow descent into obsolescence has deprived American workers of a vital institution. A well-functioning system of organized labor affords solidarity, mutual aid, bargaining power, and workplace representation, all of which can benefit workers, their families and communities, and the nation—both economically and socially. Reforming and reinvigorating the laws that govern organizing and collective bargaining should be an obvious priority for conservatives, who cherish the role of mediating institutions, prefer private ordering to government dictates, and believe prosperity must be earned rather than redistributed.

This chapter begins with a statement published by American Compass on Labor Day in 2020 and signed by a wide range of notable conservatives, including then-senator Marco Rubio and then-author JD Vance. On one hand, the argument that conservatives should embrace labor was perhaps the most radical and disruptive idea that the organization has advanced. On the other hand, it is also among the most obviously correct and among the ones that has made progress most quickly—to Teamsters president Sean O'Brien speaking at the Republican National Convention and giving input on selection of the Secretary of Labor in a Republican administration four years later.

But conservative support for labor means embracing its purpose and its potential, not its present dysfunction. In his essay "Labor's Conservative

Heart," Brian Dijkema describes what that purpose and potential are, highlighting the vital role that labor has played everywhere from Catholic social teaching to bringing down the Soviet Union. In "Rebuilding Worker Power," an essay that I wrote for the Economic Innovation Group's American Worker Project, I dive into the dysfunction of labor unions as they operate today and highlight opportunities for reform.

CONSERVATIVES SHOULD ENSURE WORKERS A SEAT AT THE TABLE

First published by American Compass on September 6, 2020.

Community is the product of people working together on problems, of autonomous and collective fulfillment of internal objectives, and of the experience of living under codes of authority which have been set in large degree by the persons involved.... People do not come together in significant and lasting associations merely to be together. They come together to do something that cannot easily be done in individual isolation.
– Robert Nisbet, *The Quest for Community* (1953)

American conservatives rightly place economic freedom and limited government among our dearest values. The defense of *markets*, though, has at times made us overly solicitous of *businesses*. As we advocate for owners and managers in their pursuit of profit, and celebrate the enormous benefits their efforts can generate for us all, we must accord the same respect to the concerns of workers and ensure that they, too, have a seat at the table. In a well-functioning and competitive market, participants meet as equals able to advance their interests through mutually beneficial relationships.

Institutions of organized labor have traditionally been the mechanism by which workers take collective action and gain representation and bargaining power in the private sector. Strong worker representation can make America stronger. Unfortunately, our nation's Great Depression–era labor laws no longer provide an effective framework, many unions have become unresponsive to workers' needs and some outright corrupt, and membership has fallen to just 6 percent of the private-sector workforce. Rather than cheer the demise of a once-valuable institution, conservatives should seek reform and reinvigoration of the laws that govern organizing and collective bargaining for three reasons:

1. Economic Prosperity. We believe that workers share more fully in our nation's prosperity when they have a seat at the table. Free markets have proved their unmatched capacity to generate growth, wealth, and innovation, but they offer no guarantee that the gains will reach all participants. We pursue and celebrate tight labor markets because we know that the result is beneficial to workers and their families and communities; likewise, we should support institutions that reinforce those effects through economic agency and self-reliance, rather than retreat to dependence on redistribution.

2. Limited Government. We prefer the private ordering of bargains between workers and management to overbearing dictates from Washington. Policymakers have stepped into the void left by workers' loss of collective representation with a vast and unwieldy edifice of employment regulation. By contrast, when workers have a seat at the table, discussions occur on a level playing field and the parties can make trade-offs tailored to their circumstances and preferences, rendering much bureaucratic oversight superfluous. Layered *atop* extensive regulation, the process works poorly; as a *substitute*, it can yield fairer outcomes that better meet people's needs.

3. Strong Communities. We consider solidarity indispensable to the health of our communities and the nation. Well-functioning private-sector worker organizations are vital mediating institutions for establishing stronger bonds among workers, facilitating mutual aid, and affording meaningful participation in the public square. Giving workers a seat at the table also fosters shared understanding and mutual respect between workers and the managers, owners, and political leaders who have become socially and economically isolated from the American mainstream.

The standard partisan arguments over labor have tended to accept our nation's current legal framework as the only one, and thus to present its expansion or contraction as the only options. Entirely different arrangements deserve consideration. In parts of Europe, for instance, "right-to-work" is the norm, but so is sectoral bargaining. On one hand, labor and management in Germany often partner on "works councils," which are illegal in the United States and opposed by American labor unions. On the other hand, such "co-determination" can also extend to labor holding seats on corporate boards, which American unions support but shareholders resist. In some places, unions manage functions like unemployment insurance and job training that we take for granted as government responsibilities. In Canada, collective bargaining offers the parties autonomy to depart from government mandates in regulating their own workplaces.

Conservatives should be willing to consider all these approaches, and others besides. We endorse no specific proposal, but believe that various combinations hold the potential for substantive reform that would advance our priorities of improving the lives of workers and their families, deepening our communities, and strengthening the nation. We are eager to pursue discussions with policymakers from across the political spectrum and representatives from all facets of the economy. Here, too, workers must have a seat at the table.

Signed

JD Vance—*Visiting Fellow, American Enterprise Institute*
Jonathan Berry—*Partner, Boyden Gray & Associates; Former Acting Assistant Secretary for Policy, U.S. Department of Labor*
Oren Cass—*Executive Director, American Compass*
Kirk Doran—*Henkels Family Collegiate Chair & Assoc. Prof. of Economics, University of Notre Dame*
William J. Kilberg—*Retired Senior Partner, Gibson, Dunn & Crutcher; Former Solicitor, U.S. Department of Labor*
G. Roger King—*Senior Labor and Employment Counsel, HR Policy Association*
Eli Lehrer—*President, R Street Institute*
Marco Rubio—*U.S. Senator (R-FL)*
Yuval Levin—*Director, Social, Cultural, and Constitutional Studies, American Enterprise Institute; Editor in Chief,* National Affairs
Terry Schilling—*Executive Director, American Principles Project*
Richard Schubert—*Former Chairman, National Job Corps Association; Former Undersecretary, U.S. Department of Labor; Former President, Bethlehem Steel Corporation*
Jeff Sessions—*Former U.S. Attorney General; Former U.S. Senator (R-AL)*
Michael Toscano—*Executive Director, Institute for Family Studies*

LABOR'S CONSERVATIVE HEART

by Brian Dijkema

Mr. Dijkema was the vice president of external affairs with Cardus and an editor of Comment.

First published by American Compass on September 8, 2020.

It is no coincidence that what finally broke the Soviet Union was a Catholic trade union—a group of shipyard workers, led by an electrician and motivated by a faith that their oppressors deemed an opiate. Christianity and its sweeping social vision enlivened the workers in Gdansk and their entire nation and, a decade later, a totalitarian superpower claiming to speak on behalf of all workers around the world had vanished. The forbidden revolution of workers bound together in solidarity around a shared vision of dignity, work, and the common good did what tanks and armed divisions had failed to do. It ended communism and gained freedom for millions. When we celebrate the triumph of Solidarnosc over Stalin's heirs, we should never forget that the movement that toppled the Soviets started because a woman was unjustly fired. It was a workers' movement before it was a political movement.

The Cold War is receding into history, but conservatives rightly hold fast to its vital lessons. One of those lessons is that the conservative mind and the conservative heart should take a keen interest in a thriving labor movement. Trade unions—associations of workers who organize together for the purpose of achieving justice in the workplace—are not, and should not be considered, the exclusive domain of the political left. Rather, the principles of a vital labor movement have more in common with the principles of the healthiest tenets of conservatism today. The institutional representatives of the conservative movement ought to take organized labor seriously.

LABOR AND THE RIGHT

Enthusiasm for a strong labor movement is anything but Marxist. Labor in America—while certainly influenced by a wide range of intellectual and religious sources—has been pragmatic and should cast doubt on any narrative that places ideology at the center of its history, past or present. It was not *simply* a matter of workers looking after their stomachs—there is plenty of concern and discussion about what constitutes life, liberty, and the pursuit of happiness in American labor history. But in most cases one finds less concern with Marx and a workers' revolution than with dignified work that provided for a well-stocked family kitchen. The same is true today. Graduate students hired as union administrators in Washington might be interested in social constructs, but most moms with SEIU membership cards are more interested in a job that allows time to help with their kids' social studies.

Even on purely theoretical grounds, thriving trade unions are a failure of the Marxist program. Karl Marx saw trade unions as integral parts of a capitalist system to be "dispensed with" as soon as capitalism was overthrown. By contrast, and contrary to common conceptions, a thriving trade union movement with a sustained focus on improving the lives of working people is indicative of robust and mature democratic capitalism, not Marxism. This is why communist countries such as China and Cuba will not tolerate free trade unions, even today. The compromise, trust, integrity, and democratic character needed to make trade unions flourish are the very things that totalitarian regimes wish to suppress.

Unions are, in many ways, a quintessentially Tocquevillian association. As the libertarian philosopher Jacob Levy notes,

> *The fact that workers have so often and in so many places sought to organize, and the fact that firms have so often and in so many places resorted to illiberal restrictions on freedom of association if not outright violence to prevent them from doing so, itself looks like prima facie evidence from the world in unions' favor. Whatever one's complaints*

against the regime of employment relations created by positive legislation such as the Wagner Act, unionization comes first, before the state action and initially in spite of state action.

Conservatives, who pride themselves on their support of liberty, emergent order, and association outside of the state, should see the spontaneous ordering and pre-political nature of organized labor as something in line with, not opposed to, their principles.

Trade unions can, in turn, bolster other social institutions—most notably the family. Catholic social teaching encourages not only that decisions be made at the level where their effects will be felt most tangibly, but that social institutions play a mutually supportive role. Good education allows for good work, good work allows for good wages, good wages provide security to form a family, a stable family provides the best context in which to receive a good education, and so on. As Andrew Cherlin and others note, labor unions have played, and still might play, an important role in providing Americans with the financial and social stability to proceed along that virtuous circle.

We know, for instance, that stable income from the state can function as a stabilizer on marriages—at least for men. Why, if we care about restraining the role of the state, should we not look upstream to institutions that secure higher wages that might also help to stabilize marriages? We know that parenting with less stress leads to better outcomes for children's educational and economic prospects but is increasingly the domain of the wealthy. Why should it stay that way? Why not support institutions that give workers real input on their work schedules?

LABOR AND THE LEFT

Most conservatives today see matters quite differently. The right-of-center's conventional narrative about labor markets is one in which individuals—totally unconstrained by any other institution—form contracts with their employer in their personal interest and in response to the laws of supply and demand. If trade unions arise, it's because an employer failed in some way—either to recognize market forces or to address workers' demands—or else because unions have coerced workers into joining. In a debate about Catholic social teaching on labor, Charles Baird encapsulated this perfectly when he said: "Good jobs are union-free jobs."

This conservative hostility is perhaps grounded in politics more so than ideology. American labor unions have in practice been owned by—or, in a sense, are the owners of—the Democratic Party. In the last presidential election, America's big unions spent hundreds of millions of dollars, the majority of which went to the Left's political causes, and Hillary Clinton received over 97% of labor's spending on the presidential race. This, despite union households favoring Hillary Clinton over Donald Trump by only 8 points according to exit polls. Among national politicians, only one Republican is among the top twenty recipients of labor's contributions. The relationship goes far beyond the cash. Most of labor's activism—from its on-the-ground support of Democratic candidates to the proliferation of labor-funded community organizations—tilts left.

As a result, most people, both right and left, believe the principles of labor—its intellectual, even spiritual roots—to be fundamentally leftist. The story goes something like this: Organized labor assumes that capital, usually in the form of the business corporation, is inherently exploitative. Both assume an adversarial relationship between the worker and the employer in which collective bargaining is but a means of achieving a ceasefire that can never yield lasting peace.

This plays out not just in constant martial metaphors—"Fight for 15!", "union busting!"—but in the legal structures of labor relations. The Wagner Act, created in the middle of the Great Depression, and which forms the backbone of American labor relations law, manifests an ideological belief that workers and owners are adversaries. Other, more cooperative or communal, structures of labor relations are, in most cases, explicitly prohibited. Instead, the law requires that workers, their unions, and the companies they work with act in opposition as they organize and bargain to reach an agreement that maximizes workers' interests—even if it comes at a cost to the company or the economy; even it means that labor uses the powers of the state to achieve those interests.

It's that last item that makes many people, especially on the Right, particularly nervous. They worry that the slight whiff of Marxism wafting around some organizing campaigns will drift into rank Marxism when unions enter the political sphere. The fact that the hierarchy of big labor in the U.S. exhibits an only thinly veiled hostility to families (the union movement has fully embraced a libertarian sexual ethic in recent years), and the "widespread indifference and even hostility toward religion among progressives and Democrats in recent years," make many conservatives even more nervous.

A BETTER FUTURE FOR LABOR

So yes, the way trade unions work in America today is unquestionably a problem. They force membership—either through the law, through thuggery, or through sweetheart deals with government. One can't deny that most of this behavior is a violation of what John Paul II calls "the subjectivity of the individual." But none of this is inevitable.

The conservative tendency to reject labor outright, rather than inquire how such a vital institution might be better ordered, is neither appropriate nor conservative. The vision of labor espoused by many conservatives (and embodied in much right-to-work rhetoric and law) leaves individuals to deal directly with companies and leaves the state to adjudicate between them. The result has been an expansion of state authority into all sorts of areas—health and safety, wages, and even, in some jurisdictions, scheduling. Is this the conservative vision? This seems more like what political philosopher Jonathan Chaplin calls "an intentional strategy at work to reshape the independent associations of civil society in the uniform image of an ever-expanding set of identical individual rights, imposed with the monopoly power of public authority" than the diffused power and plural social responsibility that are the hallmarks of conservatism.

In the Christian tradition, the subjectivity of the individual is not complete unless it is expressed socially. Thus, John Paul II also spoke about the "'subjectivity' of society." By this, he did not mean to suggest that there is some "society" that exists apart from individual subjects and whose will can be divined in the halls of government. I hesitate to say it, but I think his holiness would have agreed with Thatcher's claim that "there is no such thing as society" if it was meant in that sense. What he meant, rather, was that

> *the social nature of man is not completely fulfilled in the State [nor, of course, by himself], but is realized in various intermediary groups, beginning with the family and including economic, social, political and cultural groups which stem from human nature itself and have their own autonomy, always with a view to the common good* [emphasis added].

Now put this conception of subjectivity alongside the high view of work rightly held by most conservatives, and which is expressed so well by John Paul II: "Human work has an ethical value of its own, which clearly and directly remains linked to the fact that the one who carries it out is a person, a conscious and free subject, that is to say a subject that decides about himself."

The ethical nature of work implies that the worker is able to "decide about himself" *in the workplace*. She is not simply a tool of the corporation, nor someone whose agency is subsumed by her ability to leave the workplace if she doesn't care for it. There is more to agency than the right to exit. Ethical work assumes the subjectivity of the individual, and, per above, the subjectivity of the individual "is realized in economic groups which stem from human nature itself." Trade unions, at their best, help workers exercise this agency within, alongside, and sometimes against, the business corporation.

They also serve a key social function. It's not that unions will become social clubs (having a drink at the union hall doesn't really happen these days), but they do serve as institutions that provide a community of practice, which, in our bifurcated society, can provide real meaning. Matthew Crawford notes that the judgment received from one's fellow workers—about one's work, one's character—is one of a few remaining places of objective measurement in a world where impressions and preconceived biases rule the day. Knowing that your colleagues value your work and acknowledge your excellence is a type of more immediate and valuable social judgment of which America could use more. They might not vote the same way, but a plumber from the Bronx has plenty in common with a plumber from Boise.

Such communities can be terribly closed in some ways, but they can also serve as places of real, and unexpected, human encounter. At a 2019 conference exploring means of reviving solidarity in America, I spoke with labor leader David Rolf, who noted that, for many in the civil rights era, the trade union served as one of the few places where people who were segregated referred to and treated one another as "brother and sister." Surely, Americans can use more, not less, of this today.

Pope John Paul II's caveat, "always with a view to the common good," is key, and it is also what differentiates a conservative view of labor unions from socialist ones. Properly understood, the trade union functions as a body representing workers within other bodies whose goods must also be pursued alongside the individual interests of the worker. This view recognizes that there will be regular occasions during which employers and employees are at odds, and will work, as Levy notes, "to mitigate workplace power imbalances between managers and employees." But it also recognizes that both worker and boss are members of a community that will only thrive if the greater good is kept front of mind.

Germany provides an example of that cooperative approach. As Samuel Hammond has observed, "collective bargaining was associated with wage restraint, as German trade unions agreed to push wages below marginal productivity in an effort to boost the competitiveness of their exports." This cooperation goes beyond finances. The relationship between trade unions and businesses in skills training, for instance, is another example of the benefits of cooperation in the labor market and the workplace.

To be clear, the importance of the voluntary nature of unions does not imply that the state has no role. It does. As Pope John Paul II noted, "The state has the task of determining the juridical framework within which economic affairs are to be conducted, and thus of safeguarding the prerequisites of a free economy." And among these prerequisites is an assumption of "a certain equality between the parties." The government's task is not to interfere or to absorb, but to perform its proper role as an enabler.

A renewed labor movement will have more in common with a renewed conservative movement than it does with the current left or right. But it will also seek, find, and engage with the voices within the existing labor movement that are calling for something new—identifying points of agreement and starting there.

Conservatives should actually live out the belief that the responses to a social problem are best led by voluntary organizations. They should work to form worker associations that enable individuals and families to thrive and articulate the grounds on which to approach collective bargaining as well as the view of work and business that supports it. In doing so, the conservative movement will come to better understand the existing limits of policy on organized labor in America and can begin to build support for reforms among conservative voters. This doesn't preclude current politicians from starting the renewal on their own—they should!—but structural change will be far more likely, and far more stable, if it starts from the ground up.

In all cases, the conservative movement should listen to the stories of actual workers and attempt, in classic American fashion, to meet those needs. American conservatives are proud of America's tradition of government of the people, by the people, and for the people. In the nation's labor movement, they should see an opportunity to advance it.

REBUILDING WORKER POWER
by Oren Cass

First published by the Economic Innovation Group in August 2024 as part of The American Worker Project.

Nearly every major Western intellectual tradition until the market fundamentalism of the late 20th century understood the importance of organized labor to the well-being of workers and a well-functioning market economy.

"Upon all ordinary occasions [employers] have the advantage in the dispute, and force [workmen] into a compliance with their terms," warned Adam Smith in the 18th century.

"The laborer in an isolated condition, unable to hold out even against a single employer ... will, as a rule, find his wages kept down," agreed John Stuart Mill in the 19th, questioning the "morals" of those who did not "wish that the laborers may prevail, and that the highest limit [for wages], whatever it be, may be attained."

In the 1950s, the conservative sociologist Robert Nisbet called unions "the true supports of economic freedom." In the 1980s, St. John Paul II wrote that "the experience of history teaches that organizations of this type are an indispensable element of social life, especially in modern industrialized societies."

The labor organization, by bringing workers together in solidarity and facilitating their collective action, creates power in the labor market, representation within the firm, and an institution of civil society that operates of, by, and for the common citizen. From the conservative perspective especially, all three of these functions are indispensable.

The alternative to worker power ensuring the equitable distribution of an economy's gains is not some abstract ideal of a rising tide lifting all ships, but a more intrusive program of taxation and redistribution. The alternative to workplace representation is not the benevolent dictatorship of employers doing well by doing good, but a workplace governed by bureaucrats and their regulations. The alternative to strong mediating institutions is not Ayn Rand's individualist utopia, but an ever-expanding role for the state in the lives of its citizens.

Greater power and representation for workers can also play an important macroeconomic role in patterns of investment, innovation, and growth—and thus the trajectory for growth. The market economy's secret sauce is the alignment of private and public interest whereby the pursuit of profit advances the common good as well. But notwithstanding the unfortunately magical connotations of Smith's famous "invisible hand" metaphor, such alignment is not guaranteed.

Rather, as Smith observed, it requires that the capitalist prefer "the support of domestic to that of foreign industry" and assumes he will "give revenue and employment to the greatest number of people of his own country."

If the greatest profits are to be made offshoring production, importing foreign labor, building addictive social media applications, and speculating on Wall Street, those profits might be quite high indeed—at least in the short-run—but workers, their families and communities, and the nation as a whole will suffer. Only if workers have power can they demand cognizance of their interests, alongside those of consumers and investors, in the strategies that capital pursues. Only if offering good jobs becomes the nonnegotiable starting point for attracting labor and earning profits in America will offering good jobs be something that firms have an incentive to do.

Today, that is not the case. Domestic investment and productivity growth have been in long-term decline. In the manufacturing sector, productivity has been falling for more than a decade—American factories require more labor than they once did to produce the same output. That should not be possible in a healthy capitalism, and under such conditions, it is hard to see how jobs will improve. Of course, the economy will continue to expand the quantity of employment, but the question here is quality.

According to research conducted by American Compass, only 40 percent of jobs in the American economy meet the basic threshold for a secure job that might plausibly support a family: paying at least $40,000 annually, providing health insurance and paid time off, and offering predictable earnings and a regular or controllable schedule.

A well-functioning system of organized labor has the potential to help: by ensuring that economic gains are broadly distributed, by creating incentives to invest in productive forms of growth, and by facilitating worker engagement in production processes in ways that make such growth easier to achieve.

AMERICA'S BROKEN MODEL

To say that organized labor can help is not to say, of course, that it will. American labor unions, as they operate today, do not. In the private sector, union membership has fallen to 6 percent, which is lower than its level prior to passage in 1935 of the National Labor Relations Act (NLRA).

While Americans are eager to support the concept of labor in the abstract—they are twice as likely to have favorable as to have unfavorable views of "labor unions"—the workers who would be most likely to join and benefit from a union are largely alienated from the labor movement and unenthusiastic about participating.

Only one-third of lower- and working-class Americans want to hear politicians speaking favorably about labor and only one-third of potential union members not already in a union say they would vote for one. Labor organizers point the finger at obstructionist employers and unfair labor practices, but only 2 percent of those potential union members say they are not unionized because of threats of retaliation, and only 14 percent say the main problem is employer opposition. By far the most common reasons given are "never thought about it" and "not sure."

At root, the problem is the U.S. model of enterprise-level bargaining, which nearly all Americans take for granted as synonymous with organized labor, but which in fact is an anachronistic outlier among advanced economies. The U.S. model, codified in the NLRA, makes the process of organizing workplace-by-workplace a battle—think Norma Rae standing atop her table, turning slowly and silently with her sign reading "UNION." If more than 50 percent of Norma's coworkers vote yes, they will all become union members, her factory a unionized factory. If not, they get nothing.

For workers, the model leaves them no individual agency in union membership. In theory they can quit unionized workplaces and go to non-union shops, or vice versa, if they prefer. In practice, that option may not be available. Anti-union "right to work" activists make great hay of the situation, alarmed by the prospect of a worker having to join a union as a condition of employment. But in an economy with union private-sector union density at 6 percent, the more concerning problem by an order of magnitude is likely to be that a worker who wants to be a union member cannot find a job where that option is available.

Employers, quite rationally fearing that a unionized workforce might place them at a disadvantage against non-union competitors, have every incentive to resist an organizing campaign by any means possible. Where a union does form, its organizers having promised all manner of benefits to the new members that the employer is in no position to provide, subsequent bargaining often goes poorly. Where unions do succeed in extracting concessions, the result is likely to be capital departing the very regions, industries, and facilities where footholds are gained. Thus even successful organizing plants the seed of its own demise.

Workers like none of this. Bare-knuckle organizing fights are romanticized easily enough from afar, but they tend to be extraordinarily unpleasant within the firms themselves and to undermine the quality of labor-management relations—generally the leading driver of job satisfaction. If the end result of even a successful drive is likely to be only marginal gains, ongoing adversarialism, and a weakened employer, enthusiasm is of course low.

One of the most striking findings in labor-relations research comes from Harvard professor Richard Freeman's 1994 survey of more than 2,400 nonmanagement workers, which asked them whether they would prefer representation that "management cooperated with in discussing issues, but had no power to make decisions" or representation that "had more power, but management opposed." By 63 percent to 22 percent, workers preferred cooperation without power.

Declining union membership has triggered two vicious cycles—one regulatory, one political—that have accelerated the institution's demise and make reversal implausible. The regulatory problem is that, as worker power has declined, government has stepped in with all manner of economy-wide protections. The more that regulations raise the floor under working conditions, the less a union can promise to deliver. But for a certain brand of progressive, that trade-off has always been attractive. President Franklin Roosevelt's Secretary of Labor, Francis Perkins, famously remarked, "I'd rather pass a law than organize a union."

The not-unrelated political problem is that, as labor's influence in the market has faded, it has come to act predominantly as a progressive political force. But in a vicious cycle, that political engagement alienates workers and makes organizing much harder. By three-to-one, potential union members say they would prefer a worker organization focused only on workplace issues over one that addresses national political issues as well. Among those who say they would vote against a union, union political involvement is the top reason cited.

Samuel Gompers, the great organizer of the American Federation of Labor (AFL), warned against both these vicious cycles more than a century ago. He opposed legislating basic employment protections and believed that labor organizations must remain staunchly non-partisan. That perspective of a movement builder, not the blinkered approach of modern labor leaders milking the last drops from a dying institution, is what's needed for the labor movement to thrive again in the 21st century.

PATHS TO PROGRESS

Fortunately, the American labor movement's dysfunction is not a result of some global "megatrend" or technological change. It is not a "culture problem." The failure is a direct result of bad policy. Better policy models already in effect elsewhere provide a starting point for reform.

The obstacles are political: a Democratic Party that relies upon the existing institution for political support, efficacy be damned, and a

Republican Party that has historically aligned itself with capital and seen labor's weakness as cause for celebration. In times of gridlock, this might be cause for the greatest despair of all. But labor is the quintessential issue where the ongoing realignment in American politics is creating opportunity for progress.

Working-class voters, including union members, are streaming into a Republican Party that has become skeptical of big business, concerned about the economy's failures, and excited by the prospects of worker power.

In July, Senator Josh Hawley called on Republicans to embrace "the trade unions of the working man" in keynote remarks at the National Conservatism conference in Washington. Teamsters president Sean O'Brien addressed the Republican National Convention. Vice presidential nominee JD Vance, in his own convention speech, declared: "We need a leader who's not in the pocket of big business, but answers to the working man, union and nonunion alike."

The simplest reform would unbundle the political and economic functions of unions, as former SEIU lawyer and current Harvard professor Benjamin Sachs has proposed. No reason exists that the worker organizations codified by the NLRA to bargain with employers should also be the worker organizations that fund political campaigns. Prohibiting unions from engaging in electoral politics—for instance, with restrictions similar to those imposed upon tax-exempt nonprofits—would immediately make them more attractive to workers and a cause more palatable for Republicans to join Democrats in supporting.

One politically viable path might be to pair this reform with a legislative effort to reverse Citizens United and restrict corporate political spending. Senator Hawley has already introduced legislation to do the latter. Lawrence Mishel, longtime president of the labor-aligned Economic Policy Institute, has suggested he would take that deal.

Another promising approach would seek to create new forms of less adversarial worker representation, along the lines of the collaborative works councils popular in Germany. The NLRA prohibits such efforts on the theory that employers would use them to co-opt organizing energy and short-circuit efforts at forming full-fledged unions. But in a world where so few private-sector workers are organized and most say they would actively prefer this alternative model, it should at least be offered as an option.

An innovative proposal from Senator Marco Rubio and Congressman Jim Banks would eliminate the prohibition on works councils and establish a framework for employers and workers to partner in creating them, while also mandating that an employer going this route must also allow a worker representative on the board of directors.

But the more dramatic, systemic reform that has begun to attract attention is adoption of a sectoral bargaining model. Long a subject of discussion in think tanks and policy journals, the issue broke through to the mainstream political discourse in March when *Politico* reported that Senator Vance wanted "to see the U.S. move toward the sectoral model used in Europe, where contracts are negotiated to cover entire industries."

The sectoral bargaining model stands in contrast to the company-by-company system of "enterprise bargaining" used in the U.S. and other, predominantly Anglo-American countries. In a sectoral model, a union represents workers across an industry or occupation and negotiates on their behalf with a trade association representing the relevant employers. The resulting contract governs terms and conditions of employment industry-wide.

Sectoral bargaining avoids many of the dysfunctions of enterprise bargaining described above and tends to deliver better outcomes including higher employment levels, wages, and leisure time, and lower levels of wage inequality. Because the union is an industry-wide institution outside of any given firm, all workers are free to join or not, regardless of their place of employment. Because firms within an industry know they will all be held to the same contract, none has a reason to resist the union's presence or refuse good-faith bargaining.

In the particularly successful German model, the combination of sectoral bargaining at the industry level and works councils at individual firms avoids a race-to-the-bottom on labor standards by holding everyone to the same standards—while still affording significant flexibility and rewarding innovation. And with negotiations covering broad swathes of the economy, workers as well as employers have a strong incentive to strike reasonable deals that promote long-term competitiveness. For instance, in 2022 negotiations conducted amidst soaring inflation, IG Metall, Germany's main industrial union, agreed to decreases in real wages.

When negotiations occur at the firm level, each set of workers rationally attempts to extract maximum concessions for themselves, setting off a tragedy of the commons that can leave all worse off if the result is rapidly rising prices. But when the negotiating parties know that their decisions will directly affect macroeconomic trends economy-wide, they rationally act in workers' broader and longer-term interest.

For decades, IG Metall has also sought to hold wage increases at or below the rate of productivity gains, ensuring that Germany's export-led manufacturing sector would remain globally competitive. The practice in turn created a strong, shared incentive for employers and workers to seek productivity gains. From 1998 to 2007, compensation costs for production workers in the U.S. auto manufacturing sector rose by 24 percent, to $33 per hour. In Germany, the increase in the same sector was 51 percent, to $52 per hour. The German sector was not the one facing bankruptcy at the period's end. Economy-wide, U.S. GDP per capita far exceeds levels in Europe, but that comparison is skewed badly by the strong dollar and lower hours worked in many European countries. On a "purchasing power parity" basis and measured per hour, *The Economist* noted in 2024, productivity in many European countries is higher than in the United States, and in most it has been rising faster over the past decade—including in both France and Germany, where most workers are covered by sectoral agreements.

One other important benefit of the sectoral model is that labor unions, as institutions of civil society that any worker can join rather than company-specific organizations subject to contentious certification votes, become natural sites for the delivery of valuable benefits and services. In the "Ghent System" popular across northern Europe, for instance, unions are a popular provider of unemployment insurance and other benefits that Americans would presume must come from either the government or the employer, in turn boosting union membership. Likewise, in sectoral systems, unions play a leading role in worker training and tend to deliver better outcomes as a result.

Sectoral bargaining is not something that an advanced economy could simply adopt in one fell swoop, with 5,000 pages of federal legislation. But it provides an ideal template for experimentation.

The more modest reforms described above would be important complements to such experimentation. The industry-wide unions of sectoral bargaining are quasi-public institutions that require government's support and authorization to bargain on behalf of an industry's workers, and its funding to provide benefits and services. They cannot play those roles while simultaneously behaving as partisan political actors. By more than two-to-one, Americans of every class and every political party support reforms that get unions out of politics and into training and benefits.

Likewise, an industry in which bargaining occurred at the sectoral level would ideally be one in which firms could also create works councils to provide both flexibility in adapting broad agreements to local conditions and local representation for workers addressing workplace issues. "Systems where sector-level agreements set broad framework conditions but leave detailed provisions to firm-level negotiations," according to the OECD, "tend to deliver good employment performance and higher productivity."

Innovative policymakers should look for opportunities to experiment with the model in specific jurisdictions and industries. An ideal configuration might be a conservative governor or mayor partnering with an industry lamenting "labor shortages" or a "skills gap" and a union that has never made inroads organizing there before, to establish a local labor organization and trade group authorized to negotiate terms that would be codified industry-wide. Think "Nashville hotel staff" or "Indiana truck drivers."

Many variables require specification: Who controls the organizations and how is their legitimacy validated by the workers and employers represented? What terms and conditions are subject to negotiation and what happens when agreement cannot be reached? What other activities would the labor organization be encouraged to carry out, funded by whom, and what activities would be proscribed? Some arrangements would likely collapse, but others would succeed and could be replicated: same jurisdiction with a new industry, or same industry in a new jurisdiction.

The past 40 years have been a disaster for the labor movement. Workers have paid the steepest price, but employers, too, have been harmed by having neither a viable partner for workforce development nor consistent pressure to focus on productivity gains. Few reforms promise to be as gradual and messy, but getting labor right is indispensable to making the next 40 years better than the last 40—for workers, their families, and their communities; for workplaces and the broader labor market; and for the economic trajectory of the nation.

CHAPTER NINE

Education

Public education is one of America's great achievements and has been vital to the nation's success as a democracy, its rise as the world's dominant economy, and the flourishing of its citizens. Unfortunately, policymakers have forgotten what public education is for, pursuing decades of reform that sought to increase test scores and college attendance but served mainly to strip-mine academic talent from local communities while poorly serving the vast majority of young people. Schools cannot prepare everyone for college, nor should they. But they can do what the vast majority of Americans want them to do: Help students develop the skills and values needed to build decent lives in the communities where they live. They can provide character formation, facilitate important research, instill common values, and equip students to be productive contributors to the society. If we made those our goals, we might begin to make progress.

The first essay in this chapter, "Teach for America," is my foreword to the *Failing on Purpose* collection published by American Compass in 2021, which focused on these proper purposes. Two of the other essays from that collection follow: Bruno Manno and John Sailer describe the shortcomings of the college-for-all mindset in "The School of Self-Rule"; Yuval Levin critiques our education system's malformation of the national elite in "Making Meritocrats Moral." Both propose alternative approaches more consistent with the nation's tradition, values, and needs.

TEACH FOR AMERICA

by Oren Cass

Adapted from an essay first published by American Compass on December 6, 2021.

"The reason that our eighteenth-century founders and their nineteenth-century successors believed schools were crucial to the American future," writes education scholar E. D. Hirsch, "was not only that the schools would make students technically competent. That aim was important, but their main worry was whether the Republic would survive at all." The early American republic did not make unprecedented investments in universal public education for the sake of closing an achievement gap. That system did not become the envy of the world because it produced the highest test scores. Emphasis, per Hirsch, was on "common knowledge, virtue, skill, and an allegiance to the larger community shared by all children no matter what their origin." Touring the country in 1831, Alexis de Tocqueville found that "in the United States, the education of the people powerfully contributes to the maintenance of the democratic republic."

How far we have come, in some direction. The education reformers of recent decades have obsessed over a narrow conception of academic achievement, defined roughly as high standardized test scores and college enrollment. In 2021, Michael Bloomberg announced that he would commit another $750 million to charter schools with a goal of building "a new, stronger model of public education that is based on evidence, centered on children, and built around achievement, excellence and accountability." So embedded is this mentality that other concerns fail to register with the commentariat. "Does anyone care to make a forecast about educational outcomes in states that 'ban critical race theory' versus those that don't?" the Niskanen Center's Matthew Yglesias casually mocked. "Will the kids learn more? Less? Different outcomes for different subgroups?" The formulation begs the question. What, after all, is an educational outcome?

Several ideological trends share the blame for the shift in the public understanding of public education. Conservatives tend to point the finger at radically progressive conceptions of "equity" and revisionist history curricula that transform schools from weavers to shearers of the social fabric. But conservatives have played their own role, committed to the wishful thinking that schools sufficiently focused on improving test scores might somehow remedy all of America's other inequalities, rendering moot a range of conversations they would prefer to avoid. Through it all, the neoliberal orthodoxy embraced by both left and right, blind to anything but individual preferences mediated by markets, has worked its magic. Parents and students became "customers." Ensuring quality became a matter of quantifying and then incentivizing it. The primary goals became helping people discover themselves, pursue their passions, and lead lives free of attachments or obligations.

Of course, the reformers have failed on their own terms. Test scores went nowhere—despite a doubling of per-pupil spending, performance by 17-year-olds on the National Assessment of Educational Progress is no higher than in the 1970s. College *attendance* increased, but Harvard University's David Deming has shown that the share of young people obtaining a bachelor's degree by age 25 in 2015 was barely higher than in 1975. The high-school-to-college-to-career pipeline works for only a fortunate fifth of the population: A student is roughly as likely to drop out of high school, never pursue college, drop out of college, or complete college but land in a job that requires no degree.

Mostly what education policy has achieved is to streamline a process that strip-mines talent from the nation's communities, exports it to elite enclaves that operate as part amusement park and part indoctrination camp, and then settles it in one of a few cosmopolitan cities. That this is typically the path the reformers themselves follow, and that its output looks eerily like, well, them, could always be a coincidence. But I digress.

Beneath the tactical failures is the more fundamental error of forgetting what public education is for. Succeeding at the wrong goal would not be much of a success. The proper purposes of public education are ones that emphasize the importance of family, community, and industry to the nation's liberty and prosperity. Education policy has not just ignored these purposes, but consistently pursued antithetical ones. Indeed, the leading experts able to address them tend no longer to come from the realm of education policy at all.

The first of these purposes is empowering the common citizen. Effective public education should provide all people with a foundation of knowledge, skills, and habits atop which they can build productive lives and participate fully in the economic, social, and political life of their communities. Rigorous academics is one element of such a program, but rigorous academics to the exclusion of other content, and to the exclusion of those who lack the aptitude or aspiration to achieve its demands, is counterproductive. College prep academies have their place, but converting all of public education into one abandons the majority whose needs and interests lie elsewhere.

Second is the formation of a virtuous elite. Every nation requires leaders, every leader requires education, and so it is in the public's interest to provide an education that will prepare its elite to lead well. Institutions of higher learning once did this, but they have since disavowed any such obligation and chosen an ethic of meritocratic superiority and entitlement over one of gratitude and obligation. Coursework is regarded as a means of self-fulfillment or a prerequisite to future enrichment and often takes a backseat to a full-time bacchanalia in buildings named for hedge-fund managers. "Rather than just rail against privilege," Yuval Levin writes in "Making Meritocrats Moral," universities "should teach their students how to earn and deserve it."

A third purpose is the advancement of national power. America requires a capable workforce to foster economic growth and expand the capacity of its industrial base. Public education geared toward those tasks is indispensable, but today's leaders resent the implication that resources should be allocated in such a grubby and instrumental way, rather than to the pursuit of whatever knowledge students and faculty might find most ennobling. The word "vocational" is no longer allowed; one must call it "career and technical education." Universities gladly rely upon foreign funding and personnel, even when evidence of ongoing sabotage is overwhelming. Education policy is national security policy, and we had better start acting like it.

Finally, public education must instill civic virtues and shared allegiances. This issue is the one most fiercely debated today, but those debates mostly concern the question of whether schools should adopt curriculum that denigrates the nation and pits races against one another or maintain a more careful neutrality. But neutrality is not enough. Any cohesive and sustainable polity, but especially a democracy, requires a citizenry that takes pride in a shared identity and operates from common civic and political values. Public education, per the term's plain meaning, has responsibility for inculcating those beliefs and values and preparing young people for citizenship.

Inherent to all these purposes is the idea that public education is public—that is, it is provided for by public resources on behalf of the common good. This goes most plainly for the traditional K–12 school system, but applies as well to the college-industrial complex, most of which is overtly public and the rest of which relies on public subsidy. One might make an argument from private interest for a different approach—perhaps akin to the general experience of today—on each dimension. Plenty of kids, and too many parents, probably like the idea of college as a four-year journey of self-discovery. Many professors and students would prefer a course on "Songmaking and the Idea of Lyric" to one on a more useful topic. Some people find fulfillment in white-privilege struggle sessions. To this, the reply is simple: by all means. But don't ask public policy and resources to help.

The American right-of-center's free-market fundamentalism has prevented conservatives from directing public education toward its necessary tasks. Instead, their rhetoric relies entirely on "choice" and "opportunity." Unsurprisingly, this has fared poorly against a progressive agenda determined to co-opt the institution. A nation cannot be neutral in the content or purpose of the education that it provides its children, nor can it offer the service as entertainment for the upper-middle class. Even if it were true that our country is the worst country on Earth, that our races rightly mistrust each other, and that justice demands we hand half the land to Native American tribes and rewild the other half for roaming bison, public schools would have no business delivering the message. The Department of Education is not a suicide pact.

The good news is that, unlike the college-for-all, achievement-accelerating project of self-discovery policymakers have advanced in recent decades, public education's true purposes are achievable. Schools cannot prepare everyone for college, but they can prepare everyone for life. They can provide character formation. They can facilitate important research. They can instill common values. If we made those our goals, we might begin to make progress.

THE SCHOOL OF SELF-RULE

by Bruno V. Manno and John Sailer

Mr. Manno was a senior advisor at the Walton Family Foundation. Mr. Sailer was a senior fellow at the National Association of Scholars.

First published by American Compass on December 6, 2021.

More than half a century ago, the not-yet-Thomist philosopher Alasdair MacIntyre offered a "doom-laden" depiction of modern education. Noting that our educational system reflects "the moral content of our society," MacIntyre asserted that modernity is obsessed with "getting on."

> One gets on from one stage to the next on an endless conveyor belt. One goes to a primary school in order to pass the eleven plus in order to go to a grammar school in order to go to a university in order to get a degree in order to get a job in order to rise in one's profession in order to get a pension. And those who have fallen out are not people who have found a true end; they are mostly people who have got off, or have been pushed off, the conveyor belt.

MacIntyre's words reflect a growing disillusion with modern education. Critics have long argued that our meritocracy doesn't live up to its noble aspirations. Now, the very ideal of meritocracy has come under fire. In *The Cult of Smart*, Freddie deBoer decries our self-deceiving obsession with intelligence as a stand-in for value—which is deceptive, he argues, because academic ability is unequally dispersed. Not everyone can succeed in college. Likewise, in *The Tyranny of Merit*, the political philosopher Michael Sandel describes our meritocracy as "credentialist," harmful even to those who succeed, to say nothing of those who fall off MacIntyre's proverbial conveyor belt.

These authors crystallize a widespread unease. On one hand, many people experience education as a frenzied series of benchmarks: to get good grades, to score well on tests, to finesse admissions essays, to get into top schools, to repeat the grade-test-finesse cycle for a good job or more degrees. On the other hand, the exact goal of this education is vague. The grades, test scores, the bottom rung of a career ladder—they often seem to be the point.

Our education system does, however, advance an implicit goal, one that goes hand-in-hand with the absence of a declared *telos*. That goal could be described as therapeutic—whatever affirms one's inward self-understanding. College has, after all, come to be seen as a primary means by which to "find yourself" and to advance toward any possibility, any career, whatever you've always dreamed to be. In light of this aim, we believe that public education has lost its way.

The therapeutic aim stands in contrast with the proper goal of public education, which we might call the republican aim. If we aspire to self-rule—not dependence on autocrats for political order or landed gentry for economic survival—education inevitably plays a central role in our political life. It should be a *public* education that empowers the common person in the project of self-government.

THE PROMISE AND PERIL OF PUBLIC EDUCATION

In light of its republican aim, public education ought to serve at least two functions. The first is political, a training in the liberal arts or the art of being free. Today many define freedom as merely the absence of constraints—the freedom to do what you want. An older understanding, from which the liberal arts tradition emerged, equates freedom with the capacity for responsible self-rule. Far from being the emancipation from constraints on one's desires, freedom in this older sense involves an emancipation from those desires. As such, freedom must be learned.

Herein lies the political impetus for the liberal arts. We become free through taught habits and dispositions that empower us to govern ourselves. They are inculcated through both a reverence for the past and the specific wisdom of that older tradition of liberty. Thus, the liberal arts resist the input-output model of education, schooling as a means to the next stage.

Second, public education should serve a practical function, as preparation for becoming a contributing member of one's community. To be productive, one must be proficient in certain skills. It's hard to excel at any role, at work or in the home, if you can't read or write. Most occupations require particular talents that must be learned and practiced. Such training was traditionally contrasted with the liberal arts and referred to as a "servile" education—training which is not an end in itself. It is, after all, meant to follow the input-output model.

However "servile," this education is neither inferior nor unnecessary. It complements the liberal arts, presupposing that everyone can contribute and that they should be empowered to do so. It is a part of a cohesive public education that cultivates not only able workers and parents but also self-governing citizens, capable of supporting themselves and their families.

The republican aim of public education has, however, been gradually overcome by the therapeutic. As MacIntyre explained, the moral content of our educational system reflects the moral content of society, which he describes as fundamentally utilitarian. We are incapable of agreeing on ends, so we instead appeal to placeholders such as "the greatest good" or "public welfare." Many of our most dominant moral assumptions—the background premises to which we can appeal when making public arguments—reflect this ostensibly mandatory silence on ends. And these assumptions help explain how college has become a cultural obsession.

Our public arguments frequently fall back on an appeal to expertise, effectiveness, and professional technique—what Darel E. Paul calls "managerialism." Paul writes:

> *Managerialism sees society as a collection of organizations. Those organizations are themselves made up of smaller organized groups down to the basic group units of society. Not only does each group require internal management to realize its goals; the entire society does as well. Any positive order reached spontaneously through the interactions of*

individuals and groups is either impossible or inefficient. Positive order must be intentionally produced through expert managerial technique. In fact, this is the way all organizational goods are realized.

This is no mere deference to expertise on narrow questions of scientific inquiry. Rather, managerialism entails the delegation of common responsibility to a managerial class, reducing normative judgement to an ostensibly neutral positive measurement.

Equal in its cultural sway is what Carl R. Trueman and others have called "expressive individualism." Drawing from the work of Philip Rieff, Trueman shows how our culture valorizes the individual's deeply felt sense of identity. This tendency is fundamentally therapeutic, calling for not only the acceptance but the affirmation of each person's inward sense of self. Expressive individualism makes former Supreme Court Justice Anthony Kennedy's evergreen maxim of modern freedom both plausible and compelling: "At the heart of liberty is the right to define one's own concept of existence, of meaning, of the universe, and of the mystery of human life."

Both moral paradigms share an ostensible neutrality. Managerialism falls back on expertise and science. Expressive individualism valorizes personal choice and demands that institutions remain silent on the mystery and meaning of life. They promote the ideal type of the unconstrained individual, creating policies that remove constraints. Ultimately, managerialism and expressive individualism are but two sides of the same coin. The removal of constraints warrants an expansive managerial apparatus; the apparatus enables the removal of constraints. Those who embrace most fully the values of expressive individualism are likely to be the best managers, with only loose attachments.

These complementary paradigms provide the rationale for our fixation on college. According to managerialism, the tracked life, the "conveyor belt," is a laudable goal. Higher education functions as a pipeline to the professional-managerial class, the means by which bureaucratic expertise is disseminated. Meanwhile, college is the perfect rite of passage for the expressive individual, as students are told to find themselves and go as far as their dreams will take them. A university education is buttressed by, and further disseminates, both moral assumptions. It should be no surprise that diversity, equity, and inclusion (D.E.I.) efforts—which harness a bureaucratic apparatus and emphasize individual identity—have become ubiquitous and extensive at universities across the nation.

COLLEGE FOR ALL

The essential value of a college degree remains almost unquestionable in our political culture, bolstered by years of rhetoric that portrayed the degree as a symbol of upward mobility. In a 2014 speech, then President Obama reiterated that "where you start should not determine where you end up." In the next breath, he equated this with college: "And so I'm glad that everybody wants to go to college." The previous year, at a middle school, the president echoed what Michael Sandel calls the "rhetoric of rising." He emphasized equality of opportunity, of *unlimited* possibility for those who worked hard enough: "We've got to make sure that our young people—all you guys—have every tool that you need to go as far as your talents and your dreams and your ambitions and your hard work will take you."

Later, Obama asked the audience, "How many students here expect to go to college?" To the adults, he commented, "I expect all of them to raise their hand."

For years, this fixation on college preparation has led educators to emphasize testing and narrow academic achievement. In its most extreme forms, schools resemble Frederick Winslow Taylor's early 20th-century managerialism. Taylor took on the project of "classifying, tabulating, and reducing this knowledge to rules, laws, and formulae," so as to achieve maximal efficiency. Schools often replicate this model, reducing teaching to an input-output sequence and assessing learning by a few measurable indicators.

This is precisely the approach of many "no excuses" schools, which take our college-or-bust public rhetoric to its logical extreme. If one's only shot at a good life comes through college, schools ought to do everything they can to ensure the best test scores—controlling students' every movement for the sake of efficiency, so not a minute goes to waste. A training video from the Relay Graduate School of Education, for instance, shows a teacher guiding her students from their seats to a shared table, numbering each of their movements. When she says "one," they scoot their seats back; at "two," and they stand; at "three," they step to the right. The trainer notes the teacher's hyper-efficiency with approval; this teacher broke each step down to "the smallest chunk possible."

But the narrow focus on achievement and efficiency hardly ends once students enter college. Instead, they enter a credentialing arms race that only entrenches class divides and further engenders status anxiety. Our degree-driven meritocracy, Michael Sandel argues, never displaced a system which disperses power and wealth unevenly. Instead, it merely justified unequal distribution by rewarding personal achievement, narrowly defined by academic performance. Meritocratic winners thus feel a sense of hubris, that their wealth and power have been duly earned, while the losers are further stigmatized as backward-looking, having ultimately not tried hard enough or moved to take the right opportunities.

Merit, narrowly defined, even tyrannizes those attending elite schools and employed in elite careers. As Tocqueville described, the promise of mobility encourages the anxious desire to endlessly distinguish oneself—particularly among the winners, who have achieved the most and thus have the most to prove and to lose. Sandel observes this of his own students at Harvard, who clamor for academic and extracurricular distinction. These students would likely find themselves nodding along to MacIntyre's description of the "endless conveyor belt."

As the selective promise of mobility has been realized, it has created geographic sorting based on educational attainment. As William Bishop notes, "People with college degrees were relatively evenly spread across the nation's cities in 1970. Thirty years later, college graduates had congregated in particular cities, a phenomenon that decimated the economies in some places and caused other regions to flourish." Students who are bright, good at school, and ambitious are often pushed toward elite higher education. While some might feel local attachment or pressure from family to stay nearby, these students at least face the background noise of credentialism, fortified by movies that portray the four-year degree as a ticket to success and public policy that prioritizes college. Such headwinds push these students to go to flagship state schools or even elite private colleges.

College thus serves as the pipeline into the professional-managerial class. Beyond their field of study, students are acculturated in the language and mannerisms of this class. They are carefully sorted and ranked by admissions officers and registrars as much as by corporate recruiters and HR performance evaluators. Even the college lifestyle prepares students to live as single people in tiny apartments in New York, Austin, or the Bay Area. For small-town kids, this is the pipeline into the professional-managerial class. The process amounts to what Patrick J. Deneen calls educational "strip mining"—natural resources plundered, small towns and cities deprived, resources diverted to far-off cities.

Despite its manifold failures, college has long been treated as a policy solution to the problem of poverty and inequality. Until recently, charter schools received bipartisan support as a fix to our educational woes, and many of the largest charter networks embraced a college-centered mission. The Uplift Education network, one of the largest in the nation, intends for "70% of all our graduates to earn a college degree within 6 years of high school graduation." IDEA Public Schools surpasses that goal: "From Pre-Kinder to 12th grade, IDEA Public Schools is focused on sending 100% of our kids to college."

This is ironic—if not pernicious—because instead of helping the ordinary American, it presupposes that everyone should instead scramble for the best available opportunity, "as far as your talents and your dreams and your ambitions and your hard work will take you." Rather than bolstering the common person, the college-or-bust model gives license to scorn those "left behind." Rather than providing the impetus for better working- and middle-class jobs and more power for those without a college degree, it sets up a status pyramid scheme, where those who attend the best schools gain, while the late arrivers are told to buy in at high cost, motivated by an empty promise that their degree is of comparative value.

OPPORTUNITY PLURALISM OR IMAGO D.E.I.

Of course, our modern education system has drawn its fair share of critics. Instead of the "rhetoric of rising," a growing number of education leaders on the left embrace an idiosyncratic notion of "equity," defined in contrast with equality of opportunity. Instead of a "no excuses" approach—which emphasizes high standards and strict discipline—many reformers denigrate standards as fundamentally unfair. With these critiques entering the mainstream, one might expect college itself to be the subject of similar suspicion. The veneration of college has, however, remained largely unquestioned. In the lead-up to the 2020 election, leaders on the left quibbled over the details of a "college for all" agenda. Meanwhile, activists on the right have recently rallied around the ideal of meritocracy, leaving credentialism unquestioned.

Through all of this, the republican aim—the goal of empowering common people—is simply eclipsed. Facing the onslaught of the meritocratic scramble, the liberal arts are relegated to the goals of that arms race. As a result, schools and universities treat traditional liberal arts as if they were, in some sense, servile in nature—one input in a college application, a box to check. Ironically, elevating the "servile" arts—through, for instance, offering more pathways to the trades—might aid in the revival of the liberal arts. It would at least reaffirm that some things are worth learning for their own sake. They don't exist to help you "get on."

Our public education system would benefit from pursuing what Joseph Fishkin has called "opportunity pluralism," an alternative to our narrowly conceived equality of opportunity. Instead of striving for equal access to the single pathway of college, opportunity pluralism would ensure robust opportunities along a diverse set of pathways. College would be one of many good options—not the only good option, for those who can make it. This offers a promising alternative to the chaos of our current educational system. It also fits with that republican aim of education.

It is healthy to have a plurality of types. It is good for a political community to empower its people who work in unpretentious settings, solving practical problems, even perhaps with their hands. Yet our public education system doesn't support this kind of pluralism. Rather, we push everyone to college, foisting the therapeutic aim on everyone. It's a system designed to shape people in the likeness of the unconstrained individual, the manager—*imago D.E.I.* We should hope for more.

MAKING MERITOCRATS MORAL

by Yuval Levin

Mr. Levin was the director of social, cultural, and constitutional studies at the American Enterprise Institute and the editor of National Affairs.

First published by American Compass on December 7, 2021.

America's elite universities are both a tremendous asset and a menace to our country. They can be both these things at once because we ask a lot of them. They are expected to be training grounds for future professionals, gateways to economic mobility, sanctuaries for moral and philosophical exploration, havens for basic scientific inquiry, nurseries of expertise in countless fields, foundries of an educated elite, fonts of public spiritedness and civic learning, hothouses of political engagement, and lots more. These are all legitimate aims, even if they are not all equally worthwhile, and our universities succeed or fail at them to differing degrees. So those of us inclined to agonize over what happens now on campuses need to be specific about what American higher education is failing to do well.

The formation of elites would have to be high on that list. It's an uncomfortable subject for Americans, because we think the whole idea of elites somehow violates our democratic ethos. But "elite" almost describes a tautology: Whatever a society's frameworks for ascension to influence, power, and wealth, some people will rise and some will not. Those who do rise are that society's elite, because they have risen. Every society therefore has its elites. The question is how they are chosen, formed, empowered, and constrained. Who gets what privileges of power and status, and on what grounds?

Until relatively recently, the United States had a genuine plurality of elites, which was generally good for our democracy. The people who ran major corporations were different from the people who taught in universities, who were different from those who staffed federal agencies, produced Hollywood movies, wrote for major newspapers, or led labor unions. These groups of elites were likely to have meaningfully distinct educations, religious affiliations, political tendencies, and cultural affinities.

Today, all of those elites are likely to be much more alike. They probably all think fairly similarly about religion, culture, politics, and much else. There is now a discernible American elite class with its own cultural character, and it is in charge of most major institutions—except for those to which you have to be elected, which it controls only about half the time.

How this has happened, and how it could change, are questions that run to the core of the evolution of our culture in recent decades. But any effort to restore or re-create some diversity of elites would have to start with the reality of their consolidation and work to imbue different elite-run institutions with distinct modes of integrity and legitimacy. Such work would have to begin as better formation of the elite we have, and so by recognizing that different sectors of American society no longer really have their own elites because there is just one elite, and it is increasingly becoming its own sector of our society.

The university is at the center of what defines this elite class. Its members not only all went to college but most attended one of the top 5% or so (that is, roughly the top 200) of America's universities. Whether they like it or not, these top schools—which include public and private institutions, large and small—are where our elites are formed, and so they have an obligation to think seriously about elite formation.

Of course, that's often the last thing they want to think about. The American academy has long been uneasy about its own relationship to our society's leaders. Half a century ago, in his brilliant 1971 book, *The Degradation of the Academic Dogma*, sociologist Robert Nisbet described American academics as "an aristocracy masochistically tormenting itself with the slogans of a revolutionary democracy." There is still much truth to this description, but as America's elites have consolidated, the American academy's willful dereliction of responsibility has only become more pernicious.

Its failure threatens elites themselves as much as the institutions in their charge. The growing cohesion and malformation of American elites contributes to the dysfunctions of our broader culture and has drawn a powerful populist reaction rooted in profound resentment and mistrust. Any effort to restore trust must take seriously the unspoken but necessary task of more public-spirited elite formation and so must build institutions of elite higher education more committed to it.

ARISTOCRACY BY OTHER MEANS

Our leading universities avoid thinking too hard about elite formation by pointing to the ideal of meritocracy, which implies that elites are selected, not made. This ideal was born of a noble desire for greater fairness and social mobility: It sought to admit people to institutions of higher learning not by virtue of their birth into the ranks of the WASP gentry but in accordance with some measure of aptitude that might be quantifiable through standardized testing. Able students could thus be plucked from a variety of backgrounds and given the opportunity to rise as high as their talents could take them.

The meritocracy succeeded on these terms, at least at first. Although family-legacy admissions continue and the WASP lines are still overrepresented in top schools, there is no doubt that today's American elite is far less narrowly drawn in terms of race, ethnicity, religion, and sex. This has opened opportunities for able Americans from many backgrounds, diversifying at least the demographic roots of our educated elite dramatically and for the better.

These elites of different backgrounds nonetheless do have one thing in common: They all measure up by the standards now said to represent merit. Yet those standards are not by any means self-evidently suited to supplying us with an able and legitimate leadership class. As graduates of leading universities have come to populate the leading ranks of many more sorts of institutions than the WASPs ever ran, the standards of admission to these schools are now made to bear much more weight than they can support. And, noble though the desire to democratize higher education may be, meritocratic standards cannot nullify a simple and unchangeable fact about elites: They are inherently narrow and exclusive.

In fact, our meritocracy has turned out not to be able to avoid even the tendency of elites to become outright aristocracies—that is, to transmit privilege generationally. Thanks to both assortative mating and the powerful incentives to game the tests that grant entry into top-tier colleges, children whose parents are in the upper echelons of our society have a very strong (and growing) chance of finding themselves in those upper echelons as adults. As William Deresiewicz has noted, the portion of students at selective colleges whose families are in the top quarter of income earners in America rose from roughly 45% in 1985 to more than 65% by 2015. Our meritocracy is plainly rearranging itself into a more familiar aristocratic pattern, which leaves the larger society less and less persuaded of its claim to legitimate authority.

SATS AND THE LICENSE TO RULE

What is worse, this new aristocracy is in some important respects less reticent about its own legitimacy than the old. Because each of its members must prove his or her merit in order to gain entry to the most exclusive schools, today's elite is more likely to believe it has earned its power, and possesses it by right rather than privilege. Such merit is demonstrated by test scores and a glittering resume and is then often put to use in various forms of management and administration. The sort of elite this meritocracy produces implicitly substitutes a cold and sterile notion of intellect for a warm and spirited understanding of character as its measure of worth.

Our society, including some elites themselves, cannot escape the sense that this is an unjustifiable substitution. But rather than impose tests of character on itself, our elite responds to these concerns with increasingly intense displays of its ideal of social justice. It might adopt the language of privilege in its critiques of the larger society—and sometimes also in its masochistic torment of itself. Yet it does so without offering any means of persuasively legitimating privilege beyond pushing for more inclusive criteria of admission to elite institutions.

These efforts miss a simple point. Americans have grown skeptical of our elite's claims to legitimacy not so much because it is too hard to enter the upper tier of American life (even if it is) as because those in that tier seem to be permitted to do whatever they want. Our elite is increasingly guilt-ridden, and the broader democratic public is increasingly cynical about its leaders, not so much because too few Americans attend elite colleges as because those who do too often go on to exercise power in our society without enough restraints. The problem, in other words, is not necessarily the standards for entry, but the lack of standards *upon* entry.

Precisely because our elite does not think of itself as an aristocracy, it does not believe itself to need standards or restraints. But in a free country, trust in those with power is often a function of evident restraint—of a reason to think that a person making a claim to authority is bound by standards that effectively render him an agent of the larger society. Ironically, to strengthen its case for legitimacy, our elite might have to understand itself more as an aristocracy. As Helen Andrews has argued in an essential essay on this subject, "the meritocracy is hardening into an aristocracy—so let it. Every society in history has had an elite, and what is an aristocracy but an elite that has put some care into making itself presentable?"

What would it mean, though, for our elite to make itself presentable? It would surely require some sense of what has made it unpresentable to begin with. And our meritocracy has lacked that sense. We have implicitly mistaken an idea of merit meant to broaden the entry criteria into elite institutions for an idea of merit that could justify and legitimate authority. But authority is not legitimated merely by the ways it is obtained. Often more important in the end are the ways in which it is *used*.

A NEW ETHOS FOR ELITE EDUCATION

Here there is a crucial role for the elite universities. They must see it as their task to shape leaders who grasp that their privileged position comes with obligations to the larger society, who respect and take seriously that larger society, and who are taught to understand themselves as agents of their fellow citizens hemmed in by civic and professional constraints.

To begin with, this would need to involve an explicit emphasis on character formation and the inculcation of responsibility. Elite universities should not encourage the already prodigious self-regard of their students but should rather seek to temper and direct it. They should stop viewing those students as customers and should see them instead as rising leading citizens who require formation in a sense of gratitude, commitment to the fate of the country, and restraint in the use of power. They should work with their students' healthy discomfort with privilege, but in a way that points them toward channeling their advantages into obligations rather than rendering those students into permanent hypocrites who pretend to be powerless outsider critics while running all the country's major institutions.

This was the purpose of a great deal of the culture of our top universities prior to the last half century or so. It came to be dismissed as a mark of privilege, but it was frequently a significant (if always imperfect) constraint on the abuse of privilege. In essence, the university needs a different approach to imbuing moral purpose into its graduates. When today's academy does think about how to form its students as elites, it tells them to set themselves apart from the larger society, which is corrupt and wicked and needs leaders who will transform it despite itself. A more worthy approach to elite formation would help students see themselves as part of that larger society, which is dynamic and vigorous, rooted in deep human truths, and capable of greatness given leaders who will serve as able stewards of the public good. To speak of that society in terms of "we" and not "they" would be a start.

This would also demand a different attitude from critics of the university, of course. To see higher education as a potential source of worthy leaders in various arenas of American life would require a recommitment to the promise of the university, not a rejection of its potential or an insistence on turning the academy into yet another platform for free speech. What universities offer their students is not best understood as an opportunity to be exposed to, or participate in, unrestrained expression.

It is better understood as directed formation pursued through teaching and learning.

Beyond explicit character and civic education, then, traditional liberal education also has a crucial role to play in shaping our leaders. An elite worthy of the name requires an appreciation of the strengths and virtues of its society, and also some tools for grasping its weaknesses and vices—a way to see beyond the din of popular culture in both senses. That demands some exposure to the best of our traditions through the study of history, philosophy, religion, art, and literature. Our leading universities should at least make a serious effort to expose their students to liberal learning of a sort well suited to cultivating some appreciation of these.

A TIME TO BUILD

Needless to say, the ethic that now dominates elite higher education in America could hardly be further removed from the project of such public-spirited elite cultivation. Our leading universities are nowhere near understanding their obligations this way, and we should not expect that to change any time soon. But seeing what they lack and what they are getting wrong can inform our criticism of them—which is now too often unfocused or misdirected—and can strengthen efforts to build virtuous pockets within them where there are opportunities to do so and to develop alternatives to them that might better serve to form American elites.

Despite the fact that our elite is consolidating and its power is growing more concentrated, we are probably also entering an era of innovation and competition in American higher education. The sorts of frustrations that led to new schools being launched in the late 19th century—schools like Johns Hopkins, Stanford, the University of Chicago, and more—have emerged again and with even greater force. Some alternatives are already appearing, like the recently announced University of Austin. More will surely emerge in the decades to come, both public and private.

Tomorrow's new institutions will not displace today's elite schools, but they stand a chance of both joining and changing them, as some of those new universities of the late 19th century did. It is critical that these new paths be pursued with a sense of what a great university, and a worthy elite, could achieve for America, rather than just a sense of frustration and resentment about those we have now.

Rather than retreat from responsibility, our elite universities need to show rising generations how to embrace it. Rather than just rail against privilege, they should teach their students how to earn and deserve it.

CHAPTER TEN

Family

The family is the indispensable institution, the only one capable of producing the next generation and preparing it for the burdens of productive citizenship. Its ongoing collapse poses the greatest threat to American liberty and prosperity. How conservatives respond to this challenge will determine what kind of nation we leave the next generation to defend, and whether we will have equipped them to defend it. Yet many on the right-of-center still argue that while everyone should of course have the freedom to form families if, when, and how they want, the choice is a personal one and the government should not encourage people to make some choices instead of others.

As with the last chapter, we open here with my foreword from a 2021 American Compass collection—this time, *Home Building*, which was probably the largest and most widely read of the organization's early efforts. The second essay, from Helen Andrews, asks and answers the question "Why Bother with Family?" addressing directly the position shared by libertarians and progressives that this is not a matter of public concern. Finally, in "A Plan for Supporting Working Families," Wells King and I make the comprehensive case for a particular policy approach we call the Family Income Supplemental Credit, or Fisc. Our model provides the basis for proposals put forward by Senators Mitt Romney, Richard Burr, Steve Daines, and

Josh Hawley, as well as the framework floated by Vice President JD Vance during the 2024 presidential campaign. If a broad bipartisan consensus ever develops for an ambitious family benefit, this is how it will look.

ONE GENERATION AWAY

by Oren Cass

Adapted from an essay first published by American Compass on February 10, 2021.

At the outset of his first inaugural address as governor of California, Ronald Reagan made the vital observation that "freedom is a fragile thing and it's never more than one generation away from extinction." The beliefs, values, habits, and capacities necessary to sustain a prosperous democratic republic are not some innate feature of human nature, as both the historical record and conditions in much of the modern world affirm. We can never take for granted the need for successive generations to develop those traits anew. How does this happen?

Here, Reagan was mistaken. Freedom "is not ours by way of inheritance," he continued; rather, "it must be fought for and defended constantly by each generation." Empirically, this is untrue. Notwithstanding Thomas Jefferson's infamous exhortation that "the tree of liberty must be refreshed from time to time with the blood of patriots & tyrants" and his fear that "god forbid we should ever be 20 years without such a rebellion," most American generations have indeed inherited their citizenship in a free and prosperous country. The American people do not expend their effort building from the same starting point as their predecessors; the charge is to preserve and improve upon what they have inherited.

Reagan's emphasis on continuity and tradition in one sentence sits awkwardly beside his denial of it in the next. It is emblematic of the dissonance between conservatism and libertarianism underlying the American right-of-center's thinking, coalition, and policy agenda. The libertarian conception of individuals as free agents controlling their own fates is diametrically opposed to the conservative view that sees individuals entangled in a dense web of obligations to, and relationships with, those who came before, those with whom they must coexist, and those who will follow. Reagan's insight about freedom's fragility, and the importance of ensuring its persistence into the next generation, is perhaps the strongest argument for the conservative outlook.

To complete Reagan's thought, then, the point cannot be that freedom "is not ours by way of inheritance," but rather that we cannot bequeath it like one. The traits underpinning self-government, the market economy, and the free society do not pass biologically like a genetic sequence or legally like a last will and testament. Transmitting them onward is each generation's greatest responsibility and a process that demands much fighting and defending if young people are to be raised into responsible adults and woven into the nation's social, economic, and political fabric. Only one institution is capable of the task: the family.

For this reason, the family is antecedent to both the freedom of liberal democracy and the growth of market capitalism. An emphasis merely on advancing freedom will harm its own cause if it undermines the family in the process, which is likely if only liberty and not obligation is celebrated. Likewise, an emphasis on economic growth, if it is allowed to disrupt the family, which the market tends to do unless the community imposes constraints. Conservatives are well-attuned to the ways that liberal anti-poverty efforts can deepen poverty by eroding the imperatives of responsible family formation. We should carefully examine our own projects through the same lens.

Policymakers have failed this test in recent decades. The assumption seems to have been that so long as we generate sufficient growth and fund government benefits that meet everyone's needs, the family will flourish. That has proved wrong. From 1960 to 1996, GDP more than tripled. The safety net expanded twice as fast. Yet the number of births to married couples fell by half. That generation is now coming of age in an America beset by failed political institutions, declining trust, and seemingly unbridgeable divides, slowing innovation and investment, and left-behind communities. Whether we have the capacity to fight for and defend our inheritance is, perhaps for the first time in American history, fairly in doubt.

"FAMILY POLICY" HAS an odd and cramped definition in American politics. On the right-of-center, it tends to mean altering the tax code in various ways that might privilege child-rearing and reduce so-called "marriage penalties." Miscellaneous public-relations attempts at "marriage promotion" emerge from time to time. On the left-of-center, its focus is on keeping parents in the workforce: a series of plans like "paid leave" (until you get back to work) and "free childcare" (so you can get back to work) that are most popular with people who don't actually have children and that aim to minimize the incursion of family on the real tasks of economic growth and gender parity.

If family formation and stability, child-bearing and -rearing, are foundational to the national interest, and to the outcomes our politicians promise like liberty, equality, and prosperity, then they should get the same treatment and attention that policymakers give the economy. Whether the policy in question concerns housing, infrastructure, education, immigration, trade, taxation, investment, health care, crime, poverty, or the environment, we are accustomed to asking what the effect will be on growth, income, and jobs. The government tracks and reports quarterly progress on such measures to the decimal-point. We could, and should, ask the same questions about marriage and fertility, and await each month's release of data showing our progress.

At first, the family-policy mindset will seem almost nonsensical. Which infrastructure investments boost fertility the most, which education policies boost marriage rates, what kind of questions are those, how would we answer them, and what could we possibly do with the information? Yet our confusion should be what strikes us as strange. In what sort of society would we ask those questions about economic growth and design policy accordingly, while ignoring them with respect to the family? We have been taught that economics is a "science" whose formulas and models should guide public policy, but economists invariably disagree on what effects a policy will have, and the effects of most policies are measured in fractions of a percentage point.

Surely family policy could have at least as substantial an effect. Conservatives casually dismiss the prospect of government moving the needle on family outcomes—"that's a culture problem," goes the refrain. Yet the major legislative achievement of Republicans' two years with control of the White House and Congress was to spend $1.7 trillion for an indeterminate increase in long-run gross domestic product likely to be less than 1 percent. Perhaps we should dismiss growth as "a culture problem" and try making some progress elsewhere. How much would marriage rates rise if colleges admitted men and women in equal numbers? How many more children would be born if rush-hour commutes were twenty minutes shorter?

DEVELOPING THESE MUSCLES will take time. Much research and analysis will be required on understanding problems and crafting solutions. Policymakers will have to grow accustomed to the idea that the family is more than a talking point; it is a legitimate focus of public concern on par with topics like liberty, equality, and prosperity, for which we have such extensive political vocabulary. And then they must contemplate trade-offs accordingly: a policy that increases economic growth at the expense of family stability is not necessarily a good one; a policy that invades some personal freedoms but enables child-rearing may advance the common good.

Just one-in-four Americans report that they or their families are living the American Dream. Among those still unmarried after age thirty-five, that share falls to one-in-eight; they are twice as likely to say they are struggling to get by and worried for their future. Nearly half of parenting-age Americans say they have fewer children than they would like, most often because they cannot afford to. The vast majority agree that government should do more to support families—almost always because "families are falling behind and need help" or "more assistance to families would improve the lives of children." Our response to this challenge will determine what we leave the next generation to defend, and whether we will have equipped them to defend it.

WHY BOTHER WITH FAMILY?

by Helen Andrews

Ms. Andrews was a senior editor at the American Conservative.

First published by American Compass on February 10, 2021.

Millennials are on track to be the least married generation in American history. They are running out of time to make up for their record childlessness. That's a lot of alienation and misery, some of it unnecessary. Aren't such crises what politics is for?

Many on the right say no. The state has no business judging its citizens' household arrangements, they say. We don't want politicians declaring the number of babies being born is too low or the number of single women is too high.

If there are things that are distorting people's decision-making, then maybe we can tweak those, some libertarians admit. If young people are putting off marriage because of crushing college debt, then maybe we need some form of relief. If families can't afford housing big enough for their desired number of children, then maybe we need better housing policy.

But family policy? No. As long as no one is preventing people from marrying and having kids, then government should stay out of it. Let everyone make their own choices, and things will work themselves out.

Sydney Smith was a big believer in letting things work themselves out. In an article for the *Edinburgh Review* in 1810 on women's education, the liberal clergyman mocked the idea that anyone should worry that giving ladies too much schooling might unfit them for motherhood. "Can anything," he wrote, "be more perfectly absurd than to suppose that the care and perpetual solicitude which a mother feels for her children depends upon her ignorance of Greek and mathematics, and that she would desert an infant for a quadratic equation?"

An admirable sentiment, but is it completely true? Can we just assume that the impulse to form families is so strong that society can always trust that people will find a way to satisfy it?

Nearly 25 percent of Millennial women are now projected to have zero children in their lifetimes. Less than 5 percent of women say when asked that they want no children. That leaves the other 20 percent—millions of women who will die childless, not because they wanted to, but because they couldn't put the pieces together in time.

One factor might be the very subject Smith was discussing: education. Women have outnumbered men on college campuses for decades, resulting in an imbalance between the number of college-educated single women and the number of college-educated men available to them as partners. Yet women's standards for marriageability have remained as high as they were when the imbalance was in men's favor, wanting a partner who earns more and is at least as educated. This mismatch is one reason the share of American adults who have never married has reached a record high of 35 percent, up from 21 percent twenty years ago and 9 percent in 1970.

It's not exactly "deserting an infant for a quadratic equation." But it's not something we should ignore, either. Women's preference for having a partner who has at least as much education as they do may not be rational, but it isn't going anywhere anytime soon. If constantly expanding college enrollment is cutting off large segments of the female population from a supply of marriageable men, then that is something to weigh against any attempt to boost college enrollment even further. We can't just shrug and assume that whatever people end up doing must reflect their preferences.

Our forebears didn't. After the Revolutionary War, the young republic saw what Gordon Wood has described as a "sudden flood of didactic novels and pedagogical writings warning of the dangers of seduction." Every novel on the American market, it seemed, warned of the horrible consequences of choosing the wrong marriage partner or dallying sexually without securing a marriage commitment first. Wood chalked it up to the worries of "fathers, husbands, masters, and magistrates" that "patriarchy was in disarray." That is one interpretation. It could also be that sexual mistakes were not the kind of mistake that made male authority figures most anxious but simply the kind that they figured people were most likely to make.

There's a reason so much art throughout human history has been about choosing a sexual partner. It's the topic on which young people are most in need of instruction. Left to their own devices, their decision-making in this sphere is exceptionally bad.

Young people are impulsive, romantic, and not very good at predicting what will matter to them decades down the line. That is as true today as it was in 1776. Young people still tend to prioritize the short term over the long term, whether they are teenage girls attracted to bad boys over stable providers or thirtysomething women who put off childbearing on the assumption that they will have plenty of time to figure out family stuff after they put their careers in order.

Such myopia is not just typical of reckless teenagers, nor of the less educated women whom elites might lecture about "life choices." It's often elites themselves. Nicole Shanahan, the wife of Google cofounder Sergey Brin, is a brilliant and accomplished woman. Yet Shanahan admits that her early life decisions about work and family were made in ignorance of basic facts about female fertility. She dreamed of having it all, she told the *MIT Technology Review*. "It was eye-opening to me that there are biological factors that would limit that dream."

"Like many women who are not quite ready to start a family in their early thirties, I decided . . . to take matters into my own hands and freeze embryos," Shanahan said in 2019. "However, after three failed attempts at embryo-making and three dozen visits to in vitro fertilization clinics around the Bay Area, I learned that I was not nearly as unshakable as I thought I was."

Shanahan has since donated tens of millions of dollars through her personal charity to establish a Center for Female Reproductive Longevity and Equality at the Buck Institute for Research on Aging, to research ways to help women become pregnant later in life. (Happily, she and Brin welcomed a daughter in 2018.)

If even a woman as well-educated as Shanahan didn't have an accurate sense of the facts of biological fertility, the average woman must be at least as misinformed—and according to surveys, they are. Women overestimate their chance of becoming pregnant naturally after forty, guessing a 60 percent chance in a given month when the real likelihood is 5 percent. They also consistently overestimate the odds that a round of in vitro fertilization (IVF) will successfully result in a live birth.

We could try telling them the truth, but lots of people don't want women better informed on this subject. For some, it is a matter of self-interest. Employers prefer women to focus on their careers without worrying that their window for having children is closing—so much so that firms now pay employees to put their eggs on ice. Companies that sell consumer goods to single women like it when they have plenty of disposable income to spend on themselves.

For others, it is a matter of ideology. Feminists don't like to hear anyone talk about biological clocks. In 2002, the American Society for Reproductive Medicine wanted to place ads on buses and in movie theatres informing women of various fertility-related facts, to correct precisely the sort of false assumptions that Shanahan and educated women like her often have. One ad, for example, simply stated, "Advancing Age Decreases Your Ability to Have Children." The National Organization for Women (NOW) organized a successful campaign to get the ads pulled, not because anything in them was false, but on the grounds that they "sent a negative message to women who might want to delay or skip childbearing in favor of career pursuits."

Letting people make their own informed decisions should be the default choice of any conservative political philosophy. But in the matter of family and childbearing, if we simply trust people to make their own individual choices, we may find that people don't make choices in their own long-term best interests, as they themselves would understand if they were better informed about the facts and better able to predict their own desires later in life.

The tragedy of these choices is that, by their nature, by the time someone realizes she has made the wrong decision, it's often too late.

Yet another reason not to simply assume that if fewer people today are getting married and having kids, it's because they prefer things to work out that way.

Such misguided assumptions permeate our policy debates. Like many documents that are more talked about than read, Daniel Patrick Moynihan's famous Labor Department memo, "The Negro Family: The Case for National Action," is frequently misunderstood—not just its subtleties, but its basic argument, and not just by laymen but by experts who should know better.

A book of retrospective essays published to mark the report's fortieth anniversary, *The Moynihan Report Revisited*, states in its editors' introduction: "Moynihan's core argument was really rather simple: whenever males in any population subgroup lack widespread access to reliable jobs, decent earnings, and key forms of socially rewarded status, single parenthood will increase, with negative side effects on women and children."

That was not Moynihan's argument. His point was almost the opposite. He wrote the report after seeing a graph that has come to be known as "Moynihan's scissors," which showed welfare cases going up *at the same time that black male unemployment was going down*. Previously the two lines had run in parallel. Single motherhood used to increase when economic times were bad and jobs were scarce; after 1962, it kept increasing even when economic times were good and jobs were plentiful.

People had assumed that there was nothing wrong with inner-city family formation that prosperity wouldn't fix. The editors of that essay collection apparently still think so. But something deeper was wrong. Prosperity may be necessary, but it was not sufficient. Maybe it was cultural. Maybe it was government programs and their perverse incentives. Either way, family formation had to be treated as a *target* of policy and not just a byproduct.

Alas, such an observation is inadmissible in our day. Last November, JD Vance tweeted, "As a parent of young children and a nationalist who worries about America's low fertility I can say with confidence that daylight savings time reduces fertility by at least 10 percent."

Critics pounced on him, not for making a lame dad joke, but for supposedly endorsing white nationalism. "*Hillbilly Elegy* Author Faces Backlash over Remarks Connecting Nationalism to Fertility Rate," read the headline in Salon.com. Blue checks on Twitter murmured darkly about Lothrop Stoddard and the "'great replacement' conspiracy theory."

This was, without exaggeration, insane. But it was a good indication of where the pundit class is on family policy. The very idea that a country's government might worry about declining fertility rates is dismissed as a racist dog whistle.

Conservatives should reject that blinkered view. Declines in fertility and marriage rates can be taken not just as indications that something may be wrong with the economy or housing policy or college debt, but as problems in themselves.

Not everyone wants a white picket fence, two-point-five children, a male breadwinner, and a stay-at-home mom. There's plenty of room for pluralism. But stable families are good. Marriage is good. Babies are good. Public policy should acknowledge that. If conservatives won't, who will?

A PLAN FOR SUPPORTING WORKING FAMILIES

by Oren Cass & Wells King

Mr. King was the research director at American Compass.

Adapted from a report published by American Compass on February 18, 2021, under the title, "The Family Income Supplemental Credit."

It is an unfortunate and unavoidable reality of the modern human condition that the years during which parents are most likely to be raising children are also among those when parents can least afford it. Shortly after setting out on their own, having had little time to accumulate savings, they must embark on a course that can constrain their earnings and raise their expenses all at once. The greatest income losses and cost increases come earliest, sometimes before the first child is even born. These are not the consequences of doing something wrong or making unwise decisions. To the contrary: they are the consequences precisely of doing everything right.

Most Americans could afford the cost of raising the families they want if they had a lifetime to save for the effort. But no lender will extend them hundreds of thousands of dollars in credit, unsecured by any asset, against the hope but not guarantee that they can repay in subsequent decades. None, that is, except the nation.

If ever there were a case for a program of social insurance, mobilizing the national capacity to act collectively through public policy on behalf of shared priorities and the common good, this is it. Indeed, the case is stronger than for Social Security's promise of retirement income, which working Americans at least have decades to prepare for themselves. Here, supporting families as they raise children allows them to spend now and save later, eventually repaying their "debt" through higher tax rates as they climb the economic ladder, assuming that they are blessed with economic success themselves. Parents hold up their end of the bargain by fulfilling obligations of their own, contributing productively to the society and investing in their and their children's futures.

Many efforts in recent years have focused on creating programs to address specific pressures that households might face, like expanding paid leave and subsidizing paid childcare. These initiatives are surely well-meaning, but it's important to recognize the degree to which they reflect the priorities and preferences of a narrow, well-educated segment of the population and not of those most in need of support.

In American Compass's Home Building Survey, parenting-age Americans agreed that "the federal government should provide more support to families with children" by a three-to-one margin. Large majorities were in favor, regardless of class and family status. Ask people in favor of more support what *kind* of benefit government should provide, though, and a striking divergence appears. Among women with at least a four-year college degree, the most popular choice is free or discounted childcare and second most popular is paid family leave. Among all other groups, direct cash support is most popular. This comports with the family structures and work arrangements that most Americans seem to prefer. Among married women with children, more than half say they would prefer to have one parent work full-time while the other provides childcare at home when children are young, compared to just 14% who would prefer that both parents work full-time while relying upon paid childcare. This is also what families do: among respondents with less than a four-year degree, 60% of two-parent households with a child under five had a stay-at-home parent. Only among holders of post-graduate degrees is two full-time workers the norm.

Providing support in cash most directly helps households to fill the family-created holes in their budgets and insulates their child-rearing decisions from market pressures. It should arrive not at year's end as a tax refund, but as a monthly payment, which is the preference by a five-to-one margin of parenting-age Americans who favor a cash benefit. A mother taking a short leave and returning quickly to work will have the added income to cover the former as well as help in paying for childcare to facilitate the latter. A family that might prefer to have a parent stay home with young children can more likely afford to do so. And if the result is to allow more families to have the children they want, the nation as a whole will also benefit from higher fertility rates and a generation raised in households under less financial stress.

Family benefits are a standard feature of most Western democracies, though their structures and sizes vary widely. The United States has the Child Tax Credit (CTC), which makes families eligible for up to $2,000 per child, but delivery through the tax code hinders efforts to reach the right people at the right time. Payments are available only in a lump-sum at tax-filing time, not in monthly increments throughout the year. Moreover, in its current form, the credit can only be received as a refund against taxes paid (including payroll taxes). A low-income household with little tax liability can receive little benefit.

While the CTC has worked fairly well at its current scale, its challenge for American policymakers becomes much more pronounced with efforts to expand it further. A family with two children could receive the full $2,000-per-child credit with as little as $25,000 of earned income. But what happens if the credit doubles? Canada's family benefit, for instance, starts at a value of roughly $5,000 per child. An American family with two or three children would not have sufficient tax liability to benefit fully from a credit of that size until their income reached well above $50,000. Thus, American proposals that contemplate substantially larger benefits have to reconsider the delivery mechanism as well.

Some recent proposals from Republicans envision per-child benefits on the order of $4,000. While they vary in their specifics, all abandon the idea that the benefit is a refund of taxes owed, shifting instead to a universal model in which all families with children can receive the full benefit (at least until they reach very high levels of income). This goes too far. Working families with low incomes should be able to enjoy the benefit's full value, and reforms to advance that objective are needed. But while allowing the pendulum to swing all the way to a universal benefit may appeal in its simplicity, severing all connection to productive economic contribution violates the basic principle of reciprocity at the heart of a durable social compact. Even Social Security, after all, goes only to those who have paid in.

Whether cash payments to non-working households are a feature or bug of universal proposals depends upon the purpose ascribed to the family benefit. Payments to non-working households are incompatible with the vision for a new social compact described above, which states its purpose as supporting families already striving to support themselves but under pressure from the demands of child-rearing. To be clear, the non-working poor require support as well, and the safety net should be further strengthened to assist them. But these are different tasks, and we should not presume the same policy approach is best suited to both.

THE FAMILY INCOME SUPPLEMENTAL CREDIT

We propose a family benefit that we believe has the potential to advance conservative priorities, garner wide bipartisan support, and significantly improve the lives of American families. We eschew the term "child allowance," which smacks of condescension and conjures the image of a benevolent government-as-father-figure deigning to sponsor its troublesome dependents. The proper subject is the family, not the child, and the benefit is expressly an addition to income earned. Thus, we refer to the program as the Family Income Supplemental Credit, or Fisc, and to the payments as supplements.

Starting from our general framework, we propose a monthly payment made to the parent or guardian of a child under the age of 18. The payment amount would be $800 per month for pregnant women beginning in the fifth month of pregnancy, $400 per month from birth until the child's 6th birthday, and then $250 per month until the child's 18th birthday. A family would receive these payments per child, regardless of how many children the family has.

Many variations on these payment levels have been proposed and are worthy of consideration—indeed, the question of how to set a level is itself an important one. We worked from two useful reference points in particular: The Earned Income Tax Credit (whose maximum benefit with two children is $5,980 in 2021) provides a lower bound for the scale of support that we would aim to deliver to middle-income households. The $13,200 in "missing earnings" for middle-income households, as compared to a world where the middle quintile's share of national income had remained constant in recent decades, provides a scale for the shortfall that public policy might look to address. Under our proposal, a family with three children, two of whom are under the age of 6, would receive $12,600 over the course of a year.

The Fisc contains a work requirement in the form of a cap on how much a family can receive, relative to how much income of their own they have earned. Specifically, the Fisc's payments to a household are capped each year at the level of total income reported by the household in the prior year. Put another way, total monthly payments to a household cannot exceed one-twelfth of the prior year's earnings.

The requirement ensures that families are connected to the workforce and requires essentially that, consistent with the program's operation as social insurance, a household pay into the society before the society returns a benefit. It differs from the more complex work requirements traditionally used in safety-net programs, which are intended to connect people to work and therefore focus on the work-related activities that the recipient is engaged in at any moment in time, impose time limits on periods of non-work, and so on. Working families will meet the requirement even at very low income levels and in precarious conditions—a single earner working less than 30 hours per week at minimum wage would retain full eligibility for two children.

This approach has several important benefits. First, it retains a clear distinction between a supplement for working families and the safety net for those who cannot contribute to their own support. Opponents of work requirements will note, rightly, that this framework excludes many of the neediest households. That is entirely true and follows directly from its purpose. Likewise, opponents will surely identify various edge cases in which someone in need would find himself poorly served. Again, it is not a program designed to catch anyone who might fall through the cracks. America already operates an enormous safety net designed for such circumstances, and we are eager for discussion about how to improve its operation. But we believe that discussion is best had apart from one about support for working families, and that it should not include programs of cash payment.

Second, it strikes a balance between simplicity and integrity. While the imposition of conditions necessarily interferes with the elegance of universality, policymakers must not let an appealing form override the need for effective function. Programs should be "understandable" in the sense that the public can make sense of their details. They should also be understandable in the sense that they comport with and reinforce cultural norms and expectations to which the nation is committed. The Fisc's design is as complicated as it needs to be—participation should be connected to work—and then implements its framework as simply as possible.

Third, it offers a valuable income-smoothing function. Programs designed to incentivize work directly, for instance the Earned Income Tax Credit or a direct wage subsidy, phase in and out with each dollar earned. Someone losing a job would see that loss compounded by a reduced benefit. The Fisc is intentionally different, changing only once per year and in a foreseeable way. Someone who loses a job mid-year retains the full supplement for the year's remainder and, if enough earnings were already booked in the year, may retain it for the following year as well. Exiting the workforce in the months leading up to or after birth of a child does not affect eligibility. Only after at least a full year of no work for anyone in the household would the supplement end entirely.

Fourth, it creates an implicit marriage bonus. A worker's earnings contribute toward qualifying for the Fisc only if that worker is part of the same tax unit as the parent or guardian receiving payment. Where parents are married and filing jointly, then, the earnings of both can provide the supplement's basis. Where parents are unmarried, this is not possible. For instance, a single mother with no earnings is ineligible for the Fisc and will instead receive support via traditional safety-net programs, even if the child's father had $10,000 in earnings the prior year. If the parents are married, the household can receive a supplement of up to $10,000.

We also propose an explicit marriage bonus, raising the Fisc's payments by 20% for married parents. And we propose strengthening the safety net for expecting mothers who are ineligible for the supplement. The stage in pregnancy at which women might first become eligible offers an ideal point of contact for the safety net to engage with those disconnected from work. We recommend expanding funding for Medicaid enrollment, standard inclusion of home visits in TANF, and creation of a "baby box" program.

Finally, we believe that decisions about program administration will be vital to its success and support. The Fisc is a spending program, not a tax credit. It should be operated by the Social Security Administration (SSA), not the Internal Revenue Service. As one of us has argued previously, conservatives must abandon their unhealthy tendency to frame all legislation as tax policy and then shoehorn it into the tax code. The SSA already addresses most of the administrative challenges that the Fisc would raise, including an expansive measurement of earnings (for purposes of Social Security eligibility), calculation of benefits on the basis of prior earnings and with respect to relationships among spouses and dependents, and processing of monthly payments, including situations where dependents are reassigned mid-year.

One effect of the work requirement and this administrative model is that recipients will need to have SSNs and be legally authorized to work in the United States. Another effect is the more timely and accurate gathering of nationwide data on family structure. We recommend the creation of a Bureau of Family Statistics that would support the SSA in gathering these data, using it in program administration, and combining it with other data sources to report regularly on the state of the American family.

Programs that disburse large benefits raise reasonable concerns about improper payments and fraud. The SSA's infrastructure has proven remarkably robust for tracking earnings and disbursing payments larger than the Fisc's across longer periods of time using more complex formulas, beginning even before computerized recordkeeping. We are confident it can succeed here. We would, however, favor a robust audit mechanism and disqualification from future payments as penalty for intentional fraud.

ADDRESSING CONSERVATIVE CONCERNS

The Fisc offers a useful litmus test for how right-of-center policymakers define conservatism. Those interested primarily in cutting taxes, raising efficiency, and drowning government in a bathtub will find little to like. But for those eager to apply conservative principles to contemporary problems, an expanded social compact supported by a pillar like the Fisc deserves careful consideration. Indeed, Canada's program—perhaps the world's most generous—began as an initiative of Prime Minister Stephen Harper's conservative government, seeking to support families in a way that respected their own preferences rather than pushing all toward paid childcare.

As compared to expansive childcare and paid-leave programs that presume everyone will soon return to work, cash-based support allows parents to choose whether they would rather pay to outsource care of their children or forego some market wages but provide that care themselves. As compared to the safety net of in-kind benefits that come attached to requirements and decline quickly for working households, a broad and simple program meets immediate needs and goes nowhere when earnings rise. If fertility has fallen below replacement level, easing the path to child-rearing is perhaps the nation's most vital task.

Analysts have raised a number of objections to other, typically universal "child allowance" proposals, and here we conclude by showing why we believe the Fisc addresses each one.

1. Discouraging Work and Encouraging Dependence. A core concern animating opposition to many family-benefit proposals is the potential for cash payments to non-working families to undermine work incentives and cultural norms. One worry is that households finding themselves with more money would then choose to work less, in some cases preventing prospective workers from taking initial steps onto or up the economic ladder. Another worry is that people will become dependent on the payments and see the state as having the responsibility to provide for their families, devaluing the breadwinner's role in supporting the household and crowding out other sources of support like the extended family, the neighborhood, and the church.

The Fisc's work requirement addresses these concerns directly, drawing a clear distinction between working and non-working families and using the existing safety net to address the needs of the latter. The proposed structure does have the potential to reduce work effort for families that might choose to spend *fewer* hours in the labor force—whether the middle-income household that decides it can now make do without a second earner, or the single mother who finds it possible to go part-time and spend more afternoons with her kids. We see this as a benefit—the importance of work is in the role it assigns people as productive contributors, the habits and social interaction it promotes, and the opportunity for upward mobility it provides. This does not mean that more work is always better or that the two full-time earners or the single mother working double shifts are the desirable outcomes for public policy to promote.

2. Undermining Effective Anti-Poverty Programs. The American safety net is not just a provider of last resort. It also operates programs to address root causes of dysfunction like addiction, develop real-world employment and parenting skills, and provide wraparound support to people trying to get back on their feet. These are not things people can easily buy with cash, and in many cases the conditioning of support on participation is a vital tool to move people away from dependence.

The Fisc does not reduce or eliminate existing anti-poverty programs; to the contrary, by creating an important contact point midway through pregnancy it provides a new opportunity for engagement. Further, by increasing the rewards to workforce participation—get and keep any job and become eligible for a large supplement—it reinforces the efforts of anti-poverty programs to move people toward self-sufficiency.

3. Commodifying Family. People rightly worry that society may come to see a family benefit as a "parenting wage," which some indeed argue it should be, converting family relationships of obligation into economically tinged transactions under public oversight.

Whether a family benefit will be understood as a "parenting wage" is a matter of perception as well as design and implementation. Insisting upon work as a prerequisite for receipt makes clear that the work of being a parent is *not* what entitles one to the benefit. Framing the program as a social compact and emphasizing its role as a supplement to family income rather than a "child allowance" can help as well.

4. Federalizing Policy. Policymakers often default to federal solutions, which in many cases are the wrong ones. Varied local conditions, the importance of robust sub-federal institutions, and principles of federalism and subsidiarity all argue for deferring to state and local governments where feasible.

The safety net is a quintessential area for local policy, and we would support reforms that further localize its operation. By contrast, the federal government's unique fiscal capacity and the conceptual benefits of defining the social compact broadly (particularly given people's mobility within the country) argue for defining the Fisc as a national program. This is yet another reason for keeping separate the safety net and family benefit.

5. Slowing Growth. According to supply-side economics, the deficit-spending or tax increases required to fund an expensive new program may slow economic growth, depriving families of income rather than boosting it and ultimately leaving everyone worse off.

The Fisc's design does not differ from other family benefit proposals with respect to cost, and its social compact recommends raising top marginal tax rates. Still, the generic complaint that any new program will slow growth is overbroad and fits poorly in this context. Whether government spending will have that effect depends on how revenue is raised and what the program does. Here, transferring spending power from older, higher-income households to younger, kid-filled ones is hardly a recipe for stagnation even in the short run—the Canadian experience, for instance, suggests that the effect was highly stimulative. Further, few things would be better for long-run growth and dynamism than families having more children. "Growth" as a goal also requires modification—growth in recent decades has not been broadly shared by American families, which helps explain the need for the Fisc to begin with. A policy that leads to lower aggregate growth, at least in the short run, will still benefit the nation if it better positions working families to raise children.

6. Expanding Government. Beyond all these practical worries, and sometimes motivating them, is the principled concern that government has no business favoring some life choices—say, having children—over others, and that redistributing money in this fashion is beyond its proper purview.

The Fisc expansion of the social compact does broaden government's role and asserts a very clear, substantive preference for families and child-rearing. Libertarians uncomfortable with such things may not be persuadable on the point. It is worth noting, however, that insofar as the government already commits enormous resources across countless programs to these same ends, providing a straightforward cash benefit that empowers families to make their own choices might be the best that Milton Friedman could hope for.

Conservatives, meanwhile, face a very real test: Will we support a major government program if it is pro-marriage, pro-family, pro-life, pro-work, reinforces solidarity and a sense of mutual obligation within the nation, and meets head-on what the American people identify as one of their most pressing needs? Our hope is that the answer is yes.

CHAPTER ELEVEN

The Public Purse

Perhaps it seems odd to conclude the "People" section, and indeed the entire volume, with a discussion of taxes and spending. But in budgetary terms the federal government is primarily an insurance company providing pension (Social Security) and health care (Medicare and Medicaid) benefits to a large share of the population at any moment and nearly all Americans at some point in their lives. In the twenty-first century, the Republican Party has placed enormous emphasis on curtailing those programs to pay for large tax cuts, an agenda that is neither popular nor responsive to the nation's challenges and priorities. Failing to "reform entitlements," the so-called "fiscal conservatives" have plowed ahead with tax cuts anyway, contributing to annual budget deficits that now approach $2 trillion and a national debt so large that interest payments have begun to exceed defense spending.

Fortunately, conservatives are now rejecting entitlement cuts as a desirable pathway to "limited government." As Michael Lind explains in "The Government Should Keep Its Hands Off Your Medicare," social insurance programs like Social Security and Medicare are rightly valued by Americans across the political spectrum and a desirable element of any coherent conception of the state's role in a free society. But, I argue in "The Return of the Fiscal Conservatives," fiscal discipline remains a vital conservative principle, and a vital national imperative, as well. Something has to give, and that thing is the tax-cutting zealotry that infected conservatism in the 1990s and is only now beginning to subside.

THE GOVERNMENT SHOULD KEEP ITS HANDS OFF YOUR MEDICARE

by Michael Lind

Mr. Lind was a fellow at New America.

First published by American Compass on October 15, 2021.

There are two kinds of people: those who want politicians to "keep your government hands off my Medicare," and those who think that's the dumbest thing they've ever heard. When an angry constituent made the declaration at a town hall meeting convened by Rep. Bob Inglis during the 2009 health care debate, pundits across the political spectrum seized on it to symbolize the lamentable ignorance of ordinary people in general and populist conservatives in particular. On the right, George Mason economist Tyler Cowen called the remark, "The funniest sentence I read today." On the left, *Slate*'s Timothy Noah announced his initiative "to combat the pernicious and big-babyish meme that Medicare lies beyond government control and must remain so."

With its supercilious mockery, the overclass intelligentsia revealed an inability to distinguish between *social assistance* and *social insurance*, which both market fundamentalists on the right and socialists on the left regard as interchangeable for ideological reasons. The market fundamentalist evaluates public programs on the starkly utilitarian basis of how much monetary value flows to whom, without regard to moral justification. The socialist obsesses over moral justification but embraces a framework in which all are equally deserving of public support. To both groups, then, money is money, whatever its source. People pay the taxes they can afford and receive the benefits they need.

Most Americans disagree. Along with citizens of other modern democracies, they see a profound moral and political difference between non-contributory social assistance paid out of general tax revenues ("welfare") and contributory social insurance funded by payroll taxes or premiums ("earned benefits"), even if both kinds of programs involve government spending. Medicare may be *administered* by the government, but it is a program of, by, and for the working people who pay for and receive it.

Underlying this disconnect in thinking about the welfare state is a debate between two moral systems, which might be called the work ethic and the consumption ethic. The work ethic views membership in a community as entailing a reciprocal obligation to contribute through personal effort—whether paid or unpaid—to the community's flourishing, rather than exploiting others by free-riding on their efforts. The consumption ethic in contrast views work as merely a means to the end of personal consumption, with no intrinsic value to distinguish it from other sources of income that allow for enjoyment of the same consumer goods—private charity, government welfare, or capital gains derived from the passive ownership of assets that generate profits, rents, or interest.

From each perspective, the policy prescriptions of the other can seem outlandish. And with most Americans in the work ethic camp, and many who aspire to govern them in the consumption ethic camp, the miscommunication easily gives rise to frustration and hostility. Many of the nation's sharpest policy debates—over entitlements, health care, childcare, child allowances, and welfare—are surrogates for this clash of ethical systems. Consumption ethic economists have reams of evidence that handing out money to the poor "works," by which they mean tautologically that it hands people money. Anyone who disagrees, they conclude, must be foolish, selfish, or perhaps racist.

This does not persuade anyone, nor should it. The predominance of the work ethic is a fact of American culture and a constraint within which policymakers must operate. Programs that flout a culture's core values rarely endure or succeed. Nor should policymakers want those values to change. The attachment of pride and status to individual effort promotes worthwhile social goals, including widely shared economic growth.

The path to a more secure and generous American welfare state lies not in rejecting the work ethic and the distinction it makes between contributory social insurance and non-contributory social assistance, but rather in embracing it. An agenda that spends more of the money of the rich on the poor is understandably of little interest to the vast American middle. The goal should be to help all adults who can work to earn enough not only to support themselves and their families without means-tested social assistance but also to contribute to the funding of programs of mutual support that provide financial and social security.

THE WORK AND CONSUMPTION ETHICS

The work ethic is ancient and continues to dominate the thinking of most citizens in modern democracies about government aid to individuals. The term "Protestant work ethic," popularized by Max Weber, is misleading, insofar as it implies that most Catholics, Jews, Muslims, Hindus, and Confucians have been indolent by comparison. In fact, only a tiny minority of aristocrats and rentiers have ever been able to live without laboring to meet their material needs, along with those of their community, whether an egalitarian village or a hierarchical despotism. Once-fashionable claims that Stone Age hunter-gatherers worked only a few hours per day and led lives of leisure compared to people in agrarian and industrial societies have been criticized by recent scholarship. Among ordinary people worldwide, the work ethic is a universal tradition.

Long before widespread social insurance emerged as a phenomenon of modern industrial economies with wage-earning majorities, the work ethic shaped the rudimentary social assistance that premodern communities provided to people in need. This assistance drew clear lines between the "deserving poor"—those who cannot contribute to their own subsistence—and the "undeserving poor"—those who are idle and dissolute but capable of working. The Elizabethan Poor Law, for instance, distinguished between the deserving poor who should be taken care of by the community, whether by public provision or private charity, and "sturdy beggars" who should be compelled by economic privation or government compulsion to work toward supporting themselves and their families. The American colonies inherited this approach from Britain.

Beginning in the eighteenth century, however, humanitarian reformers, classical liberals, and some socialists rejected the work ethic for a version of utilitarianism that erases the distinction between the deserving and undeserving poor. Starting from varied philosophical premises, these groups all reached the conclusion that whether money is earned by personal effort is irrelevant. The important thing is to guarantee everyone a minimal income to be able to enjoy a minimal standard of living, defined as a certain level of consumption. This version of the consumption ethic fits nicely with the view of classical and neoclassical economics that work has no value in itself; it is merely a means to the end of personal consumption, and indeed belongs on the cost side of the ledger. Thus, no stigma should accompany unearned income, whether it takes the form of government handouts to the idle poor or passive rents to landlords, money-lenders, and capitalist investors—all groups viewed with suspicion by adherents of the work ethic like nineteenth-century American Populists, who warned of the growth of "the two great classes—tramps and millionaires" in the 1892 platform of the People's Party.

With the industrial revolution came a new category of public support: social insurance. In premodern agrarian societies, the recipients of social assistance tended to be a small number of destitute, landless laborers and their families, to whom local elites provided necessities or jobs. As a result of industrialization and urbanization, however, most people became wage earners or their dependents. These households had to pay cash for rent, food, clothing, and medical care, and could no longer rely on subsistence agriculture or domestic crafts if the breadwinner was unemployed.

For the typical worker, wages have always been too low to permit for saving in advance for all possible emergencies. Instead, the sensible and highly valued option for wage earners is to acquire insurance against unlikely and unaffordable costs like a health crisis on one hand and the prospect of income loss from unemployment or disability on the other. In some instances, these insurance products are available and indeed are purchased on the private market. But in many others, failures of insurance markets make provision implausible or prohibitively expensive.

One response in the early industrial era was the development by workers themselves of "friendly societies" or nonprofit mutual aid societies. These membership organizations, often with colorful names like the Ancient Order of Foresters or the Odd Fellows or the Shriners (Freemasons), combined the functions of modern insurance for sickness, burial costs, old-age assistance, and other expenses with the social activities of modern guilds, like regular feasting and parades. But many workers could not afford to pay dues, and nonprofit mutual aid societies often excluded people in poor health or poor financial condition to avoid adverse selection, just as commercial insurers did.

Social insurance works well only if participation is universal or near-universal, which in many cases necessitates state-compelled membership in contributory systems. If not paying premiums is an option, then the exit of the affluent and young can create a death spiral into insolvency for social insurance, just as for commercial insurance, where a dwindling number of sick and elderly people can face ever-higher premiums. For this reason, most industrial nations with wage-earning majorities adopted systems of social insurance administered by the state (although relics of mutual aid societies survive in the German sickness funds and the Ghent system of union-administered benefits in Sweden and Czechoslovakia).

But the divide between the work and consumption ethics has yielded competing visions for social insurance: the Bismarckian and the Beveridgean. The Bismarckian model, named after the chancellor of Imperial Germany who pioneered the modern welfare state to weaken the appeal of socialism to the working class, is modeled on private insurance. Bismarckian social insurance is based on contributory taxes, usually payroll taxes, and workers who contribute more receive higher benefits.

The rival model of social insurance is named after the British liberal economist William Beveridge, whose November 1942 report set forth the "Beveridge Plan" for the post-war British welfare state, a vision never completely realized in the United Kingdom or elsewhere. In the Beveridge model, public payments for health care, public pensions, unemployment insurance, and the like come out of general taxes, similar to spending on defense or infrastructure or public education. The payments to citizens should be flat and identical for all, regardless of income, or else based solely on need.

The American social insurance and assistance programs established by the New Deal in the 1930s—Social Security, unemployment insurance, disability insurance, and Aid to Dependent Children (ADC)—for the most part embodied the work ethic by creating earned benefits with eligibility based on a history of work and payroll tax contributions. ADC was designed explicitly as a program for the deserving poor on the work ethic model of social assistance, targeting widows with children in an era that took the assumption of a male breadwinner for granted.

The "War on Poverty" of the 1960s took a very different approach. ADC became AFDC ("Aid to Families with Dependent Children") and changes in both social context and policy design shifted the program's clientele to never-married single mothers who were widely seen as capable of working to support themselves. The program's social assistance was no longer consistent with the work ethic and became deeply unpopular. Public outrage at federal funding of single parents with children who did not work or have a working spouse led to the abolition of AFDC and its replacement by Temporary Assistance to Needy Families (TANF). The very features that made consumption ethic intellectuals denounce TANF as inhumane—time limits on welfare use and a requirement on adult welfare recipients to seek a job—reflected the work ethic values of the American majority, as well as their insistence on distinguishing between a stay-at-home parent supported by a spouse and one supported by the taxes of unrelated fellow citizens.

Conversely, the New Deal's contributory social insurance programs remain popular and consumption ethic complaints have generally fallen on deaf ears. Criticism of Social Security from the market fundamentalist right and the socialist left mirror perfectly their respective blind spots when it comes to the merits of its model.

Market fundamentalists fail to appreciate the advantages that government can offer over the market when it comes to a task like long-term saving and are forever proposing to replace modern systems of social insurance with tax-favored savings accounts. But the idea that Social Security's dependence on future politics is a weakness, while tax-favored IRAs and 401(k)s have the advantage of being "your money," is doubly confused. First, "your money" remains subject to future politics, too. A federal government in financial straits is more likely to tax IRAs and 401(k) accounts, which chiefly benefit the affluent, than to cut benefits to Social Security, a popular program on which most citizens rely. Second, both anticipated Social Security benefits and 401(k) accounts represent claims by retirees on the economic activity of workers. In both cases, it is the surplus produced by today's workers that lands in the pockets of retired former workers. If the economy collapses, both Social Security and mutual funds will be in dire condition. The difference is that a sovereign territorial state that can extract taxes from a diverse economy or borrow from lenders around the world is more likely to meet the expectations of retirees in a crisis than is some pile of corporate equities.

Meanwhile, socialists failing to appreciate the contributory premise of Social Security see its funding structure as "regressive." In 2021, wage earners pay payroll taxes only on the first $142,800 of labor income, and they pay no Social Security taxes at all on non-labor income like that from capital gains. Someone earning $500,000 pays only three times the taxes of someone earning $50,000, despite having ten times the income. And at the margin, the higher earner pays nothing on the next dollar earned above the limit while the lower earner still owes the full rate on additional work income.

The regressive nature of the payroll tax cap is a "feature" of Social Security, not a "bug," to use the lingo of the tech sector. Like other Bismarckian social insurance programs, the American Social Security system mimics voluntary systems of mutual aid set up by working-class citizens. Although it has redistributive elements, it is not supposed to be a social assistance program based on redistribution from the rich to the poor. In its ideal form, contributory social insurance funded on a pay-go basis is a system of horizontal transfers from today's workers to those of their own class who cannot work because they are old, sick, disabled, or temporarily unemployed. Anyone rich or poor may participate, but they do so on the same terms, making the same payments in to get the same benefits out. Conversely, the rich are under no special obligation to fund the system and hold no leverage in a threat to opt out.

Franklin Roosevelt explained his preference for a contributory social insurance system to Luther Gulick, an economist who advised the federal government, in the summer of 1941. When Gulick, like many economists then and now, complained that the payroll tax was a regressive tax on workers, FDR replied:

> *I guess you're right on the economics. They are politics all the way through. We put those pay roll contributions there so as to give the contributors a legal, moral, and political right to collect their pensions and their unemployment benefits. With those taxes in there, no damn politician can ever scrap my social security program. Those taxes aren't a matter of economics, they're straight politics.*

Far from mocking the individual who said, "Keep your government hands off my Medicare," FDR would have been delighted. Like Social Security, Medicare was designed by FDR's protégé and successor Lyndon B. Johnson to be an earned benefit based on years of work effort via payroll tax contributions.

THE CONTRIBUTORY WELFARE STATE

On a range of issues, market fundamentalists and socialists have tended to reject Bismarckian social insurance coupled with workfare in favor of Beveridgean universal income schemes, which erase distinctions that are important to the work ethic—distinctions between social insurance and social assistance, between contributory taxes and general taxes, between the deserving and undeserving poor, between individuals supported by other family members and individuals supported by the taxpayers at large. Libertarians like Milton Friedman and Charles Murray, along with many on the left, have favored replacing both social insurance and social assistance with a universal basic income in the form of direct cash handouts—in Friedman's case, in the form of a "negative income tax."

But despite having a work requirement, President Nixon's proposal in 1969 for a negative income tax as part of his Family Assistance Plan never passed the Senate. Democratic presidential candidate George McGovern's proposal in 1972 for a "demogrant" of $1,000 for every American (more than $6,000 in today's dollars) flopped as well, as did candidate Andrew Yang's similar "Freedom Dividend" during the 2020 Democratic primaries and the 2021 New York Democratic mayoral primary race. Instead, Congress created and has expanded the Earned Income Tax Credit (EITC), which has been popular with Democratic and Republican voters, if not libertarian and leftist policy wonks, precisely because it links means-tested assistance to work effort on the part of the recipient.

Disagreements about the desirability of a universal basic income reflect class as much as ideology. The UBI concept appeals to affluent rentiers with non-labor income—like tech executives whose fortunes are based on intellectual property rents, financiers who rake in fees and interest payments, and old-fashioned landlords, of whom John Stuart Mill remarked contemptuously, "They grow richer, as it were, in their sleep, without working, risking, or economizing." The vision of society as a cornucopia of unearned cash also appeals to many nonprofit grantees and academics who live on gifts by rich philanthropists or on the capital gains from university and foundation endowments. It is natural for them to ask, *Why can't everyone be a rentier or a grantee like me?*

The difference between contributory and non-contributory approaches both to social insurance and social assistance explains the divides in contemporary debates over childcare and government aid to caregivers. For believers in the work ethic, it makes perfect sense to add earned benefits like both a child benefit and a conceptually different parental caregiver benefit for an at-home parent to the existing list of contributory income maintenance programs, including Social Security, unemployment insurance, and disability insurance. In the spirit of contributory social insurance, a program that allows one of two parents to raise children at home, or allows both to work part-time, should be paid for wholly or in part by a payroll tax on the work of one or both working parents or another working family member.

This traditional social insurance approach would not be a problem in the case of a one-earner, two-parent family. But it is a problem in the case of single parents, usually single mothers. Adherents of the consumption ethic on the left, and presumably libertarian supporters of basic income as well, assert that it makes no difference whether benefits for children are linked to work by someone in the family or not; either every individual parent should have to work to receive support, or none should. Adherents of the work ethic, and normal human beings in general, distinguish between stay-at-home parents married to working spouses and stay-at-home single parents married to the federal government.

Equally perverse is the "workist" alternative, in which all parents of children, including the mothers of infants, are encouraged to be in the workforce, with their children raised by strangers in institutional commercial or public daycare. This is the policy promoted by employer lobbies that seek to increase profits by expanding the workforce rather than raising labor productivity, and their allies among elite "corporate feminists." The "maternalist feminists" like Eleanor Roosevelt, who favored protective legislation for mothers, would have been horrified by this unholy alliance against the family. So would the great labor activist Mary Harris "Mother" Jones, who declared that she was inspired to devote her life to the trade union movement in the hope that employers would pay men wages high enough that their wives could take care of their children without working.

Whatever the post-familist American intelligentsia thinks, the American electorate is unlikely to approve of paying single parents with children to stay at home, even if the same voters favor benefits for stay-at-home parents in one-earner, two-parent families. Only from the perspective of the consumer ethic, in which "money is money" regardless of its source and individuals apart from their families should be the subjects of public policy, is there a contradiction in favoring aid to married homemakers but not to single parents. From the perspective of the work ethic, the distinction is as sensible and important as that between the deserving and the undeserving poor. Society can and should be generous to single parents while promoting intact families with children as the ideal.

According to the work ethic shared by traditional labor liberals, conservative populists, and familists alike, the problem with the American welfare state is not that it is too big overall, but that social insurance is too small and social assistance is too big. The work ethic ideal is an economy in which high wages can support the high payroll taxes needed to support a contributory social insurance system, including social insurance payments for children and their parental caregivers. The combination of high market wages and generous contributory social insurance programs could also permit the downsizing of means-tested social assistance or "welfare," especially for those who can work. They should be given "workfare" jobs by the government or the private sector, perhaps in a few cases with public wage subsidies (though these must be limited to prevent employers from exploiting them).

When it comes to work and welfare, the instincts of untutored working-class people are sounder than the ideologies of libertarians, socialists, and neoclassical economists. Performing work that is useful to society and supports one's own family has intrinsic value; it is not merely a means to consumption no different in moral terms from government handouts or returns on capital investments. Earned benefits and poor relief are two different things. Unconditional cash relief for those who cannot work is necessary, but it is corrupting and demoralizing for those able to contribute to society and support themselves with their own efforts. Social Security and government-favored private retirement programs, unemployment insurance, and disability insurance should be based chiefly if not exclusively on work-related taxes or premiums. They should be thought of as state-coordinated mutual aid for a well-paid, independent, working-class majority, not as government programs paid for by the beneficence of the rich.

The combination of a family wage with contributory social insurance has never lost its appeal to the working-class majority in modern democracies. In this case, the policies that are best are those that are popular.

THE RETURN OF THE FISCAL CONSERVATIVES

by Oren Cass

Adapted from essays published by American Compass on November 2, 2023, under the title, "The Curse of Voodoo Economics"; and on June 5, 2024, under the title, "Finding the Responsible Party."

In what passes for serious commentary, pundits sagely lament and consultants expensively advise that politicians will always spend irresponsibly, deliver unaffordable tax cuts, and kick the fiscal can down the road. That's what people vote for. What are you gonna do? Just look where we are today, with budget deficits forecasted to routinely top $2 trillion and interest payments on the national debt already exceeding defense spending annually.

Yet for its first two centuries as a democratic republic, the United States of America spent within its means. From 1789 to 1849, the federal government ran a small surplus. It entered World War I with less than $1 billion in total debt and then, after borrowing billions for the fight in Europe, ran surpluses throughout the 1920s. The Great Depression and World War II generated far more debt, but thereafter revenues and spending were held in balance until 1960. By 1979, debt held by the public had fallen back from 106% to 25% of GDP. In 2000, after the Reagan-era defense build-up and victory in the Cold War, with global hegemony and unlimited borrowing capacity, debt was still below 33% of GDP and the federal budget was in its third consecutive year of surplus. Politicians, elected by American voters, can do this.

The puzzle, and the problem, is that for the past two decades they have refused. Republicans and Democrats alike have increased spending at every turn: on foolish foreign policy misadventures, new healthcare benefits and major expansions of anti-poverty programs, and massive subsidies for higher education and green energy. Republicans have repeatedly cut taxes and refused to countenance any increases, ever. Democrats have refused to acknowledge, let alone pursue, the broad-based tax increases that their spending plans require.

The Left's failure is predictable, and perhaps inevitable. Fiscal responsibility has never been a progressive priority, or even of much interest. President Joe Biden's final budget proposal dispensed with any pretense of concern for the deficit, instead proposing further *increases* to current spending levels still elevated from the pandemic. His rote calls to raise taxes on the rich, meanwhile, make hardly a dent, leaving deficits at the period's end as high as at its start. Debt held by the public would increase by 60% over ten years, to $45 trillion.

The Right can, should, and must do better. A democracy holds taxes and spending at low and sustainable levels only if the forces of fiscal conservatism counteract those of liberal profligacy. Fortunately, that role is not some dour and thankless duty; to the contrary, it anchors the case for limited government and aligns well with the preferences of most Americans. Committing to voters that new spending will also mean new taxes is the surest check on the growth in government. Taking reasonable and responsible steps to secure the nation's future is, it turns out, quite popular. New American Compass polling shows that people at all points on the political spectrum overwhelmingly agree that "the nation must be willing to take even painful steps" to address the budget deficit and that this would ideally include both tax increases and spending cuts.

Yet, over the past generation, the Republican Party abandoned its post on what fiscal restraint requires. Back in the 1980s, President Ronald Reagan signed five tax increases after his initial tax cut proved more costly than expected. But by 2011, Republican presidential candidates were all raising their hands in opposition to a hypothetical budget deal that would lower spending by $10 for every $1 of new revenue. They might have insisted on structuring and sequencing any deal to ensure the promised spending reductions occurred. The outright obstinance, however, served merely to confirm that a "pledge" they had signed never to raise taxes had replaced the national interest as their north star. The true cause of limited-government conservatism, which not only restrains spending, but also pays for the spending that does occur, had transmogrified into a half-witted anti-tax zealotry that offered the voters bread and circuses and sent the bill to their children.

The zealots have sold their strategy as somehow conservative under the banner of "starving the beast," a theory that holds depriving the government of revenue is the best way to accomplish reductions in spending. Cut taxes far enough, send the car hurtling close enough to the cliff, and eventually all will accept that steering away from disaster with spending cuts is the only option. The corollary is that raising taxes is not only painful, but also counterproductive: It merely supplies more resources to be absorbed into yet more spending. This has proved not only wrong but precisely backward. Tax cuts have repeatedly coincided with more rapid growth in government, conservative credibility has collapsed, and progressives find themselves freer than ever to advocate for continual spending increases.

The United States cannot afford for this to continue. It cannot afford further tax cuts. It cannot afford higher spending. And it cannot afford political parties clinging to absolutist positions that preclude any prospect of progress. Fortunately, there is no prisoner's dilemma here—only an opportunity for conservatives to advance their most important priorities and gain political ground by returning to their traditional principles.

TAX CUTTING EXPIRES

Republicans have professed, throughout the period of exploding deficits that began in 2001, to be the party of "fiscal discipline." At no time has this been the case. President George W. Bush, inheriting a surplus, quickly slashed taxes to their lowest level as a share of GDP since 1950 while rapidly increasing spending. By 2003, the surplus had collapsed into a deficit of more than 3% of GDP—a higher level than President Barack Obama would leave behind at the end of his second term. During Obama's time in office, House Budget Committee chairman Paul Ryan made a name for himself championing Medicare and Social Security reforms that would lower their long-term cost. But the dates for those reforms were always pushed far into the future, and none became law.

When President Donald Trump came into office in 2017, the GOP held not only the White House, but also both houses of Congress. Ryan was now Speaker of the House. But rather than reduce the deficit or implement any long-term reforms, the signature legislative achievement of those two years was the massive, deficit-expanding *Tax Cuts and Jobs Act* of 2017 (TCJA). By 2019, spending as a share of GDP was also higher than at any point in Obama's second term.

If there was an argument for TCJA more coherent than the addict's pathetic plea for another hit of the good stuff, it was that "the plan will pay for itself with growth," in the words of Secretary of the Treasury Steve Mnuchin. "We are totally confident this is a revenue-neutral bill and probably a revenue producer," said Senate Majority Leader Mitch McConnell. Suffice to say this was not true. One might construct a hypothetical scenario in which tax rates are so high that reductions generate more revenue than they lose. Perhaps that was even the case in the late 1970s, with the top individual rate at 70% and rates on corporate income and capital gains between 40% and 50%. It is not the case today. "Tax cuts pay for themselves" is one of the "10 Common Tax Myths, Debunked" by the conservative Tax Foundation.

Current tax rates and the nature of current economic challenges leave little scope or justification for yet another supply-side tax cut. True, if high marginal tax rates are discouraging economic activity, lower ones could generate a boom. When the *Tax Reform Act* of 1964 reduced the top individual rate from 91% to 77%, the take-home value of each dollar earned by a taxpayer in the top bracket more than doubled. When the top rate declined from 70% at the start of Ronald Reagan's presidency to 28% at the end, the take-home share of a dollar earned more than tripled. Those effects could be powerful.

But the case for a supply-side tax cut is contingent. To what extent are tax rates discouraging economic activity? How much would the proposed cut alter the incentives? What response would such an alteration generate? Temporarily reducing already much lower rates by a few percentage points, as in the 2001 and 2003 tax cuts or the 2017 tax cuts, may accomplish little, even as it costs quite a lot. Bringing the capital gains rate from 40% to 20% in the face of stagflation is rather a different matter than bringing it from 21% in 2002 to 16% in 2003.

A number of other factors can also complicate the "incentives" story. For instance, especially for households, a tax cut has what economists call both a "substitution effect" and an "income effect." On one hand, lower rates and the opportunity to keep more of the next dollar earned might make working hard to earn more income an attractive proposition. On the other hand, if lower rates translate into higher household income for work already being done, workers may be disinclined to exert greater effort to earn more. With additional money already coming into the bank, the household might prefer to spend relatively more time on leisure than on labor.

For corporations, the question of how and when they decide to invest has proved far from straightforward. The standard economic model holds that each firm knows its "cost of capital" and will invest in any project where the risk-adjusted return is expected to exceed that cost. Cutting the corporate tax rate effectively lowers the cost of capital or increases the expected return and should therefore cause more projects to go forward. But in practice, firms only pursue projects that clear much higher return hurdles and many have shown an inclination to return cash to shareholders through dividends and buybacks even when profitable and productive investment opportunities exist. In that context, a lower tax rate might lead simply to yet more cash handed back.

Insofar as a lower tax rate does lead firms to pursue some previously unattractive projects at the margin, the nature of those projects might also matter a great deal. The assumption that tax cuts are a wise mechanism for spurring productive investment and growth takes all investment to be equal—an extra billion dollars invested merging two firms and laying off workers, offshoring production, or building another meal-delivery app must be as good as an extra billion spent building advanced semiconductor manufacturing facilities or developing a rare-earths mine. Historically, economists have assumed just that. But in an economy that has more than enough of the former unproductive investment and far too little of the latter productive type, and where a lower tax rate will primarily yield yet more of the former, tax cuts are the wrong tool.

Conservatives should not abandon the supply side—to the contrary, the U.S. economy has severe supply-side problems that recent tax cuts have done nothing to address but that a supply-side economics properly understood would be far better positioned to solve. But the time has long since passed for abandoning the rhetoric and reasoning of tax cuts that "pay for themselves" or "unleash growth." Recitation of those dogmas in the 2020s, divorced from evidence of their plausibility, is the opposite of conservative. A committed supply-sider would look elsewhere. (See Chris Griswold's essay, "Rebuilding the Supply-Side Platform.")

Finally, the wisdom and effect of tax cuts will depend on how they are funded. If deficits rise and the government has to borrow more, any benefit of improved incentives may be offset. Debates rage among economists over how, if at all, to account for this effect. Especially on the right-of-center, where the wisdom of deficit-financed supply-side tax cuts is an article of faith, models tend to minimize the question of what a tax cut costs. At the extreme, in the analyses published by the Tax Foundation, tax cuts are literally free. They lead to higher debt, of course, but this has no impact on estimates for growth and employment and income. Simply cutting all taxes to zero would generate a remarkably favorable growth projection. That may seem implausible because it surely is. Indeed, the results of recent deficit-financed supply-side tax cuts suggest that the more skeptical models provide a better way of understanding the trade-offs.

At the 2019 Annual Meeting of the American Economic Association, Kevin Hassett, chair of President Donald Trump's Council of Economic Advisers (CEA), presented data showing that in its first year the *Tax Cuts and Jobs Act* cuts had spurred business investment and growth as predicted. So clear was this evidence "for the headline things that we model with real science," he explained, that "if you say the tax cuts aren't working then you're kind of in some kind of denial that you should think about." There was just one problem. The figures that he cited for the economy's performance in the first three quarters of 2018 were preliminary, subject to revision as the U.S. Bureau of Economic Analysis (BEA) gathered more data. As better numbers trickled in, the positive results vanished. The CEA's own charts, updated with the revised figures, would show that their models were wrong, business investment had failed to surge, and growth had perhaps even slowed. Economists across the political spectrum have likewise concluded that President George W. Bush's tax cuts in 2001 and 2003 achieved none of the desired "pro-growth" effects.

Still, conservative think tanks insist on repeating this error, to make their own budget proposals balance. In 2023, the Center for Renewing America (CRA), led by Trump administration budget guru Russ Vought, released its own ten-year budget proposal that reached balance in 2032. The document is an impressive, important marker for anyone serious about limited government. But the comprehensive set of proposed cuts does not bring spending down to current revenue levels. And yet, rather than contemplate tax increases, the proposal makes permanent the expiring TCJA cuts at an annual cost of nearly $400 billion by the last year.

So how does the CRA budget balance? It features an extra line-item titled "revenue increase from economic assumptions," crediting the government with an extra $774 billion in tax revenue delivered without any new taxes at all. This estimate derives from the assumptions that productivity growth rises 0.5% faster than the CBO baseline each year and labor-force growth rises 0.75% percent faster. Conveniently, though perhaps not entirely coincidentally, these happen to be the largest values that CBO allows a user to put into its revenue-estimating model.

The Heritage Foundation has taken a different approach in its own ten-year *Budget Blueprint for Fiscal Year 2023*. Proposing new tax cuts, the blueprint accepts that tax revenue will be lower as a result. To make up the gap, it proposes outlandish cuts—for instance, reducing Medicare spending by 45% within ten years—that have no support among Republican policymakers or voters and no chance of becoming law. Put another way, the efforts at "fiscal discipline" from conservative think tanks tend to be marketing exercises that prove they *can* balance the budget, albeit in worlds very different from our own.

THE STARVED BEAST LOOKS AWFULLY FAT

What is going on here? While none of these efforts, either in or out of government, make sense as fiscal discipline, they all fit comfortably within the so-called "starve the beast" strategy. The problem with this strategy is that it does not work, in practice or in theory. As William Niskanen, economic adviser to Reagan and longtime chairman of the libertarian Cato Institute, observed in a 2004 "Chairman's Message" for the *Cato Policy Report*:

> *This position is not consistent with the evidence, at least beginning in 1981. In a professional paper published in 2002, I presented evidence that the relative level of federal spending over the period 1981 through 2000 was coincident with the relative level of the federal tax burden in the opposite direction; in other words, there was a strong negative relation between the relative level of federal spending and tax revenues.*

The pattern appears to have held since. In the years after the 2001 and 2003 tax cuts, spending rose from 17.7% to 21.9% of GDP. After some of those tax cuts were allowed to expire at the end of 2012, spending fell from 21.9% to 20.1%. After TCJA took effect in 2018, spending rose again to 20.9% on the eve of the pandemic.

This should not be surprising. Tax policy unmoored from spending makes the spending free to voters and thus more popular with them. When spending has to be paid for, its cost is taken much more seriously. Niskanen, again:

> *The demand for federal spending by current voters declines with the amount of this spending that is financed by current taxes. Future voters will bear the burden of any resulting deficit but are not effectively represented by those making the current fiscal choices. One implication of this relation is that a tax* increase *may be the most effective policy to reduce the relative level of federal spending* (emphasis in original).

A public promised lower taxes and higher spending simultaneously has understandably little interest in fiscal discipline. A Democratic Party that believes any spending cuts will simply be channeled into further tax cuts has no interest in checking its own ambitions for bigger government.

A Republican Party that will in fact channel any spending cut into yet another tax cut has no credibility asserting that any sacrifice is required from anyone. As the Manhattan Institute's Brian Riedl observed in *City Journal* in 2024:

> *The 2001 Bush tax cuts were immediately followed with new war spending, annual nondefense discretionary spending hikes as high as 13 percent, a massive new Medicare drug entitlement, and a doubling of farm subsidies. Republicans had no credible argument against this spending after Vice President Dick Cheney declared "deficits don't matter" during the 2001 tax cuts debate.*
>
> *And I'll reiterate that the 2008–2016 GOP deficit-hawk era (under a Democratic president) ended abruptly after President Trump and Republicans cut taxes in 2017. Shortly after these reductions, a unified GOP government abandoned the Budget Control Act spending limits and hiked discretionary appropriations by 13 percent in one year (2018) and then abandoned all Tea Party–era spending-cut proposals. I had worked in the Senate and continued to speak with lawmakers after 2017. Several GOP lawmakers told me that they could no longer bring up deficits at voter town halls without voters screaming "fine, start with repealing your tax cuts."*

The more coherent and conservative approach is to put the horse back in front of the cart. Rather than cut taxes first and pursue spending cuts later, at which point the short-sighted voter will see all pain and no gain, tax cuts should be conditioned on spending cuts. *If* we get back to pre-pandemic levels generally, or cap and block-grant safety net programs, or stop paying off everyone's student loans for them, or undertake serious entitlement reform, *then* we will be able to reduce taxes by this or that amount. Conversely, *if* we accept current spending levels as the new normal, *then* past tax cuts will have to be reversed and no new ones will be on the table.

The anti-tax zealots are of course entitled to their own agenda, and indeed they would be wise to ignore and rebut all this, insofar as their objective is merely to cut taxes as far as possible, consequences be damned. But let's dispense with the fictions that they are advancing the cause of limited government, that their principles are conservative ones, and that the ends they are pursuing are rationally related to national prosperity or the common good.

THE 19-20 SOLUTION

The point of departure in most budget discussions, which prevents them from departing at all, is the question of whether we have a "spending problem" or a "revenue problem." We have cut taxes too far, Democrats say, and therefore we must focus on finding more revenue. Spending is far above historical levels and we could never raise enough revenue to cover it, Republicans say, and therefore we must focus on cutting spending. Four-year-olds fighting over the same ball have more useful discussions. Obviously, the two problems can exist together. Indeed, after an extended period of both sides behaving so irresponsibly, it would be surprising if we did not face both problems at once.

A fair-minded assessment of the data invariably concludes that both problems are indeed very real. Spending, estimated to land at 22.9% of GDP in 2024 and reach 24.1% of GDP by 2034, has reached by far its highest level outside major recessions and national emergencies. Average spending was 20.2% of GDP from 1999 to 2019 and 20.8% from 1979 to 1999. There is no precedent for sustaining spending at current levels and no plausible plan to fund it with tax increases. The Biden White House's own budget would bring tax revenue only up to 20.3% of GDP by 2034.

Revenue, meanwhile, is estimated by CBO to land at 17.5% of GDP in 2024 and average 17.7% of GDP for the coming decade. That is below the lowest spending level at any point in the last fifty years and nearly three points below average levels over the past forty. The Heritage Foundation's model manages to bring spending down this far only by, as noted above, gutting the nation's most popular programs. The CRA budget purports to achieve the same but does so only by assuming an extra $4 trillion of GDP in its denominator. Apply CRA's proposed budget cuts to the economy's size as predicted by CBO, and the remaining spending amounts to 19% of GDP.

This range of 19% to 20% of GDP emerges repeatedly as the plausible site for balance, theoretically and historically. When the budget was in fact balanced, from 1998 to 2001, revenue averaged 19.4% of GDP. The House Budget Committee under Chairman Ryan targeted revenue and spending of 19% by the 2030s in its FY2013 "Path to Prosperity" budget. The budget model that American Compass has published shows that an aggressive scenario built around substantively and politically plausible choices likewise arrives at that destination.

Remarkably, the American people intuitively land there too. Asked "how much of the deficit would you want to close by raising taxes and how much by cutting spending?" the median American selects 40% tax increases and 60% spending cuts. Mapped on to the CBO's forecasted 2025 budget gap where spending is 23.1% and revenue is 17.1% of GDP, that 40/60 split implies landing precisely at 19.5%. And unlike the politicians who insist on discussing only one or the other, nearly all Americans believe both taxes and spending should be part of the solution, with 63% believing that at least a quarter of the deficit reduction should come from each. The radical activist view that revenue must never be raised is shared by only a quarter of Republicans.

Acknowledging these realities points budget discussions down a much more constructive path. One implication, which Republicans will not like but will have to face, is that extending TCJA is the wrong fight. The deficit-expanding tax cut was irresponsible the first time around and the fiscal picture is much uglier today. Republicans are entirely correct that spending must come down for the sake of fiscal sanity, but they are entirely unserious if they believe they can achieve that goal while making their number one fiscal priority another deficit-expanding tax cut.

Conversely, if conservatives within the party are willing to assert the needed leadership, the opportunity is enormous. One vital contribution of CRA's budget is to shift the focus from difficult long-term entitlement cuts to the lower-hanging fruit of immediate cuts where spending has already grown out of control. As Vought convincingly argues:

> *When families decide to get on a budget, they do not target the largest and immovable items of their spending, like their mortgage, first. They aim to restrain discretionary spending—they eat out less, shop less, and find cheaper ways of entertaining themselves. Then they look at what makes sense for the immovables—how to refinance their debt or make major life changes. Politically, a similar approach is the only way the American people will ever accept major changes to mandatory spending. They are simply not going to buy the notion that their earned entitlements must be tweaked while the federal government is funding Bob Dylan statues in Mozambique or gay pride parades in Prague.*

Rather than pursue a "grand bargain" or establish a "fiscal commission," conservatives should choose an initial tranche of CRA's cuts and put them on the table immediately, indicating that they are prepared to accept some higher revenue as part of a deal. For instance, returning the Supplemental Nutrition Assistance Program (food stamps) to its pre-pandemic scale, eliminating the floor on Medicaid reimbursement that entitles the wealthiest states to higher federal payments, and reforming the Department of Education's student-loan programs could quickly save more than $100 billion in the first year. Returning run-of-the-mill agency budgets outside of the hotly contested areas like social spending and defense back to their pre-pandemic levels would save another $75 billion.

In part, that kind of negotiation would simply enable the horse-trading necessary to make political progress on an issue where partisans have competing and conflicting priorities. But going through the process would also deliver a more substantive achievement. At the moment, each side rightly distrusts the other—Democrats see that Republicans are looking for spending cuts to finance more tax cuts; Republicans see that Democrats are looking for tax increases to enable more spending. In that context, the first step has to be a credibility-building exercise, signaling that the game is changing to one where both sides acknowledge they are aiming for a goal somewhere between them. Legislation that actually delivered $250 billion in spending cuts and $150 billion in tax increases over the next two years, laying the groundwork for the next round of negotiations, would be worth more than twenty commissions with the bluest of ribbons.

A number of prominent Republicans appear ready to head in this direction. In 2024, Rep. Chip Roy, policy chair for the House Freedom Caucus, lamented not only that "we have my Democratic colleagues saying we can't even have a conversation about Social Security and Medicare," but also that "we have [Americans for Tax Reform] and a bunch of people flipping out on our side saying you can't even have a conversation about taxes. What in the utter hell is wrong with this body?"

"It's only fair to have both revenue and expenditures on the table," Rep. Jodey Arrington, chair of the House Budget Committee, told *Semafor* the following month. Rep. Tom Cole, chair of the House Appropriations Committee, echoed the sentiment shortly thereafter. "I don't particularly—as a Republican—like tax increases," he said. "But the reality is, I think, if you're going to have a bipartisan deal, revenue and reform, they both have to be on the table." *Politico* reported meanwhile that "House Ways and Means Committee Chair Jason Smith said Wednesday that some prominent Republican lawmakers have discussed a corporate tax hike and suggested there could be bipartisan support for one in 2025."

WHAT IF THEY SAY NO?

Of course, the other side may say no. To date, Republicans signaling a willingness to get serious have been met only with silence from Democrats who seem increasingly incapable of contemplating any curbs on their untenable ambitions for bigger government. The effect of political realignment on the progressive coalition and agenda has left it with few places to turn: As the Left has become dependent on absorbing the professional managerial class, President Obama's promise not to raise taxes on households earning less than $250,000 became President Biden's promise to protect incomes under $400,000. As the Left has embraced the cause of expansive military commitments around the world, defense cuts—always the rejoinder to the Right's demand to bring spending lower—have become difficult to advocate for with a straight face.

But from the conservative perspective, the progressive quandary is a feature, not a bug. There is no prisoner's dilemma here, with a choice to behave responsibly backfiring if the other side defects. What are progressives going to do, attack conservatives for being able to talk about tax increases as part of deficit reduction? That is the progressive position. If progressives will not be reasonable, calling their bluff clears the field for conservatives to advance their own preferred package unilaterally, while standing squarely in the middle of public opinion.

A return to fiscal responsibility is the dominant strategy, as it has always been, in American politics. When conservatives understood this, they were much more successful politically, wielded more power and thus achieved more of their priorities, limited the growth of government more effectively, and as a result better served the nation. When tax cuts became the end unto themselves, we soon forgot why we cared about them to begin with, and then that we cared about anything else. That has gone less well.

Conclusion

THE CENTER CANNOT HOLD

by Oren Cass

Adapted from the "Founder's Letters" published as part of
American Compass's Annual Report each year.

American Compass was founded in 2020, which marked the centennial of W. B. Yeats's "The Second Coming" and the line "Things fall apart; the centre cannot hold." I am no poetry buff. There are probably only two or three poems, all by Robert Frost, from which I could recite a single stanza. But that snippet from Yeats pops frequently into my mind because it describes so well the most interesting developments in our world. Things—all things—do eventually fall apart. Conditions change; knowledge expands; behaviors, beliefs, and relationships evolve; and a center squarely established at one moment in time cannot hold in another. The trajectories of individual lives, large institutions, and entire nations and civilizations are defined by what follows.

America's center is not holding. The issue is not any particular election result, or the happenstance of a global pandemic, but the expiration of the neoliberal political consensus and policy agenda that has characterized recent decades, with its globalization, deregulation, and financialization of the economy; atomization of the society; and reliance on redistribution to those left behind. The challenge manifests in symptoms ranging from the concentration of wealth in fewer hands and of growth in narrow geographies, rising "deaths of despair" and political dysfunction, declines in family and community well-being, and a stalling out of the investment and innovation that generate productivity growth and rising wages.

For Yeats, what follows is "mere anarchy... loosed upon the world." We can do better. The ability to avoid that fate is among the great virtues of our capitalist economy and republican system of government. The leaders of our institutions, by design, have incentives to detect and respond to change, and those institutions have the capacity to adapt. We ensure that prospective competitors can enter our markets, our civil society, and our politics, so that entrenched incumbents face constant pressure—and when some do snap rather than bend, replacements stand ready to fill the void.

But the process is neither an easy nor an inevitable one. The best analog comes from science, where Thomas Kuhn famously introduced the concept of a "paradigm shift" in *The Structure of Scientific Revolutions* (1962). Whereas scientists and philosophers had believed that scientific knowledge advanced steadily through incremental progress, Kuhn showed that the process was one of long static periods of "normal science," during which a community of researchers worked mostly to validate their existing paradigm, punctuated by short periods of disruption when an old paradigm failed and a new one emerged. Far from pushing this process forward, scientists will tend to defend their existing paradigm from challenge and accept new frameworks grudgingly, if at all. As the physicist Max Planck observed, "A new scientific truth does not triumph by convincing its opponents and making them see the light, but rather because its opponents eventually die and a new generation grows up that is familiar with it."

Political economy lacks the clearly stated hypotheses and experimental evidence of science, but it experiences change in a similar way. Innovative ideas harden into dogma around which politicians and economists build their careers, warding off the heresy of new thinking until they render themselves so irrelevant and inadequate to contemporary challenges that a crisis occurs, then chaos, and then a better framework emerges.

In the popular imagination, this process happens automatically, as if by magic. Adam Smith's unfortunate metaphor of an "invisible hand" leads many to anthropomorphize markets and firms, which "discover" and "allocate" and "adjust" of their own accord. Taking this myth to its extreme, Friedrich Hayek lauded the "self-regulating forces of the market," which he promised would "somehow bring about the required adjustments to new conditions, although no one can foretell how they will do this." The joke about the economist who will not bend down to pocket a twenty-dollar bill on the sidewalk because, if there were such a bill, someone would already have grabbed it, is gentle in its mocking but quite serious in its indictment.

In fact, there is no magic, only people. Bills do fall to the sidewalk, where they lie until someone does the bending and pocketing. New ideas do not burst forth from the ether; someone must think them, act on them, and persuade others of their value. The process of institutional reform is painstakingly slow and complex, demanding both the assent and effort of countless individuals, each with his own interests and priorities. All the while, inertia pushes the other way, with adherence to the status quo almost always the most appealing choice. A body at rest will stay at rest until acted upon by an outside force.

The timeless principles and creative energies of conservatism are vital to America's prospects for adaptation and renewal, but they must be applied anew, not lost in the din of tired clichés and outdated proposals recycled from some bygone world. The nation's conservative institutions have thus far proved incapable of rising to that challenge. Instead, they seem beholden to ideas generated in a previous era of renewal, which have since hardened into a market fundamentalism ill-suited to the problems of today. It is not conservative to propose a capital-gains tax cut in the face of a pandemic, deregulation of financial markets run amok, or "free trade" with a country whose stated policy is to distort markets in pursuit of industrial dominance. It is merely foolish—a recipe for things to fall apart irreparably.

Yeats concluded his stanza with, "The best lack all conviction, while the worst / Are full of passionate intensity," which captures a dynamic familiar in our politics and one that, left unchecked, will only worsen. The antidote is robust debate between good people with firm convictions. For the first time in decades, thanks to the ideas in this volume, the conservative movement is actually moving—toward a genuinely conservative economics that aims to strengthen families, communities, and the nation rather than merely maximize consumption. The success or failure of those ideas will determine the future trajectory of American politics and public policy, the American economy, and consequently our nation's liberty and prosperity.

Acknowledgments

Thanking everyone who plays an integral role in the publication of a book is hard enough. An effort to acknowledge the entire community that nurtures an organization and fuels a movement will always be woefully incomplete. But let's give it a shot.

First and foremost, someone will need to write a book someday about the members of the American Compass team, who have accomplished what no one thought possible in ways no one else had ever tried. An organization does not outperform a coalition more than 100x its size, with more than 100x its funding, unless the players are all at the absolute top of their various professions and eager to work twice as hard as anyone else, too.

Wells King and Wesley Hodges made the leap into the roles of research director and program director when the organization was nothing but a prospectus and a few months of seed funding, working tirelessly toward an extraordinarily successful launch in the midst of a pandemic that had ground the nation to a halt. Wells poured the foundations for most of what Compass works on to this day, and his own writing appears throughout this volume. Wes designed and built our entirely novel model for a membership group, which has grown from 25 to nearly 250 policy professionals who hold leadership positions across literally dozens of federal agencies, congressional offices, think tanks, and publications. These members have poured their own time and energy into supporting our work and—as importantly—each other's work, in the process creating a genuine community that we value dearly.

Chris Griswold and Abigail Ball joined shortly after our launch as policy director and communications director respectively and have led work in those areas ever since. Abby became executive director last year and now guides all of the organization's work, day to day. People wondering at how American Compass "punches so far above its weight" just need to understand that Chris can move five different bills through five congressional offices in parallel, while Abby would immediately be the best government affairs firm, strategic communications firm, or public relations firm in Washington if she launched any of the three. Emily Davis has the title of events and operations director, which in practice means that she is HR director, IT director, facilities director, finance director, and chief of staff as well. When members of the Compass team attend a swanky conference hosted by a dedicated event planning team, we chuckle to each other, "Emily could have done that. And better."

As coalition director, Duncan Braid forced open every door in the conservative movement and somehow commandeered American Compass a seat at every table, no matter how many food fights we set off. His standing-room-only training programs for young Capitol Hill staff established the gold standard that much larger and quite envious organizations tried and failed to emulate, and his monthly salon dinners for members were typically filled within an hour of the invitation going out. Policy advisors Mark DiPlacido and Gabriela Rodriguez broadened and deepened our research and recommendations, working closely with legal experts and elected officials to translate ideas into legislation. Most recently, Drew Holden, Helen Andrews, and Sam Silvestro have launched *Commonplace*, the magazine that now serves as the intellectual home for the New Right.

When we decided to produce this book, we of course decided to do so with the absurdly ambitious timeline and plainly inadequate resources that characterize every American Compass effort but seem nonsensical in the publishing world. Nevertheless, our agent, Andrew Stuart, agreed to see what he could do and somehow convinced Keith Wallman of Radius Books Group to say yes. And Keith somehow proceeded to complete the project in record time at top quality.

Whereas nonprofit boards of directors tend to be honorary parking lots for large donors, ours is a tight-knit group of the savviest advisors across all facets of American politics and policy. Mike Needham, formerly Senator Marco Rubio's chief of staff; Julius Krein, editor of *American Affairs*; and

David Azerrad, professor at Hillsdale College, all helped to conceive the organization and have served on the board throughout its first five years. Within the first year they were joined by Ambassador Robert Lighthizer, U.S. trade representative in President Donald Trump's first administration; Neil Patel, publisher of the *Daily Caller*; and Jonathan Baron, founder and principal at Baron Public Affairs.

Many others have also offered their time and energy to giving the organization its form, most notably Jacob Reses, an advisor to Senators JD Vance and Josh Hawley, and Caleb Orr, an advisor to Senator Rubio. Vance, Rubio, and Hawley, as well as Senators Tom Cotton, Todd Young, and Jim Banks, have all been extraordinarily generous in their support, going far above and beyond the typical engagement between elected leaders and a think tank to take a genuine interest and play a meaningful role in our success. Beyond the writers featured here, dozens of others made important contributions to our many projects, and many have served as Compass Advisors, helping to bring our collective ideas to the world. The membership group of young policy professionals mentioned above, now 250 strong.

Thirty years from now, this list of names will be the list that defined conservatism for a generation and reshaped American politics along the way. Yeats wrote of things falling apart, but the converse of his story is true as well. When the worst lack all conviction, and the best are full of passionate intensity, our nation moves forward.

About American Compass

American Compass is a nonprofit organization founded in 2020 with the mission to restore an economic consensus that emphasizes the importance of family, community, and industry to the nation's liberty and prosperity—

> Reorienting political focus from growth for its own sake to widely shared economic development that sustains vital social institutions;
>
> Setting a course for a country in which families can achieve self-sufficiency, contribute productively to their communities, and prepare the next generation for the same; and
>
> Helping policymakers navigate the limitations that markets and government each face in promoting the general welfare and the nation's security.

American Compass advances this mission through three complementary approaches—

> 1. Affiliation: Providing opportunities for people who share its mission to build relationships, collaborate, and communicate their views to the broader political community;
>
> 2. Deliberation: Supporting research and discussion that advances understanding of economic and social conditions and

trade-offs through study of history, analysis of data, elaboration of theory, and development of policy proposals; and

3. Engagement: Initiating and facilitating public debate to challenge existing orthodoxy, confront the best arguments of its defenders, and force scrutiny of unexamined assumptions and unconsidered consequences.

American Compass strives to embody the principles and practices of a healthy democratic polity, combining intellectual combat with personal civility. We welcome converts to our vision and value disagreement amongst our members. We work toward a version of American politics that remains inevitably partisan and contentious but operates from a common commitment to reinforcing the foundations of a flourishing society.